Legal Aspects of Documenting Patient Care

Second Edition

Ronald W. Scott, JD, MSBA, MSPT, PT, OCS

Associate Professor and Chair
Physical Therapy Department
Lebanon Valley College
Annville, Pennsylvania

D0146881

AN ASPEN PUBLICATION®
Aspen Publishers, Inc.
Gaithersburg, Maryland
2000

Library of Congress Cataloging-in-Publication Data

Legal aspects of documenting patient care / Ronald W. Scott.—2nd ed.
p. cm.
Includes bibliographical references and index.
ISBN 0-8342-1630-2
1. Medical records—Law and legislation—United States.
2. Medical care—Law and legislation—United States.
3. Medical records—Management.   I. Title
KF3827.R4S385 2000
344.73'041—dc21
99-055592

Copyright © 2000 by Aspen Publishers, Inc.
A Wolters Kluwer Company
www.aspenpublishers.com
All rights reserved.

Aspen Publishers, Inc., grants permission for photocopying for limited personal or internal use. This consent does not extend to other kinds of copying, such as copying for general distribution, for advertising or promotional purposes, for creating new collective works, or for resale. For information, address Aspen Publishers, Inc., Permissions Department, 200 Orchard Ridge Drive, Suite 200, Gaithersburg, Maryland 20878.

Orders: (800) 638-8437
Customer Service: (800) 234-1660

About Aspen Publishers • For more than 40 years, Aspen has been a leading professional publisher in a variety of disciplines. Aspen's vast information resources are available in both print and electronic formats. We are committed to providing the highest quality information available in the most appropriate format for our customers. Visit Aspen's Internet site for more information resources, directories, articles, and a searchable version of Aspen's full catalog, including the most recent publications: **www.aspenpublishers.com**
Aspen Publishers, Inc. • The hallmark of quality in publishing.
Member of the worldwide Wolters Kluwer group.

Editorial Services: Jane Colilla
Library of Congress Catalog Card Number: 99-055592
ISBN: 0-8342-1630-2

Printed in the United States of America

1 2 3 4 5

I dedicate this book with love to my wonderful wife, Pepi, and to our sons, Ron Jr. and Paul. The book is also dedicated to the late Linda McCartney, whose contributions to this world were legion. We will never forget you.

Table of Contents

Foreword

For health care professionals in all fields, proper documentation of patient care is a continual responsibility, challenge, and chore. Although documentation of patient care does not occur in order to give lawyers a livelihood, the process of creating and handling patient records does have many legal ramifications. This second edition of Ronald Scott's book, *Legal Aspects of Documenting Patient Care*, provides valuable guidance to clinicians, administrators, and students about the role of patient records in legal proceedings and the use of documentation in the management of risks associated with caring for patients.

Part of the challenge to practitioners and administrators is to keep abreast of changes attributable to economic and technological development. With respect to the financing of health care delivery, managed care in recent years has spread widely across the United States. In addition, thanks to technological developments, practitioners are increasingly able to provide services to patients at a distance, while the rapid spread of Internet usage makes the transmission of patient records vastly easier than in the age of paper-only records. This edition of *Legal Aspects of Documenting Patient Care* flags the major issues associated with the ongoing economic and technological developments that are changing the health care system.

Managed care, in one form or another, has spread rapidly. Increasingly, third-party payer coverage decisions depend upon advanced authorization from the payer (often administered by employees who are not health care professionals, or who are not educated or trained in the provider's profession). This shift in decision-making power places an added burden on practitioners. Although practitioners have always had some legal duty to assist patients in obtaining reimbursement for the care rendered by the practitioner, the shift away from the traditional fee-for-services model accentuates the practitioner's need to act as an advocate on behalf of patients—even before care is provided. In this context, adequate documentation can be crucial in enabling the practitioner to help the patient (and the practitioner) to obtain the necessary prior authorization. The current edition is written with an acute awareness of the practitioner's advocacy responsibilities in the context of managed care.

Although health care professionals always have been responsible for protecting the confidentiality of patient-related information, economic and technological changes have worked together to bring to the forefront questions of the privacy of patient records. As a practical matter, the increased involvement of third-party payers in the making of decisions about care pushes practitioners in the direction of disclosing more patient-related information. At the same time, as economic forces encourage greater disclosure, technological changes (especially the explosive growth in use of the Internet) make the transmission of patient data much easier than what would have been only imaginable a few decades ago. This combination of forces has heightened concerns about the privacy of patient records. At the writing of this foreword, the United States Department of Health and Human Services was preparing to propose important, new safeguards concerning patients' records. Privacy concerns undoubtedly will continue to spawn new legislation and legislative proposals. As a result, practitioners will face an increasing need to know not just how to document patient care, but also how to handle the records (particularly electronic records) they generate.

The basic freedom of practitioners to choose whom to treat has always been tempered by the obligation not to terminate treatment of a patient still in need of care (without giving the patient notice to enable him or her to seek care from an alternative source). This traditional professional responsibility has increasingly come to the fore as third-party payers impose more or less arbitrary limits on the care for which they will pay, leaving patients to pay out of their own pockets, find cheaper alternatives, or go without. A treatise on documentation cannot solve the dilemma of a patient who needs additional care, whose practitioner has exhausted the third-party resources available. However, this edition of *Legal Aspects of Documenting Patient Care* provides useful guidance that may be utilized to serve the patient and to protect the practitioner against the risk of liability.

Mr. Scott brings special qualifications to the task of informing students, clinicians, and administrators about the legal considerations affecting the documentation of patient care. He has practiced as both a lawyer and a physical therapist—experience that enables him to speak and understand the special language of each profession. Members of the physical therapy profession know him not only as a frequent writer but also as a dynamic and thought-provoking lecturer. The combination of his professional knowledge and experience and his passion for teaching make him particularly well suited to provide thoughtful and practical guidance to those who care for patients.

John J. Bennett
General Counsel
American Physical Therapy Association

Preface

Effective patient care documentation is as important as the delivery of care itself. That is the premise of this and the previous edition of this book. The memorialization of patient/client intake, examination, evaluative findings and diagnosis, prognosis, intervention, and discharge in the form of formal documentation serves several key functions, including compliance with professional ethical and legal mandates, the justification of third-party reimbursement for care rendered, and the permanent (or at least long-term) recordation of patient data that can serve patient, organization, and societal needs in the future.

A principal primary health professional ethical responsibility is for the provider to act as a fiduciary, or official in a special position of trust, in relation to patients under the provider's care. The creation, maintenance, and, as appropriate, dissemination of documented patient care information is one of the most important fiduciary duties owed to patients. Such documentation can mean the difference between life and death for patients. From a legal perspective, what appears in patient care documentation is considered by courts and other entities as the best evidence of what transpired between a patient and his or her primary health care provider, especially regarding the appropriateness of a diagnosis and interventions carried out on a patient's behalf by a provider. In this sense, patient care documentation determines whether the legal standard of care has been met or breached by a health care provider in a health care malpractice proceeding.

To be of optimal utility, patient care documentation created by a primary health care clinical professional must be accurate, comprehensive, concise, objective, and timely. In cases where an interdisciplinary team of health care professionals renders care to a patient, such documentation must also be expeditiously communicated to other colleagues intervening on that patient's behalf and having an imminent need to know the information contained therein.

This book takes a decidedly legalistic focus in its overview of the topic of patient care documentation. This slant is taken in part because as a health law attorney, I have witnessed on multiple occasions the devastating consequences of poor, nonexistent, or altered patient care documentation—to patients and their significant others, to health care providers and organizations, and to society at large. A legal focus also serves to educate (or remind) health care professionals of their formidable documentation responsibilities incident to patient care delivery. Even under the current managed care paradigm characterized by time constraints and a primary focus on revenue maximization, patient care documentation cannot be given short shrift, because legal and professional ethical practice standards have not altered substantially to accommodate this business model. Under any potential patient care documentation format—acronym (e.g., SOAP), narrative, or template—the exact same legal standards that applied when fee-for-service health care delivery predominated still apply under managed care.

While a legalistic approach to patient care documentation may educate or remind health care providers, organizations, and systems about their legal duties, a fine balancing act must ensue in practice, in which providers must avoid creating patient care documentation that appears overly self-protective or risk management focused. Such an approach (in lieu of a patient welfare approach to patient care documentation) creates an inference of sublimation of a provider's or organization's duty owed to its patients in favor of self-interest, which may increase the likelihood of health care malpractice liability for providers and organizations. There are appropriate circumstances under which patient care documentation takes a risk management, or self-protective, focus, and these are discussed in the text.

The outline of the second edition of *Legal Aspects of Documenting Patient Care* follows that of the first edition. Chapter 1 provides an overview of malpractice legal proceedings and tort reform initiatives. Chapter 2 discusses the purposes and (three) formats for patient care documentation and presents 25 selected documentation problems, errors, and suggestions, with case examples. Chapter 3 focuses on the patient care record as a legal and business document and stresses the importance of avoiding spoliation, the wrongful alteration or destruction of patient records. Chapter 4 addresses documentation issues related to obtaining and memorializing patient or client informed consent to diagnostic and therapeutic examinations and interventions. Chapter 5 presents a generic model for patient care quality and risk management that stresses the importance of effective documentation and information management. Chapter 6 addresses salient documentation issues from advance directives to incident reporting to reimbursement to telehealth, among others.

I hope this text meets the needs of health care professional students, clinicians, and organization/system administrators. The information contained herein is intended as general legal information and not as specific legal guidance for any individual practitioner. Such specific advice can only be given by one's personal legal counsel, based on (ever-evolving) state and federal law requirements and guidance. Best wishes for clinical practice success!

Chapter 1

Overview of the Legal Environment and Documentation-Related Health Care Malpractice Issues

This chapter presents an overview of the law of health care malpractice, including discussion of professional negligence and the legal standard of care, expert witness testimony, vicarious liability for the actions of others, and patient abandonment, among other important legal issues. The chapter also explains in nonlegalese language the basic processes associated with health care malpractice claims and lawsuits, with special emphasis on pretrial depositions. The chapter ends with a discussion of tort reform initiatives designed to stem the number of health care malpractice claims and lawsuits.

THE HEALTH CARE MALPRACTICE CRISIS

For the past few decades, the United States has experienced what has been labeled a health care "malpractice crisis,"[1] characterized by large numbers of legal actions and larger civil malpractice verdicts in favor of patient-plaintiffs and against health care providers. This phenomenon has affected not only medicine but every primary health care professional discipline that provides direct patient care services, including nurses, physical and occupational therapists, and physician assistants, among many others. This chapter introduces general legal principles and presents an overview of health care malpractice law.

Primary health care providers face a high degree of malpractice exposure, not only because they treat patients when they are most at risk—sick or injured and often in pain—but also because of many other factors. External factors that increase providers' malpractice exposure include a greater sense of consumerism among the patient population; intensified federal and state regulation of health care delivery; and a metamorphosis in the health care milieu away from informal, personalized care in favor of increasingly competitive, "business-like" delivery of health care. Many disciplines, including physical therapy, have undergone internal professional changes that may increase their members' health care malpractice liability risk exposure. Some of the internal factors that may create greater legal risks for physical therapists as a representative primary health care discipline include the expanding scope and breadth of professional practice; the highly visible position of the profession in the health care delivery system; the trends toward direct access practice or practice without physician referral in most jurisdictions; clinical specialty certification; and the publication of the practice guide, the *Guide to Physical Therapist Practice*.[2] Other health care disciplines face similar, as well as unique, practice issues with liability consequences.

Health care professionals and clinical managers can do many things in practice to minimize the incidence of claims of health care malpractice and malpractice lawsuits. Of paramount importance is excellence in communications between health care providers and patients and among health care providers treating patients. In communicating with patients, providers must remember to explain what they are doing during clinical examinations. Providers also must explain examination and diagnostic test results to patients and explain them in simple layperson's language. Patients not only want information about their health status and care but are entitled to it as a universal legal principle and fundamental human right. Under the legal concept of informed consent, health care providers must convey to patients sufficient information about their health status to allow patients to make informed choices about whether to accept or decline recommended interventions. Effective clinical documentation of primary provider-patient communication processes, especially regarding informed consent, is crucial to managing malpractice risk exposure.

In addition to effective communication with patients, health care providers must also communicate effectively and systematically with other health care professionals who are either concurrently treating a given patient or who will treat that patient in the future. The principal means of communicating information among health care providers is through patient care documentation. Accurate, timely, thorough, and concise documentation can be the deciding factor for whether a patient lives or dies. Effective documentation also has "professional" life-and-death consequences for health care providers charged with malpractice. In a malpractice trial, tried perhaps many years after care was rendered, what is written in the treatment record may constitute the only objective evidence of whether care given to a patient-plaintiff by a malpractice health professional-defendant met or breached minimally acceptable practice standards.

Besides effective communication and documentation, other strategies can be used to help lessen the risk of malpractice actions. These include simple things such as treating patients with empathy and compassion; practicing only within one's personal scope of clinical competence and within the legal parameters of one's profession; consulting with other health care providers whenever necessary; and establishing within health care facilities effective quality and risk management programs to monitor and evaluate patient care and to manage malpractice risk exposure.

> *Effective documentation in the treatment record may constitute the only objective evidence of whether care given to a patient-plaintiff by a malpractice defendant met practice standards or was substandard.*

Reflective of these considerations, legal issues concerning physical therapy and other nonphysician health care specialties have received greater attention by legal and health care authors in the recent past, including the publication of textbooks by at least two physical therapist-attorneys. Also, professional associations, including among others, the American Health Lawyers Association, the American Medical Association, the American Nurses Association, the American Occupational Therapy Association, and the American Physical Therapy Association, are sponsoring more professional seminars on selected legal topics such as risk management, expert testimony, and the legal standard of care.

MALPRACTICE DEFINED

Legal writers and scholars have used two approaches to defining health care malpractice. Under the traditional approach, the definition of health care malpractice includes only conduct that constitutes professional negligence—the overwhelming basis for imposition of malpractice liability.[3]

Under a broader approach, however, every potential legal basis for imposition of health care malpractice liability, including professional negligence; breach of a therapeutic contractual promise made by a provider to a patient; patient or client injury from dangerously defective care-related equipment or other products (strict product liability); strict (absolute, non–fault-based) liability for abnormally dangerous care-related activities; and patient or client injury that results from intentional provider misconduct in the course of patient care, may be included in the definition of health care malpractice.

Most of the above bases of malpractice liability-negligence, intentional conduct, and product and strict liability are classified as "torts" (French for "wrongs"), a class of legal actions that includes most private physical and mental injuries except breach of contract actions. Torts are classified as private actions, because they involve injuries personal to private parties, in contrast to crimes, which are public actions, or wrongs against society as a whole.

Two Formulations for the Definition of Health Care Malpractice

Traditional narrow definition: Professional (care-related) negligence only

Broad definition (trend): Any potential legal basis for imposition of liability, including:

- *professional negligence*
- *breach of a patient-professional contractual promise*
- *liability for defective care-related equipment or products that injure patients or clients*
- *strict liability (absolute liability without regard for fault) for abnormally dangerous care-related professional activities*
- *intentional care-related provider misconduct conduct*

The broad definition of health care malpractice is superior to the traditional definition in several respects. From a risk management perspective, its inclusiveness helps to focus the attention of health care system and organization managers, educators, and clinicians on more parameters than just professional negligence. Also, it serves to make everyone in the health care system aware of the fact that the legal system exists to protect the broadest range of rights of patients and clients.

PROFESSIONAL NEGLIGENCE

Professional negligence by health care providers involves delivery of patient care that falls below the standards expected of ordinary, reasonable practitioners of the same profession acting under the same or similar circumstances. Professional negligence involves, then, care that falls below the minimal acceptable standards for practice, or substandard care. To be professionally negligent means that the provider did or failed to do something in the course of patient examination, evaluation, intervention, or follow-up that other similarly situated health care professionals would not accept as constituting minimally acceptable care. Put still another way, professional negligence is legally actionable carelessness. Negligent patient care documentation by a provider, when it causes patient injury, constitutes legally actionable professional negligence-based health care malpractice.

Whether care is negligent is usually determined at trial by expert testimony by one or more professional peers. To qualify as an expert, such a witness must be familiar with (1) the care-related procedure in issue in the case and (2) the standard of care of the defendant-health care provider's discipline in the relevant geographical frame of reference at the time that care and alleged patient injury took place.

Qualifications of an Expert Witness Testifying on the Legal Standard of Care

In-depth knowledge of:

1. the health care examination, evaluation, or intervention-related issue in the case; and
2. the applicable standard of care at the time that care was rendered

---

A patient suing a health care professional for malpractice must prove four elements at trial: (1) that the provider owed the patient a professional duty of care; (2) that the provider violated or breached the duty owed; (3) that the violation of the standard of care caused physical and/or mental injury to the patient; and (4) that, as a result, the patient is entitled to money "damages" in order to make the patient as whole again as possible. The standard (or burden) of proof for proving each of these required elements in civil malpractice trials is "preponderance of the evidence," which equates to "more likely than not" that the trier of fact (jury or judge acting as fact-finder in a judge-alone trial) believes that the patient-plaintiff's evidence presented at trial is more credible than that of the health professional-defendant.

The Four Requisite Elements of Proof for a Patient-Plaintiff in a Health Care Malpractice Trial:

1. *The provider owed the patient a special duty of due care;*
2. *The provider violated the special duty owed;*
3. *As a result, the patient was injured; and*
4. *The patient is entitled to legally recognized money damages.*

ORDINARY NEGLIGENCE VERSUS PROFESSIONAL NEGLIGENCE

Many clinical situations involving patient injury do not involve professional negligence, but only ordinary or general negligence. Ordinary negligence, even when it occurs in the health care clinical setting, does not constitute health care malpractice.

A common form of ordinary or general negligence involves what is termed "premises liability." From falling on a slippery floor surface to being run into by a wheelchair or stretcher to being struck by an ambulance, ordinary premises negligence involves the kinds of careless mishaps that can occur in any physical settings—from a retail store to a college or university to a public street or sidewalk. Ordinary negligence, then, is not health care malpractice, as it is not directly care-related. For that reason, with ordinary negligence, an injured patient usually need not introduce expert testimony to attempt to show a breach of the professional standard of care, because everyday situations such as slips and falls are within the common knowledge of lay jurors, who thus do not need experts to explain the mechanism of injury to them.

PROFESSIONAL STANDARD OF CARE

When cases do involve allegations of professional negligence, the plaintiff must usually establish the applicable standard of care and its breach by the defendant-health care provider. There are three different formulations of the standard of care in effect within various jurisdictions in the United States. Under the traditional view, health care professionals are compared with reasonably competent peers practicing only in the exact same community. This standard originally was applied to prevent prejudicing rural health care providers who lacked comparable access to the modern technology and resources available to urban-based colleagues. Modernly, this standard is no longer applicable in most states.

The current majority rule is to compare a defendant-health care professional with reasonably competent peers practicing in either the same or similar communities. In one reported physical therapy malpractice case, *Novey v. Kishawaukee Community Health Services*, the court ruled that an occupational therapist lacked legal competence to testify about whether a physical therapist met or breached the standard of care, because occupational therapy and physical therapy are different "schools of medicine."[4] This case potentially has broad implications for health care professionals attempting to testify for or against health care professional-litigants of different disciplines on the litigant-professional's legal standard of care. (The extent of influence of the *Novey* decision on future cases depends on whether state or federal judges in cases outside of the state choose to adopt the decision as precedent. State court judges hearing cases outside the state in which a case is heard are not bound by law to follow the decision reached.)

The trend regarding the standard of care is to apply a state- or nationwide standard to all health professionals of a given discipline and compare a defendant charged with health care malpractice with reasonably competent peers acting under the same or similar circumstances, without regard to geographical limitations. Courts (by case law) and legislatures (by statute) are imposing this standard more and more, because of standardization of education and training and because of advances in communications technology that remove the former disadvantages of rural or isolated practitioners. The standard of care for board-certified clinical specialists is also a uniform national standard of care.[5]

Three Formulations for the Legal Standard of Care for Health Care Professionals

The three formulations for the legal standard of health care clinical practice all compare the defendant in a health care malpractice case with reasonably competent peers and ask whether such a peer would or could reasonably have acted like the defendant under the same or similar circumstances as existed in a pending lawsuit. The three formulations differ only in their geographical frame of reference.

1. *Traditional rule: Compare defendant with peers in the same community.*
2. *Modern majority rule: Compare defendant with peers in the same community or in similar communities, state- or nationwide.*
3. *Trend: Compare defendant with any or all peers, state- or nation-wide, acting under the same or similar circumstances.*

RES IPSA LOQUITUR: INFERENCES AND PRESUMPTIONS OF HEALTH PROFESSIONAL NEGLIGENCE

Occasionally, a health care malpractice plaintiff will be unable, for reasons beyond the plaintiff's control, to prove that care-related injuries were caused by a breach of the duty of professional care by the defendant. For example, a comatose patient who is injured during surgery cannot testify about the cause of the injuries. Under such circumstances, courts will infrequently permit negligence to be (voluntarily) inferred (or [mandatorily] presumed in some states) against a health care professional-defendant, under a legal principle called *res ipsa loquitur* (Latin for "the thing [i.e., injury] speaks for itself").

If negligence is merely inferable, a jury is free to infer negligence against the defendant or not, at its will. If, however, negligence is legally presumed, then the burden shifts to the defendant to produce sufficient evidence to rebut the presumption of negligence. For example, assume hypothetically that a comatose patient sustained a broken femur during or about the time that a defendant-registered nurse administered passive range of motion. If, under *res ipsa loquitur*, negligence is inferred, the jury deciding the case is free to disregard the inference, irrespective of whether the nurse's attorney puts forward evidence in an attempt to rebut the inference of negligence. If, however, negligence is presumed, the legal burden shifts from the plaintiff to the nurse's counsel to introduce evidence to rebut the presumption of negligence. Such evidence might consist of testimony of a radiologist who read the patient's radiographs while the patient was an inpatient (called a fact, or percipient, witness) that the patient suffered from severe osteoporosis, which might have caused the femoral fracture.

For the doctrine of *res ipsa loquitur* to apply and relieve the plaintiff of carrying the sole legal burden of production of evidence in a case, three factors must be present. First, the plaintiff's injuries must be the kinds that normally do not happen absent negligence on somebody's part. Second, the defendant-health care provider must have exercised exclusive control over the instrumentality that caused the plaintiff's injuries. Finally, the plaintiff must not have been contributorily negligent in causing the injury in issue.

Res Ipsa Loquitur—When Negligence Is Inferred or Presumed without Proof by the Patient

1. *The patient's injury was the kind that normally does not occur absent negligence;*
2. *The defendant-health care provider exercised exclusive control over the treatment or modality that caused the patient injury; and*
3. *The patient was not contributorily negligent in causing the injury.*

One reported physical therapy malpractice case, *Greater Southeast Community Hospital Foundation v. Walker,*[6] concerned a patient burned by a hot pack. In that case, the trial court allowed an inference of negligence under *res ipsa loquitur*. On appeal, the court reversed (disallowed) the verdict at the trial level in favor of the patient because testimony at trial had raised a question as to whether the patient had manipulated the hot pack during treatment. With such a question unresolved, it was ruled that it was improper to invoke *res ipsa loquitur* because the hot pack might not have been under the therapist's exclusive control, but also under the patient's control, and the patient might have been contributorily negligent for having manipulated the hot pack.

DEFENSES TO HEALTH CARE MALPRACTICE ACTIONS

Two important defenses available to defendant-health care professionals, among many others, are the statute of limitations and comparative fault. The former is a procedural defense, and the latter is a substantive defense.

Statutes of Limitations

Statutes of limitations are legislatively enacted laws in effect in every state that limit the time period within which a private plaintiff in a civil case, or a prosecutor in a criminal case, may commence a lawsuit. There are often special rules applicable to health care malpractice, which vary from state to state. Generally, though, the "time clock" begins to run against a patient when the patient discovers or reasonably should have discovered that he or she was injured and knows the source (but not necessarily the cause) of the injury. The running of statutes of limitations may be interrupted or "tolled" by such factors as continuous treatment by a defendant-provider or infancy or mental incapacitation of a plaintiff.

One reported physical therapy case, *Myers v. Woodall*,[7] concerned different statutes of limitations in effect in the state of the lawsuit for professional and ordinary negligence. What resulted was that the patient, who was allegedly injured while being transported to physical therapy, was held to have the right to sue the aide who transported the patient to physical therapy, but not the physical therapist or the hospital, because the professional statute of limitations had expired. The phenomenon of shortened statutes of limitations for health care malpractice actions, like statutes of repose, is a result of tort reform legislation designed to curb the number of health care malpractice legal actions.

Comparative Fault

Another major defense in health care malpractice legal actions is comparative fault. Comparative fault involves consideration by a judge or jury, not just of a health care professional-defendant's conduct, but also that of the patient-plaintiff. Under comparative fault principles, a defendant's liability may be reduced, or in a few jurisdictions precluded altogether, if the plaintiff violated the expected standard of reasonable care for his or her own safety. There are two formulations for assessing a plaintiff's fault. In contributory negligence jurisdictions, a plaintiff's case is dismissed and the plaintiff has no legal remedy if he or she was in any way contributorily negligent in causing his or her injuries—even one percent or less at fault. Because this "all-or-nothing" rule is so harsh, it has been subject to many exceptions, such as who had the "last clear chance" to prevent patient-plaintiff injury. It is not currently the law in the overwhelming majority of states.

Most states use comparative negligence as their rule when assessing a plaintiff's conduct. In most states using comparative negligence, a plaintiff may still prevail in a legal case if he or she was either (depending on the jurisdiction) less than 50 percent at fault or 50 percent or less at fault. The few comparative negligence jurisdictions allow a plaintiff to recover irrespective of degree of fault. This concept is called "pure" comparative negligence. In a pure comparative negligence state, a patient who was 90 percent at fault for his or her own injuries and who sustained $2 million in damages might still recover $200,000 (10 percent of $2 million).

VICARIOUS LIABILITY

Vicarious liability addresses (in addition to partnership liability) circumstances under which an employer, such as a health care organization or system, bears indirect legal and financial responsibility for the conduct of a person, such as an employee. The concept of vicarious liability dates back to ancient times and, in legal circles, is often referred to by its Latin name, *respondeat superior* ("let the master answer").

Employer Vicarious Liability

The basic rule of vicarious liability is that an employer is indirectly liable for the job-related conduct of an employee when the wrongdoer ("tort-feasor") is acting within the scope of his or her employment at the time the negligence occurred. Therefore, when a hospital-based primary health care provider is alleged to have committed professional negligence or care-related intentional misconduct such as sexual battery while treating a patient, the hospital employing the provider may be required to pay a money judgment if the provider's negligence or intentional misconduct is proven in court.

An employer's indirect responsibility for an employee's negligence does not excuse the individual provider who actually committed the negligence from financial responsibility. The tort-feasor is always personally responsible for the consequences of his or her own conduct. The concept of vicarious liability, however, gives the tort victim another party (usually with more available assets) to make a claim against or to sue. When an employer is required to pay a settlement or judgment for the negligence of an employee, the employer then has the legal right to seek indemnification from the employee for this monetary outlay.

One might ask if it is fair to impose liability on an employer who is innocent of any wrongdoing. In balancing the considerations between an innocent patient-victim and an equally innocent employer, the legal system weighs in favor of the patient. There are several good reasons for this. First, it is the employer, not the patient, who is best equipped to control the quality of care rendered by its health care providers. Second, the employer earns revenue from the official activities of its employees and contractors and should, therefore, bear responsibility for the activities that generate such revenue. Third, the employer is better able to bear the risk of financial loss—through economic loss allocation (e.g., purchasing liability insurance and, to a lesser degree under managed care and cost-containment, establishing prices for health professional services) as part of the cost of doing business.

An employer may be held vicariously liable for wrongdoing by others who are not employees. In the relatively few cases addressing the issue, courts also have imposed vicarious liability on hospitals for the negligence of volunteers, equating unpaid volunteers with employees. For this reason, hospitals and clinics using the services of volunteers should carry liability insurance for volunteers' activities and include them in orientation to relevant policies and procedures, including work place safety measures.

Partnership Vicarious Liability

Another area of vicarious liability involves general partnerships, wherein each partner is considered to be the legal agent of the other partner. Absent an unambiguous express agreement to the contrary, each partner normally is vicariously liable for the other partner's negligent acts or omissions committed within the scope of activities of the partnership.

Exceptions to Vicarious Liability

Intentional Misconduct

There are several important exceptions to vicarious liability. Although an employer may be liable for employees' negligence, the employer may not be legally responsible for unforeseeable intentional misconduct committed by its employees. An example of such unforeseeable intentional misconduct in the health care setting might include the commission of sexual battery on a patient by an emergency room security guard or another patient. (Such conclusions about vicarious liability are acutely case-specific and involve considerations of whether the employer undertook all available reasonable steps to ensure patient safety.)

Independent Contractors and Their Employees

Another exception to vicarious liability concerns independent contractors, including contract agency health care providers and their staffs. The legal system distinguishes employees, for whom an employer generally is legally responsible, from contractors, for whom an employer generally is not legally responsible. This distinction is based primarily on the degree of control the employer exercises over the physical details of the professional's work product.

In some cases, courts may hold employers vicariously liable even for contractors' actions under a legal theory called apparent agency. When a contract health care provider in a clinic is indistinguishable from an employee in the eyes of patients, for example, the law may treat the contract health care provider as an employee for purposes of vicarious liability. Therefore, prudent health care employers should take appropriate steps to ensure that patients know when they are being treated by contract professionals rather than by employees (e.g., by requiring contractors to wear name tags that identify their status as contract personnel and/or by posting photographs identifying employees and contract professionals in a clinic reception area).

Primary Employer Liability for Actions of Employees and Contractors

A health care organization or system may be directly or primarily liable for employees' or contractors' conduct. Such liability exists independent of any vicarious liability that may also apply. An employer is directly liable under the legal concepts of negligent selection and retention, for example, for the wrongful actions of employees or contractors whom the employer reasonably should have (1) rejected for employment, (2) carried out remediation for deficiencies, or (3) discharged from employment.

Under law, hospitals and private clinics have certain responsibilities that they may not delegate to employees, professional medical staff, or independent contractors, under a legal concept called "corporate liability." Such responsibilities are called "nondelegable duties." Under corporate liability theories, courts have imposed various nondelegable duties on hospitals, including, among others: (1) a duty to use due care when selecting, privileging, and reprivileging physicians and surgeons and when evaluating the credentials and privileges (as applicable) of other primary health care providers; (2) a duty to ensure that premises and medical equipment are safe and adequate for patients, visitors, and staff; (3) a duty to establish patient care quality standards for their organizations and departments and divisions and to monitor and evaluate the quality of patient care on an ongoing basis; and (4) a duty to monitor continuously the competence of professional and support personnel within the facility.[8]

LIABILITY FOR PATIENT ABANDONMENT

Legally actionable abandonment of a patient occurs when a health care provider improperly unilaterally terminates a professional relationship with a patient and may be classified either as professional negligence or intentional misconduct, depending on the circumstances of the abandonment of the patient. Many patient care-related activities can constitute actionable abandonment, from momentarily leaving a patient unattended to refusing to work overtime during an emergency. While a health care provider has almost absolute discretion in electing whether to form a professional relationship with a patient, certain legal rules must be complied with to terminate an existing patient-professional relationship properly. The law imposes a special duty of care on a health care provider caring for a patient, similar to the special duty owed by an attorney to a client or a parent or guardian to a child under his or her charge.

Patient abandonment is a more salient issue because of managed care, under which considerations of cost containment may cause third-party payers to limit patient care to a set number of visits. Health care clinical professionals, not administrators or clerical personnel, are legally charged to determine the duration of patient care. Clinicians must seek appeal of administrative length-of-care decisions adverse to their patients and in contravention to their clinical judgment. Careful and appropriate documentation of justifications and rationale for such appeals (in patient records and memoranda not filed in patient care records) are crucial to minimize the likelihood of patient abandonment liability for clinical health care professionals.

Termination of the health care provider-patient relationship is justified when the patient makes a knowing, voluntary election to end the relationship, either unilaterally or jointly with the provider. The provider may *unilaterally* terminate the professional relationship with the patient when a medical condition under care has resolved. Unilateral termination of the relationship by the provider also properly may occur when, in a rehabilitation health professional's judgment, the patient has reached the zenith of his or her rehabilitative potential. Such a situation requires careful documentation in the patient's care record that will pass legal scrutiny should a health care malpractice action arise. (How to document such a situation and others discussed herein are addressed in later chapters.) Also, a health care professional must always communicate the fact that the patient has been discharged to a referring entity, any time a patient has received care pursuant to a referral.

Negligent Abandonment

If a patient claims that he or she was discharged prematurely, then the legal action that results may be a professional negligence-based health care malpractice action. As with any other health professional negligence case, the plaintiff-patient will have to prove four elements by a preponderance, or the greater weight, of evidence: (1) that the provider owed a duty of care to the patient; (2) that the provider violated the duty by negligently unilaterally terminating the professional relationship prematurely; (3) that the provider's improper discharge of the patient caused harm to the patient ("causation"); and (4) that the patient suffered legally cognizable damages, such as pain and suffering, additional medical expenses, and lost wages, that warrant the award of money damages in order to attempt to make the patient whole.

Intentional Abandonment

In contrast to negligent abandonment of a patient, a health care provider may also be charged with intentional abandonment of a patient, which carries with it more serious adverse consequences. As an intentional tort, intentional abandonment carries with it the possibility of a punitive (exemplary) damages award should the patient prevail at trial. In most cases, the defendant's professional liability insurer will not be obligated (or even permitted) to indemnify the insured if the intentional conduct is adjudged to be sufficiently egregious to justify the imposition of punitive damages against the defendant-health care provider.

Intentional abandonment might involve situations in which a patient is discharged for reasons such as failure to pay a bill, a personality conflict with a health care professional, or an insurance denial of reimbursement for further care. Under such circumstances, the provider must, at a minimum, give advance notice to the patient of the provider's intent to terminate the relationship; give the patient a reasonable amount of time to find a suitable substitute health care provider (if applicable); and assist the patient in finding a suitable substitute health care provider. Any information about the patient—examination findings, diagnosis, or intervention-related data—must be communicated to the substitute care provider expeditiously. The provider transferring the patient must be sure to document in the patient's record the patient's relevant status at the time of discharge. As a risk management measure, such a provider transferring a patient should also carefully memorialize in documentation the steps undertaken to assist the patient in finding a substitute care provider in an office memorandum, which should be retained for the period of the statute of limitations and then only disposed of under advisement of the provider's or health care organization's legal counsel.

Substitute Health Care Providers

Two special situations bear mentioning. One basis for an abandonment complaint might be that a health care provider left a patient in the care of a substitute health care provider while the original provider went on vacation, to a conference, or elsewhere on personal business. In settings in which patients contract for care with specific named clinicians, such as may occur in the private practice setting, such providers must be sure to obtain and document the patients' informed consent before transferring care to substitute health care providers. In hospital and health maintenance organization (HMO) settings, by contrast, patients do not normally contract for care with specific nonphysician health care providers, such as physical and occupational therapists, nurses, dietitians, social workers, and others, so the issue of abandonment during vacations and other periods of coverage does not normally arise for these providers in such settings.

Abandonment Issues in the Limited Scope Practice Setting

Another problem concerns providers such as psychologists, social workers, physical and occupational therapists, nurse practitioners, nutrition care professionals, and other health care professionals who operate limited scope practices. Consider as an example a physical therapist specializing exclusively in the care of pediatric and adolescent patients with orthopedic or sports-related injuries. Is such a provider at liberty to refuse to treat an unrelated condition involving a current patient? The answer is probably "yes"; however, the clinician must inform the patient before forming the professional-patient relationship of the limited nature of his or her practice and gain the patient's informed consent to undergo limited scope care. Effective documentation of the patient's informed consent to limited scope care can be crucial in avoiding health care malpractice liability should a claim or lawsuit arise.

When a Health Care Professional May Be Required To "Abandon" a Patient

Certain circumstances may require a treating health care professional to disengage from caring for a patient, such as when the provider terminates his or her employment with a hospital or clinic or when a patient's third-party reimbursement for care terminates. Depending on the circumstances in each particular case, such a provider may be required to continue necessary care on a *pro bono*, or free-of-charge basis, even when third-party reimbursement terminates. Providers and health care organizations should always consult with their attorneys before discharging patients still in need of care under such circumstances.

BASES OF LIABILITY OTHER THAN NEGLIGENCE

The vast majority of reported health care malpractice legal cases involve allegations of professional negligence by providers. This is so in large part because courts are reluctant to allow patients to sue for non–negligence-based breach of contract in the health care setting, in part because of the special status relationship between health care professionals and patients. Similarly, courts hesitate to permit patients to sue health care providers over injuries from defective products because the delivery of health care is generally viewed as the rendition of a professional service, not the sale of a product. This fact, however, is changing as more and more health care professionals market and sell products in their clinical practices in order to generate necessary revenue in the managed care practice environment. In such cases, courts may permit imposition of strict product liability when dangerously defectively designed or manufactured health care products injure patients, their family members, and other third parties.

Few health care malpractice cases generally are premised exclusively on the issue of a lack of informed consent. Still, this area of legal responsibility is of great importance for all clinicians because every primary health care provider is legally and ethically responsible for obtaining patients' informed consent before treatment. This important area of malpractice law is explored in greater detail in Chapter 4.

OTHER SETTINGS AND CONSEQUENCES OF MALPRACTICE ACTIONS

Criminal Proceedings for Conduct That Also Constitutes Malpractice

Besides a civil malpractice lawsuit, a health professional alleged to engage in gross negligence, reckless conduct, or intentional misconduct may face criminal legal proceedings[9] and adverse administrative actions before licensure boards and certification entities. Criminal actions, such as civil malpractice lawsuits, are judicial proceedings but differ in that a state or federal prosecutor brings the criminal case against the defendant on behalf of public interests, rather than the interests of an individual victim. Because the prospective penalties are more severe, the standard of proof—beyond a reasonable doubt—is much higher than the preponderance of evidence (or greater weight of evidence) standard generally in effect in civil court.

The consequences of a finding of liability in a civil malpractice trial and a finding of guilt in a criminal trial are also different. If a civil defendant is adjudged liable, the patient-plaintiff normally is awarded compensatory money damages for expenses such as lost wages, medical expenses, pain and suffering, loss of enjoyment of life, and property losses. Normally, a civil defendant's insurer indemnifies the insured and pays off such a money judgment. In egregious cases involving reckless or intentional misconduct, a civil jury or judge may award punitive damages to a plaintiff, for which a defendant's insurer might lawfully refuse to indemnify. The penalties for a criminal defendant found guilty of a crime normally are limited to incarceration (or the threat of incarceration, i.e., probation) and a monetary fine.

Administrative and Professional Affiliation Actions

Adverse administrative actions affecting licensure and/or certification and the ability to practice one's profession may be taken by state administrative licensing agencies and certification entities and, in the case of licensure, typically require a hearing to protect the constitutional due process rights of the respondent (equivalent of defendant). Private professional association actions affecting professional association membership may likewise result from health care malpractice actions that involve professional ethical infractions.

MALPRACTICE TRIAL PRACTICE AND PROCEDURES

Roles of Health Care Professionals in Malpractice Proceedings

A health care provider can take one of three roles in a civil malpractice proceeding: fact witness, expert witness, or defendant. The fact witness is probably the most familiar role. Also called an eyewitness or percipient witness, the fact witness possesses relevant firsthand knowledge about the issues and merits of a legal case important to one or both sides. A percipient witness might include a health care clinician, aide, or chaperone who carried out or observed patient care activities involving a patient-litigant. Like experts and defendants, fact witnesses may be called upon to answer questions in interviews or under oath in depositions by one or both parties in a case during the pretrial, case-building "discovery" phase of the trial process. Fact witnesses normally do not have the discretion to withhold their testimony or admissible opinions, and they normally testify subject to a subpoena or court order. Fact witnesses are normally reimbursed according to fixed (low) statutory fee schedules, rather than being allowed the opportunity to negotiate higher fees with the party calling them to testify, as are experts.

Primary nonphysician health care professionals find themselves more frequently in the role of health care malpractice defendant, as disciplines other than medicine are increasingly swept up in the malpractice litigation crisis. As a party defendant, a health care professional faces serious adverse professional and personal consequences should a verdict be rendered against him or her, including monetary loss, loss of reputation and goodwill, and adverse administrative actions at the state and federal levels. This fact is not presented with the intention to frighten health care providers but rather to familiarize them with the legal system and its processes and to make them aware of the need to seek out and obtain legal representation expeditiously whenever a potentially compensable event such as a patient injury ripens into a claim or lawsuit. It is vitally important to follow legal counsel's advice and, in particular, to refrain from talking about any potential or actual legal action against you with anyone except counsel or counsel's agents (e.g., paralegal professionals and investigators working for the health care provider's attorney). The same admonition applies to written correspondence about a pending case when you are a health care malpractice defendant. Don't send any out, without legal counsel's review and concurrence.

Pretrial Proceedings

A health care provider must notify his or her facility legal department, personal insurance representative, and personal attorney (if applicable) immediately on receipt of any legal papers concerning a patient's care. When a lawsuit is filed, the first papers served normally are the "summons" (notice of lawsuit) and the "complaint" (specifying an incident allegedly causing patient injury and the amount of money damages sought). An insurer will expeditiously assign legal counsel to the case to file an "answer" to the patient-plaintiff's "pleadings."

Once the complaint, answer, and other responsive papers have been exchanged and filed with the court having "jurisdiction" (control) over the case, pretrial discovery begins in earnest. The parties to the lawsuit may require each other (but not each other's witnesses) to answer formal questions called "interrogatories." The defendant-health care provider may even be called on by the plaintiff to concede liability in what is called a "request for admissions." Documents, including patient treatment records, will be requested by the patient's attorney, and other tangible evidence, such as instrument and equipment used in the course of treatment, may have to be produced for inspection by the plaintiff's expert(s).

Depositions: Procedures and Precautions

The deposition is probably the most familiar discovery device because many health care professionals have undergone deposition as witnesses or potential or actual malpractice defendants in the past. A deposition consists of sworn testimony of a party or potential party to a lawsuit, or of a fact or expert witness. It is usually taken in the office of the attorney representing the "deponent" (person being deposed) or in another seemingly informal environment. To reduce stress, try to avoid being deposed at your health care organization, where, among other things, interruptions by staff, patients, vendors, and others might affect your concentration on the legal proceedings.

Irrespective of where a deposition takes place, do not as a deponent be lulled into a false sense of security because of the apparent informality of the deposition process. A deposition is a serious legal proceeding, the consequences of which are as important as trial testimony. A court reporter transcribes every word—formal and informal—that every participant in the deposition says. The transcribed deposition may later be introduced at trial, especially to refute trial testimony as inconsistent with prior sworn testimony given at the deposition.

If health care professionals reading this section take just one piece of advice from it, it is that they should never undergo a deposition either as a witness or defendant without prior consultation with and preparation by an attorney. This does not mean that every deponent needs to have an attorney present to represent him or her at deposition. Bear in mind, though, that a health professional deponent called merely as a witness to an event one day may be named as a health care malpractice defendant the next day as a result of deposition testimony. One of the primary purposes of depositions is for attorneys for both plaintiff(s) and defendant(s) to discover relevant facts that will lead to evidence that will enable them to prevail at trial or facilitate a pretrial settlement of the case.

Health Care Professionals as Expert Witnesses

The overwhelming majority of malpractice (and all other legal) cases are disposed of through means short of resorting to trial, principally through pretrial settlement. Should a health care malpractice case progress to trial, however, the verdict will probably turn on expert testimony. Health care professionals may qualify as experts for many purposes (e.g., as rehabilitation consultants on a patient-plaintiff's rehabilitation or vocational needs or potential). However, the principal area in which they testify as experts in malpractice proceedings is as clinical experts on whether a defendant-health care provider's treatment of a patient-plaintiff met or breached the legal standard of care.

An expert witness on the standard of care may testify for either the patient-plaintiff or for the health care provider or organization-defendant. To meet the legal standard of care and avoid being adjudged negligent, a clinical health care professional caring for a patient must exercise that special knowledge and skill characteristic of reasonably competent peers acting under the same or similar circumstances. More specifically, a health care professional must use examination, evaluative, diagnostic, prognostic, and intervention techniques and procedures that constitute at least minimally acceptable professional practice. Always bear in mind that legally acceptable care equates to minimally acceptable standards of practice, not necessarily what is optimal or even average.

Before testifying as an expert on a professional standard of care, a witness must first be qualified as legally "competent," based on expertise concerning the specific aspect of patient care at issue in the case. Oftentimes, the opponent's attorney will offer to stipulate to the qualifications of an expert witness. In such a case, the judge and jury do not have an opportunity to hear about the expert's academic background, professional publication history, or other individual attributes and achievements. Counsel proffering a witness as an expert may wish, in such situations, to seek the court's permission to enter the witness's qualifications into the record anyway. This exposure to the expert's qualifications will enhance the credibility of the expert in the eyes of the fact finder and may lead to the fact finder giving greater weight to the expert's testimony and opinions during deliberations on liability.

All health care professionals should consider it a civic duty to honor a request by an attorney or a court or other public agency to testify as an expert on the standard of care in a case or administrative legal action. If health professionals from the same discipline as a defendant under charges do not come forward and assume responsibility for so testifying, members of other disciplines may fill the void and opine on another profession's practice standards, perhaps in an incomplete or incorrect manner. Attorneys and judges in individual cases will normally seek out appropriate expert witnesses from academic and clinical settings or through referral by litigants and others in the trial process.

With tens of millions of civil lawsuits filed or pending in state and federal courts in the United States, far ahead of all other civilized nations, there clearly is a serious litigation crisis. In larger or relatively more litigious states, civil cases, including health care malpractice lawsuits, take many years to come to trial.

THE NATIONAL PRACTITIONER DATA BANK

Since September 1990, whenever money (in any sum) is paid to a patient-plaintiff or his or her representative, either in settlement or by way of a court judgment in a health care malpractice case, information about the responsible health care provider must be forwarded to the Department of Health and Human Services for inclusion in the National Practitioner Data Bank (NPDB). This data bank was established pursuant to the Health Care Quality Improvement Act of 1986.[10]

Another important purpose of the data bank is to compile data concerning adverse licensure and credentialing actions involving licensed health care providers. Together, malpractice payment reporting and adverse actions reporting are intended to create a record that follows licensed health care professionals included in the data bank wherever in the United States they might seek employment.

Employers of licensed health care professionals are required under the statute to query the data bank regarding new employees and at regular intervals thereafter. The information is deemed strictly confidential and normally is not "discoverable" by patients or their attorneys. Nor is NPDB information available to the general public.

TORT REFORM

Most state legislatures have undertaken, since the advent of the litigation and health care malpractice crises, measures labeled as "tort reform" to decrease the number of civil lawsuits. Some of the tort reform measures enacted by various states include:

- Requiring that a health care malpractice plaintiff undergo an administrative hearing on the merits of his or her case before proceeding to trial.
- Capping maximum noneconomic money damages for pain and suffering and loss of enjoyment of life.
- Limiting attorney contingent fees (contingent fees are based on percentages of recovery fees bargained for between attorneys and clients).
- Reforming *joint and several liability* to prevent one defendant from being required to pay an entire judgment when that defendant is only partially responsible for a plaintiff's injuries.
- Setting absolute time limits—based on the date of injury or manufacture of a product—within which legal action must be commenced (called *statutes of repose*).
- Relaxing the *collateral source rule,* under which juries are prevented from learning of a plaintiff's collateral sources of compensation for injuries, including insurance coverage or partial payments by other defendants.
- Penalizing attorneys and their clients for initiating lawsuits deemed to be frivolous, especially in the federal courts.
- Withholding from plaintiffs (and depositing in state treasuries) a percentage of any "punitive" (punishment) damages awarded to them by juries in product liability actions.[11]

CONCLUSION

All health care professionals, organizations, and systems are affected by the litigation and health care malpractice crisis, characterized by increasing numbers of claims and lawsuits, including those brought by patients claiming injury. The overwhelming majority of health care malpractice cases are based on allegations of professional negligence or substandard delivery of care. Whether a health care provider retrospectively met or violated minimally acceptable practice standards is normally determined through testimony of expert witnesses or reference to relevant professional texts, peer-reviewed journals, and practice standards, guidelines, and protocols.

Employers of health care providers may be vicariously or indirectly liable for employees', volunteers', and even independent contractors' commission of health care malpractice. Health care organizations may also be independently liable for violating nondelegable duties owed to patients and others, including the duty to select and retain only competent health care professionals; the duty to maintain safe premises and equipment; and the duty to oversee the quality of patient care provided in their facilities. Clinical managers and practitioners also need to carefully establish procedures delineating the circumstances under which health care providers may disengage from further care of patients in order to minimize allegations of negligent or intentional patient abandonment. This issue is particularly important under cost containment-focused managed care

Health care providers must expeditiously notify their facility risk managers, insurers, and personal legal representatives whenever an incident occurs in the clinic that might conceivably ripen into a claim or lawsuit. Such occurrences are called potentially compensable events. A claim of health care malpractice ripens into formal legal civil proceedings when a defendant-health care provider receives a summons and complaint specifying the basis of the alleged malpractice and a demand for money damages or other relief.

One of the most important pretrial proceedings is the deposition, in which parties and witnesses to malpractice lawsuits undergo examination under oath by the parties' attorneys. Never go into a deposition, either as a witness or defendant, without prior consultation and preparation by legal counsel. The deposition serves several important functions, including locking in sworn testimony weeks, months, or years before trial and discovering facts that might lead to relevant evidence in the case.

The consequences of health care malpractice legal actions are potentially devastating for both patients affected by substandard care and health care professionals whose reputations and personal well-being are affected by such allegations, whether or not the allegations are true. Licensed health care professionals on whose behalf malpractice judgments or settlements are paid face the additional penalty of having their names included in the National Practitioner Data Bank, maintained by the federal Department of Health and Human Services. For these reasons, and for the protection of patients and health care professionals alike, management of health care malpractice risk in clinical practice, particularly through creating and maintaining accurate, complete, objective, and timely documentation of patient care activities, is critically important.

The United States (regrettably) is the most litigious nation on earth. In an effort to stem the numbers of civil lawsuits initiated in state and federal courts, courts and legislatures are taking actions to dampen the malpractice fervor through procedural and substantive restrictions on plaintiffs' ability to bring civil tort lawsuits. Such measures collectively are called tort reform. Resort to alternative dispute resolution—mediation and arbitration—is another means of lessening the number of formal civil lawsuits in the long pipeline.

REFERENCES

1. B.R. FURROW ET AL., HEALTH LAW, 3RD ED. (1997).
2. GUIDE TO PHYSICAL THERAPIST PRACTICE, (1997), Alexandria, VA: American Physical Therapy Association.
3. R.G. Peterson, *Malpractice Liability of Allied Health Professionals: Development in an Area of Critical Concern*, J. ALLIED HEALTH, Nov. 1985, at 363–371.
4. Novey v. Kishawaukee Community Health Serv., 531 N.E.2d 430 (Ill. App. Ct. 1989).
5. Shilkret v. Annapolis Emergency Hosp. Ass'n, 349 A.2d 245 (Md. 1975). *See also* Restatement (2d) of Torts, § 229A, comment (d), which implies that all professionals who hold themselves out as possessing superior knowledge or skill beyond that common to generalists in their profession are judged according to a uniform national standard of care.
6. Greater Southeast Community Hosp. Found. v. Walker, 313 A.2d 105 (D.C. 1973).
7. Myers v. Woodall, 592 P.2d 1343 (Colo. Ct. App. 1979).
8. K.A. Kearney & F.L. McCord, *Hospital Management Faces New Liabilities*, HEALTH LAW, Fall 1992, at 1–6.
9. P.R. Van Grunsven, *Medical Malpractice or Criminal Mistake? An Analysis of Past and Current Criminal Prosecutions for Clinical Mistakes and Fatal Errors*, DE PAUL J. OF HEALTH CARE LAW, 1998; 2(1):1–54.
10. 42 U.S.C. § 11101–11152.
11. M. Geyelin, *States Claim Share of Awards in Liability Suits*, WALL ST. J., Mar. 3, 1993, at B1, 11.

SUGGESTED READING

R.L. Gitchell and A. Plattner, *Mediation: A Viable Alternative to Litigation for Medical Malpractice Cases*. DE PAUL J. OF HEALTH CARE LAW, 1999; 2(3):421–459.

D.L.LEITNER, MANAGED CARE LIABILITY, (1996); Chicago: American Bar Association (Tort and Insurance Practice Section).

R.E. Ostel, *The National Practitioner Data Bank: The First Four Years*. 110 PUBLIC HEALTH REPORTS 383 (1995).

R.W. SCOTT, HEALTH CARE MALPRACTICE: A PRIMER ON LEGAL ISSUES, 2ND ED (1999); New York: McGraw-Hill, Inc.

R.W. SCOTT, PROFESSIONAL ETHICS: A GUIDE FOR REHABILITATION PROFESSIONALS, (1998); St. Louis, MO: Mosby Year-book, Inc.

R.W. SCOTT, PROMOTING LEGAL AWARENESS IN PHYSICAL AND OCCUPATIONAL THERAPY, (1997); St. Louis, MO: Mosby Year-book, Inc.

REVIEW: CASE STUDIES

The following case examples involve hypothetical situations and are not based on actual health care malpractice cases, published or unpublished. The characters are fictitious and are not intended to represent or resemble any actual health care provider or entity. Any resemblance to actual cases, situations, individuals, or entities is coincidental and unintended.

1. A is a physical therapist caring for B, a patient with a medical diagnosis of cerebrovascular accident. B was properly referred to A by C, a physiatrist, for rehabilitation. After conducting an appropriate examination, formulating evaluative findings, reaching a physical therapy diagnosis and prognosis, and selecting appropriate interventions, A calls B's insurance company for authorization for care. A requests a minimum of 10 visits to care for B. An insurance clerk with B's managed care insurer authorizes only 3 visits based on an administrative algorithm. What steps must A, as fiduciary to B, take to obtain appropriate care for B?

2. X, a hand care patient of Y, an occupational therapist, admits to Y that X is feigning a work-related hand injury to "milk" the workers' compensation system. What documentation steps should Y take?

SUGGESTED ANSWERS AND DISCUSSION

---

1. A should, in similar cases, routinely employ a series of sequential steps: (1) request reconsideration from the clerk at XYZ; (2) demand

to discuss the case with a health care professional reviewer; (3) appeal a denial of necessary care; (4) consider self-pay, lower cost, and/or *pro bono* care, as appropriate; (5) make optimal use of available clinic and home care time to achieve patient care goals; and (6) document, in patient care records and memoranda, as appropriate, discussions with the insurer and deliberations/courses of action regarding care options for B.

2. Y probably is not prevented by legal privilege, and may have a legal duty to disclose X's workers' compensation fraud to authorities. Y should document the circumstances of X's disclosure in an incident report and seek immediate further guidance from his or her supervisor (if any), organization administration (if any), and organization and/or personal legal counsel.

Chapter 2

Clinical Documentation: Methods and Management

This chapter overviews critically important concepts related to the nature and processes of health care clinical documentation. The main purposes of health care documentation are discussed, with emphasis on the principal purpose of health care documentation—the communication of vital health-related information about patients to other health care professionals having an imminent need to know. The chapter also explores the three principal formats for notation and the essential contents of patient treatment records required to meet the legal standard of care. The chapter concludes with discussion of 25 select documentation problems, errors, and suggestions, including case examples.

INTRODUCTION

No business activity in the United States, except perhaps for national defense, is as critically important to the welfare of the citizenry, or as costly, as the delivery of health care. Literally tens of millions of inpatient and outpatient visits—many with life and death consequences for patients—are logged annually throughout the United States. Annual health-related expenditures in the United States are approximately $1 trillion[1]— 14 percent of the gross national product. No business endeavor, including national defense, routinely requires the comprehensive and accurate documentation of client (patient) service (history, examination, evaluation, diagnosis, prognosis, and intervention) to the degree that the health care delivery system does.

As part of the legal duty owed to patients, every primary health care provider is required by legal, professional, and business ethical standards to record clinically pertinent historical, examination, evaluative, and intervention-related information about patients and to maintain that information in the form of patient treatment records. Besides primary health care providers (i.e., those licensed independent practitioners who can legally interact with patients without the requirement of a prior examination and referral by another health care provider), other health care professionals interacting with patients in supportive or consultative roles have the same duty to record patient information (if they are privileged under law and by their organizations to document) and ensure that it is safeguarded.

Who can legally document information in patient records is a matter of federal and state law, organizational or systems policy, and customary practice. For inpatient records, therapeutic orders are normally written by medical physicians and surgeons attending individual patients. In most cases, no one except a physician can record information in the "Physician's Orders" section of an inpatient record, except where so permitted by law and custom, such as when a dental surgeon writes relevant orders for care for a specific patient. In outpatient patient care settings, however, especially in clinical settings in which no physician may be present, intervention orders are routinely written by primary health care providers other than physicians, for example, by physical and occupational therapists, speech therapy professionals, dietitian, nurses, and others.

Patient care records take many forms. Two primary classifications of patient care records include inpatient records and ambulatory, or outpatient, records. (Some authorities consider emergency treatment records as a separate category of patient care records.) While in the past, original patient treatment records were required by law to be handwritten in all jurisdictions, modernly, both inpatient and ambulatory records may be created originally and maintained, either in whole or in part, on a computer in most states.

It is difficult to enunciate a precise definition for a patient care record. In simplest terms, a patient care record is a memorialization of a specific patient's health status at a given point in time. The patient treatment record includes clinically pertinent information that is clear, concise, comprehensive, individualized, accurate, objective, and timely. It serves both as a business document and as the legal record of care rendered to the patient.

From business and clinical perspectives, as well as from a legal standpoint, documentation of patient care is as important as the rendition of care itself. This axiom holds true for the protection of patients and health care professionals alike. For health care providers, patient care documentation is substantive evidence of the nature, extent, and quality of care rendered to patients; while for patients, it serves as a permanent record of their health status, which may, among many other purposes, serve as a historical record for future lifesaving intervention.

> *Documentation of patient care is as important as the rendition of care itself.*

PURPOSES OF PATIENT CARE DOCUMENTATION

The patient care record serves a myriad of important purposes. Primary health care professionals and health care organizations act as fiduciaries, or persons and entities in a special position of trust vis-à-vis patients under their care. Therefore, logically, the primary purpose of patient care documentation is to communicate vital information about a patient's health status to other health care providers concurrently caring for that patient and having an imminent need to know the information contained therein. This principle operates either in an inpatient or ambulatory care setting. The clinical information entered by one health care professional in a patient's record is assimilated by other providers into their intervention plans and incorporated with their goals for patients, to ease discomfort, speed recovery, and maximize function and independence.

Despite what may be suspected by some to be the primary purpose for patient care documentation—self-protection from patient-initiated claims and litigation—this is clearly not the case. That kind of negative approach to documentation serves no positive purpose and only instills fear in health care professionals. Such fear, in turn, fosters an atmosphere of costly defensive health care practice.

A defensive posture regarding patient care documentation may actually increase the chances of malpractice exposure. Patients and their significant others can readily sense a health care provider's defensiveness. They justifiably find distasteful the kind of formal, cold, business-like relationship that inherently results when a health care professional puts fear of malpractice exposure (or other self-interest, such as revenue maximization) ahead of the patient's welfare. If patients come to believe that their health care providers are excessively focused on self-protection from litigation exposure or other selfish considerations, then they may be more inclined to pursue legal actions if and when an adverse outcome results from intervention.

There are many other important, recognized purposes of patient care documentation.[2] Documentation of patient care serves as a basis for planning and for ensuring continuity of care in the future for patients currently under care, particularly for those inpatients who, after discharge, will require health professional intervention at home. By memorializing a patient's health status at any given point, documentation also serves to create a historical record of a given patient's health, from which data can be extracted for, and utilized in, future contingencies, ranging from emergent life-threatening crises to disability determinations.

Documentation also forms the basis for monitoring and evaluating the quality of care rendered to patients as part of a quality management program. Such programs are required of health care facilities accredited by entities such as the Joint Commission on the Accreditation of Healthcare Organizations (Joint Commission), the Commission on Accreditation of Rehabilitation Facilities (CARF), the National Committee on Quality Assurance (NCQA), and others, including local, state, and federal public oversight entities.

Besides its utility as a database for monitoring and evaluating the quality of patient care, patient care documentation is useful as a productivity measure of provider workloads, and to assess whether health care providers are practicing effective utilization management of human and nonhuman health care resources. It also serves, through identifying deficiencies, to ascertain whether there are needs for training for health care providers, from communication skills to substantive aspects of patient care.

As a business document, the patient care record is also evaluated by governmental third-party payer entities such as Medicare, Medicaid, TriCare (for military beneficiaries), and state and local governmental entities, and by insurance companies and other payers to determine levels of reimbursement for patient care. Documentation of patient care, then, is the primary means of justifying reimbursement for treatment. The treatment record also provides information that is useful for scientific and clinical research and for education.

Besides being a business document, the patient care record is a legal document as well. In the event of a health care malpractice claim or lawsuit, providers' documentation of patient care activities provides substantive and relatively objective evidence of the care that was rendered to the patient claiming malpractice. Documented evidence of care recorded in the patient's record provides expert witnesses with a basis from which to form a professional opinion on whether a provider or multiple providers met or violated standards of practice and legal standards of care. Patient care documentation serves many other legal functions, too, including, among others, its use as substantive evidence of work or functional capacity in workers' compensation and similar administrative proceedings.

As an additional legal issue, documentation of patient informed consent protects patients, providers, and health care organizations and systems by serving as written evidence that a patient actually understood the risks and benefits of specific interventions and made a knowing, informed choice to undergo examination and accept recommended interventions. Documentation of a patient's desires in the event of that patient's mental incapacitation through "advance directives" serves also to memorialize patient decisions, evidence respect for patient autonomy, and protect health care professionals who must carry out the patient's valid advance directives.[3]

Purposes of Patient Care Documentation

1. *Communicates vital information about a patient's health status to other health care providers concurrently caring for that patient and having an imminent need to know the information contained therein.*
2. *Acts as a basis for patient-care planning and continuity of care.*
3. *Serves as the primary source of information for monitoring and evaluating the quality of patient care rendered.*
4. *Provides information for reimbursement and utilization review decisions.*
5. *Identifies deficiencies and training needs.*
6. *Serves as a resource for research and education.*
7. *Serves as a business document.*
8. *Serves as a multi-purpose legal document.*
9. *As a legal document, provides substantive evidence on whether providers' care rendered, and health care organizations' oversight of patient care activities, met or violated legal standards of care.*
10. *Specifically concerning informed consent and advance directives, memorializes patient informed consent to examination and inter-*

> *vention, as well as patient desires regarding life-sustaining measures, through advance directives, in the event of a patient's subsequent mental incapacitation.*

CONTENTS OF PATIENT CARE RECORDS

Required contents of patient care records vary greatly, depending on, among other considerations, state and federal laws and regulations, accreditation standards, organization and system requirements, and patient care settings. For hospitalized patients, for example, patient records are typically divided into two parts: (1) intake, or admissions, data, including the relevant patient histories and assessments, physical examinations by admitting physicians (including admission studies and tests) and other primary health care professionals, and the admission diagnosis or diagnoses, and (2) the clinical record, in which progress notes, consultations, laboratory tests, diagnostic imaging studies, operative and anesthesia reports, and discharge summaries are written.[4] Contents of ambulatory patient care records display greater variation.

FORMATS FOR PATIENT CARE DOCUMENTATION

Because communication of patient information to other health care professionals concurrently caring for that patient is of such critical importance, clinicians must ensure that their documentation of a patient's health status is understood by others on the health care team. This section discusses acceptable formats for communicating patient information to others. Practical considerations for effective documentation are considered in the next section.

There are practically only three general patient care documentation formats: narrative format, template (or report) format, and acronym/ initialism format. The simplest form of patient care documentation is in narrative, or free form, format. The prose form of literary composition, used by students in papers, theses, and dissertations, is the most common example of narrative format. Template or report format utilizes word and phrase prompts and blank spaces to generate and record data. The functional outcome report and most computerized documentation systems are primarily in template format. The acronym/initialism format employs alphabetic letters to form words (acronyms) or initialize data. "SOAP" is an example of the acronym format; "P-S-P" (Problem-Status-Plan) is an example of initialism format. The three basic patient care documentation formats may be combined into hybrid formats, and all three are equally amenable to being accessed by computer.

Each of these three formats offers relative advantages and disadvantages. The principal advantages of the narrative format are that it is the most flexible of formats and does not limit the amount of data that writers can annotate. Its disadvantages are that it does not compartmentalize information into readily discernible categories and that it facilitates verbosity by writers. The template or report format's key advantages are that information is neatly compartmentalized and standardization maximized through its use. Its disadvantages include that it may facilitate underdocumentation (e.g., when all blank spaces are not addressed) and that special circumstances may be difficult to address, or may be relegated to a miscellaneous section on the form. Acronym/initialism formats share the compartmentalization advantage that characterizes the template or report format. S-O-A-P format (discussed in greater detail below) is so universally utilized by health care providers and organizations that its use may facilitate faster processing of information by users and thus enhance communication. Its primary disadvantage is that, except for S-O-A-P users, its format may be unfamiliar to other users.

During the past several decades, the problem-oriented model has become the gold standard for patient care documentation.[5] The problem-oriented approach highlights key information, including historical information about a patient and his or her chief complaint; clinical examination findings and objective observations of the examining clinician; the diagnosis (or diagnoses) or evaluative findings; and a proposed plan of intervention for the patient. In essence, both acronym/initialism and template/report formats are problem-oriented. Narrative patient care documentation, on the other hand, often makes critical patient information difficult to locate expeditiously.

More on S-O-A-P

In S-O-A-P format, patient information is compartmentalized into four main sections of an initial note: the subjective element ("S"), the objective element ("O"), the assessment ("A"), and the plan ("P"). Collectively, these elements are the problem-oriented S-O-A-P note documentation model. Under the S-O-A-P note format, health care professionals can quickly access pertinent information recorded by another provider who conducted a prior examination of a patient by referring to the four elements of the S-O-A-P note.

The "S," or subjective, element of a rehabilitation-setting initial S-O-A-P note includes the following information: (1) a patient's medical diagnosis (or diagnoses); (2) a summary of the patient's relevant health history taken from the patient interview and from a review of the patient's available records; (3) the patient's expression of his or her condition, including parameters of symptoms, such as the nature (constant, intermittent) and quality (minimal, moderate, severe) of pain, the presence or absence of sensory symptoms (e.g., paresthesia, anesthesia, and loss of normal proprioception [perception of joint position in space]), ambulatory, balance, and coordination statuses, level of independence, and mental status; and (4) the patient's medication list, subjective reactions to medications being taken, and any allergies—documented or reported. Some clinicians create a separate section for the patient history and do not include it under the "S" element of a S-O-A-P note.

The "O" element of the rehabilitation-setting initial S-O-A-P note includes objective examination data and findings about the patient. These data might include skin appearance and tone; muscle, sensory, and neurological examination results; the patient's activities of daily living (ADL) status; results of a gait analysis; analytical skills test results; reflex test findings; and laboratory test and diagnostic imaging report results.

The "A" element of the rehabilitation-setting initial S-O-A-P note represents the evaluating health care professional's clinical assessment, based on objective examination findings and subjective input from the patient and others and on available patient health records. The "P" element of the rehabilitation-setting initial S-O-A-P note delineates the clinician's intended plan of intervention for the patient. In this section, the clinician might also document that the patient gave informed consent to the examination and recommended intervention. If, in addition to being examined, the patient receives initial treatment or other intervention, then the objective and subjective results of such intervention should also be summarized under the "P" element of the initial note.

A fifth alphabetical initial may be added to the traditional S-O-A-P format, that being a "G" for goals. Outcome criteria, or patient goals, represent expectations of and for the patient, and are often subdivided into short-term goals (often abbreviated STG) and long-term goals (LTG).

Do Stated Treatment Goals Equate to a Legally Binding "Therapeutic Promise"?

A legal issue that sometimes arises in health care malpractice proceedings is whether patient goals established by a clinician in a patient care note represent a guarantee, or warranty, of a specific therapeutic result, for which the failure to achieve the goal may be labeled a breach of a therapeutic promise, resulting in contract-based liability on the part of the provider and/or health care organization. The answer to this question is generally no. Patient intervention goals are not promises made to a patient, but rather, are the written manifestation of the health care provider's professional judgment. As such, goals merely represent the provider's professional opinion about expected outcomes of intervention. Health care providers are cautioned, however, that the actual communication of therapeutic promises to patients may very well create a binding legal obligation to meet the promises made, or to face liability for breach of contract if they are not achieved.

Summary of S-O-A-P-G Initial Patient Care Note Format

S: Contains historical information (medical, medication, occupational, familial, and social) relevant to a specific patient's health condition or complaint, related by the patient to the primary health care professional and extracted from the patient's health record.

O: Contains the results of objective tests and other examination findings, including relevant laboratory and diagnostic imaging results.

A: Contains the evaluative assessment and clinical diagnosis/diagnoses.

P: Contains the proposed plan of intervention for the patient, and may include documentation of the patient's informed consent to examination and intervention. If initial intervention ensues, then a summary of results is also recorded.

> *G: Contains short- and long-term goals (patient-generated expected outcomes) of intervention.*

Problem-Status-Plan Initialism Format

A variation of the S-O-A-P problem-oriented patient care documentation format often used for recording patient progress notes is the problem-status-plan, or "P-S-P" format. Under this format, a re-evaluation note will include the patient's problem(s) and prior evaluative findings and diagnosis (or diagnoses) under "P"; the patient's subjective expression of his or her condition after treatment and the objective findings of the re-examination are listed under "S"; and the revised plan of intervention is listed under the second "P." As with the S-O-A-P format, some clinicians prefer to add a "G" element to this format as well, to memorialize their revised outcome criteria, or goals, based on the patient's needs and desires.

Problem-Status-Plan (P-S-P) Documentation Format for Patient Re-evaluations

P: Contains a summary of the patient's prior evaluative findings and diagnosis (or diagnoses).

S: Contains subjective and objective information about the patient's condition on re-examination.

P: Contains the modified patient intervention plan, based on the current clinical findings.

Examples of the formats discussed above appear in the appendix at the end of this chapter.

The examples of standardized documentation formats presented in this chapter represent only some of the many formats in use by health care providers, individually and collectively. No one format is "the" correct format for meeting the required legal standard of care for patient care documentation. As long as a particular format used by health care professionals working in concert promotes effective communication about their patients' health and conditions, then the format is legally acceptable and within the legal standard of care. Considerations of third-party payer documentation requirements for reimbursement, although not a health care malpractice legal issue per se, are critically important, too, for the financial viability of health care professionals, organizations, and systems. Existing and developing computerized documentation formats facilitate the simultaneous compliance with regulatory and procedural documentation requirements of multiple third-party payers, and are highly recommended for use by providers and facilities.

RISK MANAGEMENT CONSIDERATIONS FOR EFFECTIVE PATIENT CARE DOCUMENTATION

Patient Care Documentation: The First Draft Is the Final Work Product

Imagine that you are an author of fiction novels. Several hours after signing a "contingent" book contract based on an outline proposal, your prospective publisher calls you on the telephone and demands that you begin writing immediately and submit a final product within one week. As an added burden, imagine that the publisher tells you that you will be allowed only one draft of the novel, upon which a firm publication decision will be based. Impossible? Ludicrous?

Now imagine that you are a health care provider working in the emergency department of a regional trauma center. A critically injured patient is transported to your facility without notice. While other members of the team begin to examine the comatose patient, you begin to record the patient's vital signs on an admission form. The patient suddenly goes into cardiac arrest, and cardiopulmonary resuscitation immediately ensues. With all of the tension and haste inherent in this situation, your recording of the information shouted to you by surgeons and nurses reflects your state of nervousness. The entries are scribbled, and words, syllables, and rough diagrams take the place of full sentences and careful illustrations that otherwise would be standard procedure.

Now imagine that the patient's condition deteriorates, and she dies while in the emergency department. A health care malpractice lawsuit is filed, and it proceeds to trial. The attorney for the patient's estate and her survivors offers the emergency room admission record into evidence. The conduct of the medical team will probably be judged in large part on the basis of that record of care that, of necessity, was written in an atmosphere of haste and tension, without any opportunity for drafts or revisions. Similar circumstances occur in emergency departments, operating suites, and other locations throughout health care organizations literally tens of thousands of times each day.

Although not every patient care encounter demands that documentation of care be conducted "under the gun," in almost every situation health care clinical professionals interacting with patients are prohibited from revising or refining their initial examination or intervention patient care entries, because to do so would constitute *spoliation*, or the intentional destruction or alteration of patient care documents with the specific intent to hide or change their clear meaning. The conduct of health care providers, unlike with most other professionals, is routinely evaluated and judged on the basis of a first "draft" of their work product—that is, the patient care record.

Patient Care Documentation Problems, Errors, and Suggestions

Because the consequences of patient care documentation entries are so critically important to effective management of health care malpractice risk exposure, this section presents 25 common patient care documentation problems, errors, and suggestions, designed to minimize the incidence and effects of incomplete or legally substandard documentation. Some of the problems identified herein may seem so trivial and their solutions so obvious that they do not merit mentioning; however, very often in health care malpractice proceedings, the simplest, seemingly trite documentation mistakes have the most serious adverse impact on legal case outcomes. No one should think that his or her intelligence is being insulted by some of these apparently simplistic guidelines for patient care documentation because the recommendations presented may help to prevent a finding of liability for health care malpractice and all its adverse consequences.

Twenty-Five Documentation Problems, Errors, and Suggestions

  1. Documentation problem: Illegible notation
  2. Documentation error: Failure to identify (or correctly identify) the patient under care

3. *Documentation error: Failure to annotate the date (and time, depending on customary practice) of patient care activities*

4. *Documentation problem: Use of multiple or inconsistent documentation formats by providers in a facility*

5. *Documentation error: Failure to use an indelible instrument to record examination, evaluation, diagnostic, prognostic, intervention, or outcome data about a patient under care*

6. *Documentation problem: Pen runs out of ink midway through a patient care record entry*

7. *Documentation problem: Line spacing in patient care record entries*

8. *Documentation problem: Signing patient care record entries*

9. *Documentation problem: Error correction*

10. *Documentation error: Unauthorized abbreviations*

11. *Documentation errors: Use of improper spelling, grammar, and the use of extraneous verbiage not affecting patient care*

12. *Documentation problems: Physician orders: transcription problems; examining and intervening on behalf of patients without written orders, where legally required*

13. *Documentation error: Untimely documentation of patient care activities*

14. *Documentation error: Identifying or filing an incident report in the patient care record*

15. *Documentation problem: Failing to delineate patient care rendered or identify clinical information supplied by another provider*

16. *Documentation error: Blaming or disparaging another provider in the patient care record*

17. *Documentation error: Expressing personal feelings about a patient or patient family member or significant other in the patient care record*

18. *Documentation suggestion: Document observations and findings objectively*

19. *Documentation suggestion: Document with specificity*

20. *Documentation error: Recording hearsay ("second-hand" input) as fact*

21. *Documentation suggestion: Exercise special caution when countersigning another provider's, student's, or intern's patient care notation*

22. *Documentation error: Failure to document a patient's informed consent to examination and intervention*

23. *Documentation suggestion: Document thoroughly patient's/family's/ significant other's understanding of, and safe compliance with, discharge, home care, and follow-up instructions*
24. *Documentation suggestion: Carefully document a patient's non- compliance with provider directives or recommendations*
25. *Documentation suggestion: Carefully document a patient's or family member's/significant other's possible contributory negli- gence related to alleged patient injuries or lack of progress*

Documentation Problem: Illegible Notation

If there is one comment that patients make most often, it probably is that their physicians and other health care providers do not write legibly in their health records. It might not surprise you to hear that health care profession- als themselves also often cannot decipher one another's patient care record entries, causing them either to have to consult with the writer of an entry for "translation" or, worse yet, to disregard the illegible information or even an entire entry.

Even in emergency situations, there is no excuse for documenting patient care illegibly. Keep in mind that the primary purpose of patient care documentation is to communicate vital information about a patient to other health care professionals concurrently caring for that patient and having an imminent need to know.

How many times have you had to struggle to try to decipher another health care provider's handwriting on an intervention order, in a consulta- tion report, or in another document? Have you ever had to spend time trying to decipher your *own* prior patient care entries? Assuming that the latter situation has occurred on at least one occasion for all of us, imagine how embarrassing it would be to be asked by a patient's attorney during a deposition to read one of your own garbled notation entries and not be able to do so. Or worse yet, to be asked to read it aloud before a judge, a jury, and 40 to 50 spectators at trial. The devastating effect that such a situation would have on a health care malpractice defendant-health care provider's or organization's case is self-evident.

Clinical managers and health care organization and system administra- tors must take whatever administrative steps are necessary to ensure that health care professionals within their domains of supervision and control write legibly. This may entail developing alternative documentation sys- tems not based on handwritten notation for providers who cannot be made compliant. For example, the use of dictation and transcription of entries is a viable alternative to handwritten documentation for such primary health care professionals. Use of computerized documentation systems can also alleviate the problem of illegible patient care documentation. When these systems are unavailable, individual providers who cannot write or print legibly should type their patient care entries. As a last (and drastic) resort, the retention of clinical privileges in a facility can and should be conditioned on the ability to communicate legibly with other providers and support personnel.

Providers themselves should also self-police to ensure that their handwritten patient care documentation is legible and neat. When necessary, print or type entries instead of writing in cursive. Remember that a negligent failure to communicate patient treatment information is itself a form of health care malpractice and a legitimate basis for primary (direct) liability for resultant patient injury.

> *When a health care provider's illegible documentation of patient care information is the proximate cause of delayed treatment or patient injury, the failure to communicate effectively constitutes actionable health care malpractice.*

Documentation Error: Failure To Identify (or Correctly Identify) the Patient Under Care

Failure to identify, or correctly identify, a patient under care in documentation is another form of negligence that can lead to malpractice liability. Every page of a patient's record must contain the patient's full name written in indelible ink or in the form of a stamp. Each page should also contain appropriate personal identifying information about the patient to facilitate expedient communication with the patient or relevant others.

As a primary health care provider or supportive professional writing patient information on a document, you bear primary ethical and legal responsibility for ensuring that the patient written about is correctly identified on the document. As a matter of customary practice, do not relinquish control over a piece of paper involving patient care that you have written an entry on unless the patient's name and identifying information is on it.

Documentation Error: Failure To Annotate the Date (and Time, Depending on Customary Practice) of Patient Care Activities

Failure to annotate the date (and, where required, the time) of patient care can be a supporting factor in the imposition of health care malpractice liability. Accounting for the chronology of patient care is especially crucial for physicians and nurses administering medications to patients when a duplicate dose of the medication in issue might be toxic to the patient. Providers such as physical and occupational therapists, whose practice and utilization management standards set limits for the number of permissible interventions in a given time period must also carefully annotate the dates (and perhaps times) of interventional activities. Date entries must always include the day, month, and year. To avoid confusion over A.M. and P.M. where treatment times are annotated, consider adopting the systematic use of military time (e.g., 0001 to 2400 hours).

Documentation Problem: Use of Multiple or Inconsistent Documentation Formats by Providers in a Facility

Effective communication of patient care information among health care providers is most efficaciously facilitated when providers all "sing from the same sheet of music." Clinical managers, department and service chiefs, and facility/system administrators must ensure that providers are using documentation formats that are universally understood by other providers in the facility/system where the relevant documentation may be used. The best way to ensure this is to standardize documentation formats, requiring primary health care providers, for example, to use the S-O-A-P (Subjective-Objective-Assessment-Plan) format for initial patient examination notation and the P-S-P (Problem-Status-Plan) format for patient follow-up and discharge notation. Alternatively, a facility or system may mandate the use of a common template or series of template forms for patient care documentation. Obviously, some degree of flexibility must be built into any standardized documentation system. However, the use of enigmatic formats or data by individual providers should be prohibited as a matter of policy. If professional colleagues cannot decipher your patient care notation, "what we have here is a failure to communicate."

Documentation Error: Failure To Use an Indelible Instrument To Record Examination, Evaluation, Diagnostic, Prognostic, Intervention or Outcome Data about a Patient under Care

Another commonplace documentation error involves the use by providers of writing instruments other than indelible ink, such as pencils, erasable ink, and felt-tipped pens, whose patient care entries are easily obliterated or smeared. When patient care entries are made in pencil or erasable ink, the temptation to "correct" or otherwise alter entries—especially in the face of a potential legal action—is heightened. As a preventive measure for the protection of all concerned, do not write or allow providers under your control to write patient care entries in any medium except indelible (black or dark blue) ink. Even where there is no evidence of alteration or spoliation of records in a health care malpractice case, an inference of negligence might be ascribed by a jury or judge to a facility in which the use of erasable notation is tolerated.

In a similar vein, always ensure that computerized patient care entries are saved on the computer before leaving the relevant software program. Administrators should systematically provide for "automatic save" features to prevent the loss or subsequent alteration of crucial patient care data when an operator leaves a computerized patient care documentation program.

Documentation Problem: Pen Runs Out of Ink Midway through a Patient Care Entry

What do you do if, when writing a patient care entry, your pen runs out of ink? Well, obviously you must complete the entry with a second pen (hopefully with the same color ink). You should precede the second part of the entry, however, with a brief parenthetical phrase, stating that your first pen ran out of ink at that point. Be sure to initial the parenthetical comment.

The parenthetical comment is necessary to prevent a later inference of spoliation of records in the event of any legal action involving the patient in whose record patient care activities are being documented. An example of how to document a change in writing instrument partway through documenting an entry appears in Exhibit 2–1.

Exhibit 2–1 Documenting a Necessary Change of Writing Instrument during a Patient Care Record Entry

Consider the case in which a registered nurse's pen runs out of ink midway through the entry of a narrative-format nursing progress note made at a shift change. The change in pens used to write would be documented as follows:

Nov. 23, 20xx/1445: Patient resting comfortably. Dyspneic breathing / (Note: Original pen ran out of ink. MKM, RN) / no longer observed. Normal skin color. RR = 14/min. (signature and title).

Documentation Problem: Line Spacing in Patient Care Record Entries

As will be elucidated in greater detail in the next chapter, spoliation or alteration of patient health records is a growing problem,[6] with serious ethical and legal implications for health care professionals and organizations. One effective method that clinical managers and facility/system administrators can use to decrease the temptation on the part of providers to add information to prior entries is to establish a policy requiring that providers documenting patient care write on every line. (Note: In many of the illustrations throughout this book, spaces appear between lines of documentation but are interspersed solely for the purpose of highlighting different elements of the entries. Such spacing should not be construed as the recommended spacing for patient treatment documentation.)

Documentation Problem: Signing Patient Care Record Entries

By signing (or initialing) a patient care entry, a provider authenticates and acknowledges legal and professional ethical responsibility for the information contained in the entry. It goes without saying that one should have special pride in his or her signature, so providers are urged to sign patient care entries legibly and neatly. From a risk management perspective, a legible and neat signature may also serve to create a positive impression in the minds of others reviewing the record. In the event of a subsequent health care malpractice proceeding involving the record, a judge and jury viewing a record with a neat signature may rightly conclude that its author was as careful and precise in caring for the patient-litigant as in signing his or her name.

Along with one's signature, the author of a patient care entry should include his or her professional title (e.g., MD, DO, PT, RN, LPN, OTR/L,

SLP, DC, etc.). Irrespective of how neat a signature is, a stamp with the provider's full legal name and title should be affixed in the vicinity of the signature. State or federal law, facility/system policy, and local or national customary practice may dictate inclusion of other information in a legal signature, including the provider's professional license number.[7]

State or federal law also dictates whether a rubber stamp impression of a provider's signature or a computer-generated electronic signature constitutes a valid legal "signature." Computerized records are discussed in greater detail in Chapter 6.

Documentation Problem: Error Correction

To err is human. To correct errors properly in patient care records is good risk management. Despite a good faith effort to document accurately the first time around, everyone will make mistakes occasionally when documenting patient care data. Mistakes can range from using an incorrect term in an entry to writing a patient's entry on a page labeled with another patient's personal data.

Individual health care professionals who write patient care entries, clinical managers, and facility/system administrators should develop standardized rules for correcting patient care entries in records and on other official documents. One method that is commonly used is to draw (or trace along a straightedge) a single line neatly through the erroneous material and then initial it. Providers should also consider indicating the date and time of the correction, even though error correction normally is made during the same sitting as the original erroneous entry.

A basic rule that must be obeyed is to avoid hiding a mistake. Do not obliterate any patient care entry by scratching out what is written. Do not erase any entry. Similarly, the use of correction liquid to obliterate a prior entry in patient care records is a prohibited method of error correction. The purpose of patient care record error correction is to prevent a potential miscommunication of information, not to hide or obliterate what is being edited.

Even writing over an entry a second time for the innocent purpose of making lighter ink more readable is discouraged, because a patient-plaintiff's attorney or a judge or jury reviewing the record at a later date may reasonably be suspicious that an improper entry alteration had occurred. Ensure that what you write in a patient's record is clear, bright, and neat the first time around.

Criminologists are expert at detecting alteration of patient care record entries, and such evidence, in the face of a denial of record alteration, is devastating to a health care professional's credibility generally and to the defense case in health care malpractice proceedings. Specialists can readily distinguish the ink from two different pens, even when the color appears identical to the naked eye and can even opine on whether entries were made at different times on the basis of penmanship and writing style.

What should a provider involved in a health care malpractice case say if he or she has committed an error in patient data entry correction, such as obliterating a prior entry? By all means, the provider concerned must coordinate with legal counsel on what specifically to do and say about the mistake during deposition, at trial, or otherwise. In all cases, he or she must not deny the mistake if asked about it during official proceedings. To do so would be to give false testimony—a criminal offense in most cases.

Authorities writing on the subject recommend different approaches to commenting on why error correction is being carried out. One acceptable method of correcting patient care entry errors is simply to draw through the erroneous material and initial and date the deletion, as discussed above. Some authorities recommend the commonly used technique of handwriting the word *error* above the correction.[8] Others urge providers not to use the word *error* to prevent an inference of clinical negligence associated with the entry error from arising in a judge's or jury's mind.[9] Some authorities recommend using words such as *mistake* or *mistaken entry* ("M.E.," if this is a recognized abbreviation), instead of *error*.[10] Still others recommend writing a brief note in the margin adjacent to the correction indicating why it was made.[11] The most prudent approach to annotating error corrections is to avoid it altogether, so as not to create an adverse inference of sloppy patient care in the minds of judges or juries in health care malpractice proceedings.

Examples of acceptable techniques for patient treatment entry error correction appear in Appendix 2–B, Exhibits 2–B–1 and 2–B–2.

> *The purpose of patient care notation error correction is to prevent a potential miscommunication of information, not to hide or obliterate what is being edited.*

Documentation Error: Unauthorized Abbreviations

In the busy managed care environment of contemporary patient care, nothing is more at a premium than time. Using acceptable abbreviations in patient care notation is a smart way to facilitate communication and save precious minutes that writing each and every term and phrase out long-hand would entail. The selective use of abbreviations facilitates communication and improves patient care because it is easier for other providers caring for a patient being written about to scan shorter notes containing known abbreviations than to labor through longer narratives without abbreviations.

Clinicians, however, need to exercise caution when using abbreviations to ensure that others understand what information they intend to convey. To ensure uniformity and universal comprehension, clinical, facility, and system managers must develop standardized lists of approved abbreviations and require providers to use only those abbreviations. The list or lists of facility-approved abbreviations must be widely disseminated to all those personnel who do or might write, interpret, transcribe, and review patient care notation, including clinicians, students, medical records personnel, and administrative, secretarial, and clerical personnel.

Facility/system administrators should seek broad input from all potential users when formulating the lists and must ensure that approved abbreviations lists remain current. An ongoing systematic review of existing approved abbreviations is highly recommended.

Special caution must be exercised when one abbreviation may have two or more common meanings, such as "AC," for acromioclavicular, alternating current, or anterior cruciate. If the intended meaning for such an abbreviation is not crystal clear to potential readers, then the writer must spell the word out to ensure comprehension by all.

The potential adverse consequences of using unintelligible abbreviations can be as serious as carrying out patient care in a negligent manner. If providers relying on cryptic patient care documentation misinterpret vital patient information and take injurious courses of action toward a patient as a result, then both the drafter and reader of that erroneous information may face health care malpractice liability.

An example of a rehabilitation service approved abbreviations list appears as Appendix A.

Documentation Errors: Improper Spelling, Grammar, and the Use of Extraneous Verbiage Not Affecting Patient Care

As with illegible notation, improper word spelling and the use of incorrect grammar by health care professionals reflects negatively on them individually and on departments, services, facilities, and systems. These vocabulary errors may create an impression of carelessness, which, if inferred and extrapolated by judges or juries in health care malpractice legal cases, may contribute to findings of liability. Examples include misspelled words like "mussels" (for muscles) and uteriss (for uterus).

Always have readily available both a medical and standard dictionary for reference when writing patient care and related documentation. Clinical managers and facility/system administrators should also consider developing lists of lay and medical terms that are frequently misspelled, and disseminating them to staff for training use.

Regarding extraneous verbiage not affecting patient care, a basic rule of thumb to remember is that only information related to patient examination, evaluation, diagnosis, prognosis, or intervention belongs in a patient care record. As an example, it would be wholly appropriate to record in the subjective portion of a S-O-A-P note a patient's verbalization of his or her pain symptoms. It would be inappropriate to comment in the record irrelevant information about another health care provider's demeanor during official exchange about patient care (e.g., "Mar. 12, 20xx/0400: Called Dr. Smith regarding patient's c/o stomachache. Dr. Smith *seemed irritated about receiving the call, but* ordered Maalox for the patient prn— Regina Doe, RN")[italicized material to be deleted].

Documentation Problems: Physician Orders: Transcription Problems; Examining and Intervening on Behalf of Patients without Written Orders

Nurses and nurse practitioners, physician assistants, physical, occupational, and speech therapists, and other primary health care providers working in either inpatient or ambulatory care settings who read doctors' and other referring providers' preprinted or typed orders normally have no difficulty interpreting their meaning. However, handwritten orders written in haste—particularly during emergency situations—are often illegible. Health care professionals caring for patients pursuant to such referrals must be sure to clarify any ambiguities before carrying out orders, rather than making possibly erroneous assumptions about what is meant, to prevent patient injuries and potentially compensable events that could ripen into legal actions for health care malpractice.

Facility and departmental managers must establish policies that encourage providers who interpret physicians' orders to seek clarification of orders that appear ambiguous. These policies should be in writing and should be disseminated to all providers covered by their provisions. The policies should delineate appropriate methods for questioning such orders and spell out acceptable procedures for challenging suspected erroneous orders. Providers should remember to document carefully their inquiries and physician responses regarding ambiguities in diagnostic and treatment orders.

State law, facility policy, accreditation standards, and local custom govern the practice of caring for patients under verbal versus written physician's orders. Referral orders involving referring providers and consultants also raise important documentation issues. For most health care providers, the law requires written referral orders to treat patients referred by physicians and others for care. Even when allowed by law, clinicians such as physical therapists in direct access states who evaluate patients under verbal referral orders should always require the referring physician, dentist, or other provider to authenticate such orders expeditiously with signed written orders to enhance communication and protect both the referring provider and the clinician to whom the patient is referred. A sample form letter for requesting such orders appears in Exhibit 2–2.

Documentation Error: Untimely Documentation of Patient Care Activities

No factor contributes more to effective communication among health care providers simultaneously caring for patients than does the timely documentation of care. Failure to timely document important patient clinical information that other providers can use to prevent or alleviate patient suffering, or to effect speedier recovery or optimal function, is a form of professional negligence.

Ideally, timely documentation of patient care occurs concurrently with the rendition of care. In reality, however, patient care notation is often made at the end of a work shift. The further in time documentation of care occurs from the actual rendition of care or observation of a significant patient event or condition, the less accurate it becomes.

Exhibit 2–2 Sample Request for Written Referral Orders To Accompany Verbal Referral Orders

---

Anytown Community Hospital
Anytown, USA
Physical Therapy Clinic

May 1, 20xx

FOR: Dr. _____

SUBJECT: Written referral orders re _____

Patient dx: _____

Dear Dr. _____ :

Please sign the enclosed referral order and return it to me in the enclosed stamped envelope so that we may complete our records and commence treatment. Per your request during our telephonic consultation of April 29, 199x, I have evaluated _____ . I am enclosing the report of my examination and evaluative findings.

Thank you for your prompt response.

Sincerely,
Reginald P. Hasenfus, PT
Chief Physical Therapist

Attorneys examining health care providers in depositions or at trial often successfully challenge the accuracy of their documentation of patient care based on untimely notation. They persuasively argue before juries and judges that a provider's memory of critical events—like that of any percipient witness to an event—fades with the passage of time. Notation of care or patient status made hours, days, or even weeks after the fact, then, is less credible than when it is documented contemporaneously with care or observation.

Equally untimely as documentation made too long after care is rendered is documentation that is made before care is actually rendered. Consider, for example, the following hypothetical situation:

A, a clinical physical therapist at ABC General Hospital, examines patient B for a complaint of interscapular myofascial pain. As part of the plan of care, A initiates moist heat, myofascial mobilization, ultrasound, and active range of motion exercises for patient B. Before patient B is finished with her first treatment session, A completes his initial patient care note, stating in part that "B had no adverse reaction to the initial treatment." Several minutes later, C, A's physical therapist assistant, informs A that B sustained a skin burn from the moist heat treatment. To correct his initial misimpression of patient B's tolerance of treatment, A must then either write an addendum to his original note or cross out and correct the erroneous portion of the original note. In either case, A's credibility is diminished, and if the incident devolves into a lawsuit, a jury or judge would probably be less likely generally to believe A's testimony about patient B's care than if the erroneous comment about patient B's status had not been improperly and incorrectly written in advance.

The physical therapist in this example could have prevented the loss of credibility regarding his testimony about patient B's overall care by having waited until patient B completed her initial treatment session to document her post-intervention status.

Occasionally, providers will be required to document entries that are made some time after care has been rendered or after important information about a patient's status has already been observed. Such a late entry may necessarily occur when the provider may not have ready access to the patient's record or, as in the above hypothetical situation, when additional clinically pertinent information about the patient becomes available only after the initial note is completed. A late entry should always be labeled as an "addendum" or "follow-on entry" to avoid a later inference that spoliation or improper alteration of the patient's record occurred. Also, a late entry should be labeled with the date and time that it is written. If a late entry does not build on the entry immediately preceding it, then some reference to the prior entry being amended must be made in the body of the late entry.

An example of how to document correctly the original and late entries illustrated in the hypothetical situation above appears in Exhibit 2–3.

Documentation Error: Identifying or Filing an Incident Report in the Patient Care Record

Patient, visitor, and staff injuries unfortunately will occur from time to time in health care settings, regardless of precautions taken by clinical managers, clinicians, and support staff. When such nosocomial injuries

Exhibit 2–3 Example of Documenting a Necessary Late Patient Treatment Entry

---

ABC General Hospital
Physical Therapy Department

Oct. 31, 20xx

S: 49 y o, F, dx: right interscapular myofacial pain syndrome, referred by Dr. Johansen of Pain Clinic for "evaluation and appropriate treatment." Hx of FOOSH, Oct. 20, 20xx. No fx in RUE, acc to X-ray report in pt.'s OPR, dtd. Oct. 21, 199x. Meds: Motrin, Robaxin. No rad, neg. sensory sx, acc to pt. Neg. prior hx.

O: GMT NL, BUE, FAROM BUE and C sp. Reflexes 2+/symm., BUE. SLT intact BUE and C & T sp. Neg. deformity; 12 trigger points of pain along sup. and med. R scapular border. Posture NL.

A: Myofascial pain syndrome, R interscapular region.

P: MH, US, myofascial mobilization, AROM B scapula and C & T sp., in clinic x 5. Tol. initial rx very well, w/o complaints.

G: Decrease pain sx 50% x 2–3 wks; I pain-free ADL x 4–6 wks; prevent recurrence.

ADDENDUM: Oct. 31, 20xx/1400: Initial evaluation/rx entry of this date stated that pt. tolerated MH and US "very well." However, approx. 5 min. subsequent to note being written at 1330, pt. reportedly sustained a skin burn from MH over R medical scapular border, as reported to me by Carl Modality, PTA. Burn appears bright red, painful, small 2" diam. unbroken blister. I called Dr. Johansen and reported findings; pt. treated w/ice pack x 30 min, per Dr. Johansen VO. Pain and redness resolved. F/U w/Dr. Johansen in A.M. or prn earlier.   —Bob Therapist, PT

---

occur, careful objective documentation of information that the provider writing about the injury perceives is critically important. Careful, complete documentation of an injury serves at least three purposes: to promote optimal quality care to the injured party; to serve the risk management function of protecting the facility from unwarranted liability exposure; and to form the basis for further training of staff members to try to prevent similar incidents in the future.

Whenever any adverse event involving actual or potential injury to a patient, visitor, or staff member occurs, a formal incident report should be completed and forwarded through the clinical manager to a centralized risk management office for review and retention. An incident report also must be completed whenever a medication error occurs or when a patient or visitor makes a formal complaint about a facility, system, or its staff.

Administrators and clinical managers should educate their staffs that the completion of an incident report under such circumstances is the norm and will not, in and of itself, constitute a stigma against any provider potentially responsible for an adverse event. Staff members should also be educated as to why an incident report is so critically important. Because memories fade relatively quickly after an event is perceived, it is vital to document right away what happened to an injured party.

Writers of these reports, clinical managers, and facility/system administrators can feel secure in knowing that incident reports, like other quality assurance/improvement/management or attorney-work product documents, normally enjoy qualified immunity from release to patients, their attorneys, and others seeking to obtain them.[12] However, because incident reports necessarily contain more detailed administrative information than a concomitant patient care note concerning care rendered to an injured party, they should not be filed in the injured party's patient care record.

Also, to avoid drawing a patient's or attorney's attention to the fact that an incident report has been filed, providers must be careful not to mention in the patient care record that an incident report has been filed. This precaution is not advocating "hiding the ball." Documentation of the existence of an incident report has no place in a patient care record because an incident report contains purely administrative and not clinical information.

Advice on techniques for designing and drafting incident reports and suggestions about their contents appear in Chapter 6.

Documentation Problem: Failing To Delineate Patient Care Rendered or Identify Clinical Information Supplied by Another Provider

Not every observation or finding described by a clinician in a patient examination, evaluation, or intervention note concerns observations or findings that the clinician perceived firsthand. Very often, other health care professionals, support staff, and other persons supply clinically pertinent information about a patient that is incorporated into primary documentation of care. Patient care carried out by another provider, as well as clinical information supplied by another person to the writer of a patient care note, should be clearly attributed to the source person.

Failure to denote another person's responsibility for clinical information supplied to the writer of a patient care note may result in legal responsibility being ascribed exclusively to the note writer for the information at issue. This may be the case even when the information clearly could not have emanated from the writer, for example, where a surgeon or radiologist furnishes information about a patient's medical status to a nurse, physical or occupational therapist, or other nonphysician provider caring for the patient.

Consider the following hypothetical case:

> X, a staff occupational therapist at Anytown General Hospital, conducts an initial musculoskeletal evaluation of patient P, pursuant to a proper written order from Dr. Z. Patient P's diagnosis is right carpal tunnel syndrome, status-post carpal tunnel release 7 days ago. Patient P is referred for "evaluation and appropriate exercises." During her evaluation of patient P, X telephones Dr. Z for consultation, after patient P reveals to X that she fell onto her outstretched right hand two days postoperatively and is now experiencing local sharp pain at the proximal thenar eminence. X suspects a carpal fracture. Patient P's chart contains no information about recent right wrist radiographs. Dr. Z advises X that she just examined patient P yesterday and ordered x-rays of her right wrist, which were negative. Dr. Z tells X to proceed with postoperative range of motion exercises. X documents in her evaluation note that patient P's right wrist x-rays were normal, without ascribing responsibility for the information to Dr. Z. X also fails to document Dr. Z's verbal instructions to her to proceed with treatment. X proceeds with treatment, which consists of home active exercises. On her one-week recheck, patient P's right proximal wrist pain has increased significantly and she is tender to palpation over the scaphoid bone. X walks to the radiology department, where she reviews patient P's prior right wrist x-rays with Dr. R, a radiology resident. Dr. R had just officially read patient P's x-rays and documented the results two days ago; they show a scaphoid fracture. When X reveals this finding to patient P, patient P becomes infuriated with X over the erroneous prior reading of her radiograph and threatens to sue. Even though Dr. Z most probably will concede that she misread patient P's radiographs and communicated to X that they were normal, an ambiguity still exists in X's initial evaluation note, in which it appears that X personally read patient P's radiographs as normal. This misinterpretation of X's evalu-

ation note could have easily been prevented had X documented patient P's radiographic findings in the objective section of her note as follows: "X-rays of R wrist taken Mar. 19, 20xx, by Dr. Z and read as normal. (Information obtained telephonically from Dr. Z on Mar. 20, 20xx)." The following phrase should also have appeared in the assessment portion of X's initial note: "P. cleared by Dr. Z for AROM exercises."

Similar misinterpretations over who is responsible for patient care or diagnostic information can also occur when assistants, aides, residents, interns, and students on clinical affiliations relate clinical information to providers who are privileged to document in patient care records, and the writer fails to denote who actually provided the care or furnished the information. For example, consider the following hypothetical situation:

A physical therapist assistant administering therapeutic exercises to a rehabilitation patient relates to the supervising physical therapist that the patient displayed anterior shoulder pain during active arm exercises. The proper course of action for the supervising physical therapist (who is not present at the scene) is to annotate that finding in a progress note and credit the physical therapist assistant as the source of the information. Such a note might appear as follows:

Dec. 23, 20xx/1900 P: 67 y o M, dx: s/p R CVA w/ residual L UE weakness.

S: Shawn Jones, PTA, reported telephonically that pt. c/o increased L ant. shoulder pain with PNF; no apparent subluxation, swelling, or other objective signs reported. I was at another location. Directed Mr. Jones to d/c exercises for now and instruct pt. and wife to cont. w/ MH or CP, according to pt. preference, prn.

P: Will reexamine pt. this p.m. for new L UE pain complaint.

—Philomena Therapist, PT

Whenever a primary health care provider receives and documents clinical information about an adverse change in a patient's condition derived from another professional or support person, the primary provider becomes obligated to re-examine the patient expeditiously or risk professional negligence-based health care malpractice liability exposure for patient injuries for the negligent failure to appropriately monitor the patient.

Documentation Error: Blaming or Disparaging Another Provider in the Patient Care Record

Information that disparages another health care provider, or blames any provider for a patient's condition—either expressly or by implication—has no place in the patient care record. Such information has no clinical relevance to patient care. One type of entry often seen in patient care records that has an implication of blame is notation that documents missed patient appointments.

Consider the following hypothetical situation:

> Patient Y underwent an arthroscopic debridement and repair of her torn left medial meniscus yesterday. At ABC Hospital, postoperative arthroscopic knee procedure patients go to physical therapy one day preoperatively for preoperative examination and patient education about the postoperative exercise program. In this case, a miscommunication between the orthopedic ward and physical therapy prevented patient Y from being seen preoperatively. Although all three providers involved—the orthopedic surgeon, the charge nurse for the orthopedic ward, and the orthopedic physical therapist—could give in to the temptation to document patient Y's missed preoperative physical therapy appointment defensively, it would be unproductive and perhaps inaccurate to cast aspersions on each other for the mistake. Examples of inappropriate entries in this case would include the following three examples:
>
> Example 1: Apr. 1, 20xx/1400
>
> P: One-day post-op L arthroscopic medial meniscus debridement and repair.
>
> S: Minimal swelling; no drainage. Pt. reluctant to do isometric quadriceps sets. *PT neglected to see pt. for pre-op teaching.*
>
> P: To PT today for post-op rehab per protocol.
>
> G: D/C crutches in 1 wk; FFAROM L knee X 2–4 wks; I pain-free ADL X 6–8 wks.   —Otto Ortho, MD
>
> Example 2: Apr. 1, 20xx/1500
>
> S: 32 y o M, computer programmer, s/p L arthroscopic medial meniscus debridement and repair yesterday. To clinic via w/c. Referred for post-op rehab per protocol. Meds: Tylenol prn (none since 11 A.M. today).

O: Alert; seems disturbed over his missed app't for pre-op education. In bulky dressing; removed; no drainage. AAROM, L knee: 0/65 degrees; min. swelling. N/V intact. Rest of LQ screen WNL.

A: s/p L arthroscopic medial meniscus debridement and repair yesterday. Ready for post-op rehab; crutch walking PWB (50%). *Note: Missed pre-op app't was due to the ward failing to send down a preop consult.*

P: CW today, begin QS, SLR, AAROM; progress per protocol. Pt. is I on crutches, at approximately 50% PWB, level and stairs; understood and safely carried out all instructed activities.

STG: D/C crutches in 1 wk; FFAROM L knee X 2–4 wks.

LTG: I pain-free ADL X 6–8 wks.   —Ron Therapist, PT

Example 3: Apr. 1, 20xx/1415

P: One-day post-op L arthroscopic medial meniscus debridement and repair.

S: Dr. Ortho just ordered pt. to PT today for post-op rehab. Pt. visibly upset p/ Dr. visit because of missed pre-op PT eval. app't. *It was my fault that pt. didn't get to PT pre-op. I saw Dr. Ortho's standing pre-op order but forgot to send pt. to PT because I was involved w/ six other admissions. Sorry!*

P: To PT now in w/c for post-op rehab and crutch gait trg. PWB (50%) per protocol.

G: I CW PWB X 1 day; I pain management; prevent wound infection.
                                        —Regina Smith, RN

The three hypothetical patient care notes above illustrate several important points. Dr. Ortho should not have displayed his anger over the missed preoperative teaching appointment in front of the patient. He also should not have documented in his progress note that the physical therapist was negligent in failing to see the patient preoperatively. (This conjecture was, in fact, inaccurate.)

Dr. Ortho's reaction to the patient's missed appointment and the documentation of his speculation as to its cause started a chain reaction of patient dissatisfaction and defensive documentation by other providers on the team that was irrelevant, disruptive to patient care, and unproductive. The end result may well be (depending on the outcomes of this patient's care) that the patient files a complaint, claim, or even a legal and/or administrative action because of what occurred. If that occurred, then the defensive documentation illustrated above would be very helpful in support of the patient's health care malpractice case.

Just as Dr. Ortho and Mr. Therapist should not have blamed physical therapy and nursing, respectively, for the missed appointment in the patient's care record, Ms. Smith should not have conceded blame for the incident in the patient's record. Again, her admission has no clinical relevance and therefore no place in the patient care record.

Problems of this type are best addressed informally between members of the patient care team in the setting of an interdisciplinary quality management committee meeting. The focus of such a meeting is primarily on how to resolve the *problem*, not on targeting individuals. If more formal action is required, then the surgeon or another team member should initiate an incident report, wherein reasons for the missed appointment can be more freely detailed. Of course, an incident report would be required if the patient suffered injury as a result of the missed appointment. The incident report, as a quality assurance/improvement or attorney work-product document, is normally immune from release to the patient or the patient's attorney under state or federal law.

Even in an incident report, however, a provider is not free to defame another provider by making a false accusation that damages the defamed provider's professional reputation in the eyes of others in the relevant health care community. Purely personal defamatory remarks are legally actionable as intentional *torts* (wrongs).

Defamation has two varieties: libel and slander. Written defamatory remarks about another provider, such as might appear in a patient care record, incident report, or other document, constitute *libel*. Also included within the definition of libel are defamatory statements made on computer, videotape, or other relatively permanent media. Spoken defamation is called *slander*. If a defendant is found liable for defamation, then the damages might include not only compensatory money damages for loss of the victim's personal and professional reputation, but also punitive, or exemplary, damages intended to punish a wrongdoer. In many states, the defendant may be personally responsible for payment of the judgment in such a case, where the defendant's insurer is statutorily relieved of responsibility for indemnification for judgments involving malicious intentional torts and/or punitive damages.

> *Defamation[13]: a communication to a third party of an untrue statement about a person that damages the defamed person's good reputation in the community. Although normally a person claiming to be defamed must prove any losses suffered as a result of the defamation, damages may be presumed, and may not need to be proven, for victims who are professionals and businesspersons. The two classifications of defamation are:*
>
> - *Slander: oral defamation*
> - *Libel: written or other semi-permanent modes of defamation*

Documentation Error: Expressing Personal Feelings about a Patient or Patient Family Member or Significant Other in the Patient Care Record

Just as patient care documentation entries can disparage health care providers, inappropriate statements written about patients in their records may also constitute actionable defamation. Health care providers documenting patient examinations, evaluations, or interventions must exercise special caution to avoid making inappropriate personal comments about patients under their care. For example, [actual observed] attributions such as "malingerer," "supratentorial symptoms," "manipulator," and "pseudo-intellectual" are all inappropriate. Such comments, if discovered by the patient, will justifiably sour the patient-professional relationship and make the patient more litigation-prone, for health care malpractice and defamation causes of action. In such a case, the health care provider will be in the nearly impossible position of trying to establish at trial during the defense case that the documentation in issue accurately characterized the patient.

Despite the fear of a defamation action, a health care provider is ethically obligated to document findings that negate a patient's assertions of symptoms. This, however, must be done very carefully. Statements such as "objective examination normal" and "palpation, even to light skin touch, results in severe pain response by patient" are, if accurate, appropriate. More risky, but perhaps still appropriate, comments are ones such as evaluative conclusions that state "rule out subjective exaggeration of symptoms, based on normal objective findings" and "rule out secondary gain." Conclusions based on conjecture, such as "objective findings do not justify subjective complaints," are inappropriate and dangerous and must be avoided.

Providers must also be vigilant when they transcribe statements made by patients during examinations and interventions. Any statement made by a patient that is documented in the patient care record must appear in quotation marks. For example, if a patient says to a physical therapist during an examination for a complaint of work-related low back pain that his back does not hurt him now, then the therapist should quote the patient, rather than paraphrase the patient's remark, in the subjective section of the evaluation note. When documenting such a statement that is clearly contrary to the patient's self-interest[14], the provider should have the patient confirm the statement before writing it in the patient care record. Although it may seem to be defensive health care, consider having a witness present when the patient confirms such a statement. Ethically, however, such a statement requires documentation in the patient care record, because it is clinically pertinent information about the patient.

In the rare case in which a patient plainly asserts that he or she is falsifying symptoms (i.e., committing fraud) to bolster a legal case or to dupe an insurance company or workers' compensation board, the provider should immediately report that finding to his or her supervisor, organizational administrator, or legal counsel for further action.

Documentation Suggestion: Document Observations and Findings Objectively

Subjective information belongs exclusively in the subjective ("S") section of a patient care note. Clinical information documented in other sections of the note ("O," "A," and "P") must be written in objective, unambiguous, and, to the extent possible, quantifiable terms to promote clear, effective communication with other providers. Providers should avoid documenting ambiguous conclusions about a patient's status, such as "appears within normal limits," "apparent muscle tightness," and "tolerated treatment well," as well as ambiguous intervention plans, such as "routine strengthening exercises" and "conservative measures."

Documentation Suggestion: Document with Specificity

Similar to clinical information that is ambiguous and lacks objectivity is information that lacks specificity. When generalizations are made or when information that clearly can and should be quantified is not, providers miss an important opportunity to communicate effectively about their patients to other providers.

For example, if an occupational therapist conducting two-point discrimination sensory testing of a patient's hand writes "within normal limits," then other providers reading the findings can only guess at their meaning. The preferred way of documenting such findings would be to quantify in standard terms (here, millimeters) the patient's discrimination of two static or moving sharp points and report results (pictorially and numerically) for specific locations on specific fingers.

Another example concerns a hypothetical physician's assistant conducting reflex testing of a patient during a neurologic examination. If the physician assistant reports "reflexes WNL," then other providers reading the note have no clue as to which reflexes were tested or what "WNL" means. More specific and meaningful would be the following report: "Biceps, Triceps, and Brachioradialis reflexes 2+/symmetrical/ brisk in both upper limbs."

Documentation Error: Recording "Hearsay" (Second-Hand Input) as Fact

Documenting "hearsay" as if it were fact is a common and dangerous practice that can leave health care providers in a position of increased vulnerability to health care malpractice and defamation liability exposure. *Hearsay* is a legal term of art used to describe any extrajudicial (out-of-court) statement offered as evidence in court for the truth of the matter asserted in it.[15] Regarding patient care documentation, hearsay describes a statement made by one person and adopted as fact by another person. That is, hearsay describes secondhand input.

Take, for example, the case in which a physical therapist, P, who intervenes for patients bedside on hospital wards, enters patient Q's room. Q is a 65-year-old male patient, status-post left cerebrovascular accident, with right hemiparesis and poor standing balance. Q is not yet ambulatory. On entering Q's room, P notices Q lying on the floor next to his bed, moaning. The bed rail is down. Sitting on a chair next to the bed is Q's wife, R. When P asks R what happened, she replies, "The bed rail was down and he rolled out of bed." P calls loudly for help; Q is examined by Dr. S and found to be unhurt, except for two minor bruises on his right elbow and right femoral greater trochanter. Q's status would be correctly described in progress notes by P and Dr. S as follows:

June 25, 20xx/1425

P: L CVA; R hemiparesis; bedside PT pt.

S: Pt. found lying on floor next to bed. Dr. S examined pt. and stated pt. is "fine, except for 2 small bruises, one on R elbow, one on R greater trochanter." Dr. S ordered PT held for today.

P: Hold PT today, recheck status in A.M.

G: Progress to standing X 1 wk.—Endie Tee, PT

June 25, 20xx/1428

P: L CVA; R hemiparesis.

S: Mr. Tee, PT, reported that pt. found on floor next to bed. Examination WNL, except for 2 small bruises, one on R elbow, one on R greater trochanter.

P: Hold PT for today; monitor V/S q 4 hrs X 24 hrs. Re-examine in A.M.   —Vigil Lant, MD

Note that each provider only documented as firsthand the clinical information that he personally perceived. The physical therapist and physician each correctly attributed hearsay information provided by the other appropriately in his note. Also note that neither provider made mention in patient care documentation of how patient Q might have alighted from his bed. That information was correctly excluded from their documentation. Such information should instead be documented in an incident report. Because Q's wife supplied that information, her hearsay statements must be appropriately recorded in the incident report. This example will be revisited when incident report documentation is discussed in greater detail.

Another example of hearsay involves information related by a patient presenting for examination with incomplete prior documentation of the patient's status. Consider, for instance, the case in which a physical therapist is examining a patient pursuant to a written physician referral, with a diagnosis of left lateral (humeral) epicondylitis. The therapist does not have any reports about radiographs. The patient volunteers that the referring physician took radiographs of the left elbow and read them as normal. If the therapist relies on that information in his or her examination, evaluation, and diagnosis, it must be properly attributed to the patient as the source of the information. It would, therefore, be incorrect for the therapist to write "X-ray WNL" as part of the examination. Instead, the therapist would correctly document in his or her patient care notation as follows, including reference to patient as source for information about the left elbow x-ray and the patient's allergic status:

Aug. 5, 20xx

S: 45 y o F, dx: L lat. epicondylitis; referred for evaluation and appropriate rx.

O: Alert, cooperative. FAROM BUE; GMT NL BUE. Neg. swelling peri-L lat. epicondyle. SLT intact BUE. Min. TTP L proximal lat. epicondyle. Mod. c/o pain L lat. epicondyle w/ resisted L wrist extension and passive L wrist flexion. Per pt., X-ray of L elbow, taken by Dr. X, Aug. 3, 20xx, reported to her as WNL by Dr. X. (No report available; Dr. X and staff on vacation.)

A: L lat. epicondylitis.

P: HCP X 5 (pt. reports "no allergy to HC"); gentle AROM, progress to PREs. No objective signs, or patient complaint of problems, with rx.

G: Decrease sx 25% X 2 wks; I pain-free ADL X 2–4 wks; prevent recurrence through ADL hints.   —John P. Doe, PT

Documentation Suggestion: Exercise Special Caution When Countersigning Another Provider's, Student's, or Intern's Patient Care Notation

Staff physicians, clinical preceptors, and other primary health care providers are frequently called on to serve as clinical instructors for health professions students. In that role, providers routinely countersign patient care notation made by students under their supervision. In most cases, such authentication is required to make the student's documentation legally acceptable. Providers who countersign another person's patient care notes are urged to proofread carefully what is written because, like a guarantor who cosigns for a loan for another person, the countersigning health care professional assumes legal responsibility for the information contained in the note.

If the supervising clinical instructor or mentor observes incomplete or inaccurate information in a student's or intern's patient care note, then the supervisor is obligated to correct the note before signing it. This may be done by having the student correct discrepancies in the documentation or, as supervisor, by correcting the note and initialing the modifications made. Once countersigned, a student or intern's patient care note is legally adopted by the supervising health care professional as his or her own note. The preceptor then shares legal responsibility for what is written therein.

> *Once countersigned, a student or intern's patient care note is legally adopted by the supervising health care professional as his or her own note. The preceptor then shares legal responsibility for what is written therein.*

Documentation Error: Failure To Document a Patient's Informed Consent to Examination and Intervention

The concept of informed consent recognizes the fundamental human rights principle that every adult patient with full mental capacity has the right of control over health care decision making and must be given sufficient clinical disclosure information by a health care provider to make an informed choice. For many procedures, such as surgical procedures, state statutory law spells out documentation requirements that serve as legally sufficient evidence of a patient's informed consent to intervention. For most routine health care interventions, however, there are no statutory formats to comply with to document patients' informed consent. Providers, therefore, must devise their own formats for documenting patients' informed consent to routine health care interventions. Informed consent to treatment generally and suggested formats for documenting informed consent in particular are discussed in greater detail in Chapter 4.

Documentation Suggestion: Document Thoroughly Patient's/Family's/Significant Other's Understanding of, and Safe Compliance with, Discharge, Home Care, and Follow-up Instructions

In a managed care environment, characterized by diminished reimbursement for health care services, the legal standards of care for physicians; nurses; physical, occupational, and speech therapists; orthotists and prosthetists; and other health care providers includes the issuance of written home care instructions to patients on discharge from the hospital or from clinical ambulatory care. Providers are urged to retain master copies of standardized home care instructions given routinely to patients and/or families/significant others caring for patients at home. These forms should be an integral part of a clinic procedures manual.

Service chiefs and risk managers should ensure that staff clinicians provide written, personalized home care instructions to every patient. If issuance of these written home care instructions becomes a standard clinical practice, then even in the absence of documentation of their issuance, providers testifying at a health care malpractice trial years after their issuance can truthfully testify that the issuance of written home care instructions is universal and "customary practice." Such evidence of customary practice, even when the provider cannot recall a specific case or patient, is usually admissible as substantive evidence of compliance with the custom in an individual case.

As with informed consent, a provider should document that a patient and/or family member or significant other understands, safely carries out, and accepts responsibility for compliance with a home program of care. The provider should also document any special precautions or limitations on the patient's activities, as well as follow-up care instructions. It may constitute patient abandonment to not offer necessary follow-up to a home care patient.

Such documentation in a patient discharge note might appear as follows:

Oct. 31, 20xx

P: L CVA, R UE hemiparesis.

S: Alert, cooperative; independent in ADL; FAROM w/ NL GMT BUE. SLT intact BUE. Reflexes 2+/symm. BUE. Normal R UE propriocep-tion.

P: Discharge to home. Written instructions for home exercises, includ-ing PNF and AROM exercises, issued to pt. Pt. to stop program if severe pain, swelling, or loss of sensation occurs, and report symptoms to me immediately. Pt. understands all, agrees to comply with program as outlined in handout, and safely demonstrated all recommended home exercises. F/U 2–3 wks or prn.

G: Increase R UE strength to enable pt. to perform household duties X 1–2 mos.   —J. Ray, OTR/L

> *Documentation of home care/follow-up instructions issued to a patient/family member/significant other responsible for home care on discharge.*
>
> *List of required elements:*
>
> - *Written home care instructions issued.*
> - *Patient/family member/significant other advised about any special precautions or limitations associated with the home care program.*
> - *Instructions for follow-up re-examination, as indicated.*
> - *Written documentation that patient/family member/significant other understands and consents to the home care program, acknowledges responsibility for compliance with it, and demonstrates the ability to carry it out competently and safely.*

> *It may constitute patient abandonment to not offer necessary follow-up to a home care patient.*

Documentation Suggestion: Carefully Document a Patient's Noncompliance with Provider Directives or Recommendations

Documenting patients' noncompliance with care is an important risk management tool to protect health care providers individually and their employing health care organizations from health care malpractice liability in the event that a claim or lawsuit ensues, resulting from alleged injuries incident to care. Providers should carefully document noncompliance events involving patients under their care, such as refusal to comply with the facility's "no smoking" policy or comply with dietary restrictions; refusal to ask for ambulatory assistance where the patient cannot ambulate independently (with or without assistive devices); refusal to use ambulatory assistive devices when ordered; and refusal to take medications as ordered or to carry out exercises or other important interventions. Careful, thorough, objective, nondefensive documentation including specific therapeutic orders violated and dates, times, and circumstances of patient noncompliance should be included in such notation.

Documentation Suggestion: Carefully Document a Patient's or Family Member's/Significant Other's Possible Contributory Negligence Related to Alleged Patient Injuries or Lack of Progress

In some instances, health professional negligence can be inferred or presumed if patients are injured under circumstances in which they normally would not suffer injury, absent a provider's probable negligence. Such circumstances might include patient falling while transferring or ambulating, falling from the bed onto the floor, medication overdoses, burns while under heat or ice treatment, and tissue ischemia from tight compression garments, casts, or orthoses.

Under the legal concept of *res ipsa loquitur*, professional negligence might be presumed against a health care provider in the above situations unless there is documented evidence that the patient or a family member/ significant other caused or contributed to the patient's injuries. Like everyone, a patient can be contributorily negligent (i.e., fail to conform to the standards required by law for his or her own safety and protection from harm).

Health care providers must carefully document a patient's refusal to comply with recommendations and instructions, as well as a patient's misuse or tampering with exercise equipment or other therapeutic devices, such as electric heating pads or neuromuscular stimulation devices. When a patient is contributorily negligent and suffers injury as a result, the patient cannot normally invoke *res ipsa loquitur* as an aid to proving a case of health care malpractice.

CONCLUSION

Documentation of patient care is as important as the rendition of care itself. This chapter introduces patient care documentation management and methodology. The most important reason to document patient examination, evaluation, diagnosis, prognosis, intervention, and follow-up care is to record pertinent clinical information about the patient and communicate it to other health care providers caring for the patient, now or in the future. Secondary reasons justifying effective patient care documentation include, among others, identifying training needs, justifying reimbursement for care, and serving the risk management function of memorializing the examination and interventions performed on a patient's behalf and by whom. A suggested standardized format for patient examinations/evaluations is the S-O-A-P-G (subjective-objective-assessment plan-goals) format. For progress and discharge notes, health care providers and organizations are urged to consider using the more streamlined P-S-P (problem-status plan) problem-oriented format for recording patient care information. This chapter includes detailed discussion of 25 selected documentation problems, errors, and suggestions for improving patient care documentation. The goal that providers must strive for is to document findings and observations of clinical relevance accurately, clearly, comprehensively, and in a timely manner. Documentation should be objective, specific, and nondefensive. The end result of a carefully designed documentation program is optimal quality patient care.

> *The end result of a carefully designed documentation program is optimal quality patient care.*

REFERENCES

1. J.D. KLEINKE, BLEEDING EDGE: THE BUSINESS OF HEALTH CARE IN THE NEW CENTURY (1998); Gaithersburg, MD: Aspen Publishers, Inc. p.3.

2. *See, e.g.*, S.S MURPHY, LEGAL HANDBOOK FOR TEXAS NURSES (1995); Austin, TX: University of Texas Press, ch. 10.

3. E.J. Larson & T.A. Eaton, *The Limits of Advance Directives: A History and Assessment of the Patient Self-Determination Act.* WAKE FOREST LAW REVIEW, 1997; 32(2): 249–293.

4. M.W. CAZALAS, NURSING AND THE LAW, 3RD ED. (1978); p. 52.

5. *See, e.g.*, L. Weed, *Medical Records That Guide and Teach*, 278 N. ENGL. J. MED. 593–600 (1968).

6. *See* R.L. Prosser, *Special Communication: Alteration of Medical Records Submitted for Medicolegal Review*, 261 JAMA 2630–2631 (1992).

7. *See generally*, JOINT COMMISSION ON ACCREDITATION OF HEALTHCARE ORGANIZATIONS, COMPREHENSIVE ACCREDITATION MANUAL FOR HOSPITALS (1999), ch. IM (Management of Information).

8. *See Documentation: Subtle Skills Can Never Be Overemphasized,* HOSP. RISK MGMT., November 1990, at 141.

9. *See* P.W. Iyer, *Thirteen Charting Rules To Keep You Legally Safe,* 91 NURSING 44 (June 1991).

10. Iyer, *Thirteen Charting Rules.*

11. *See* E.D. JOSEPH ET AL., DOCUMENTING AMBULATORY CARE 16 (1986).

12. Quality assurance documents, including incident reports, are protected from routine release in federal health care facilities. *See* 10 U.S.C. § 1102. Similar qualified immunity for quality assurance/improvement documents also exists pursuant to most state statutes.

13. *See generally* E. Weinstock, *Defamation, Dentists and Dentistry*, 2(2) DEPAUL JOURNAL OF HEALTH CARE LAW 325–359 (1998).

14. A statement against one's own pecuniary or proprietary interests is admissible in legal proceedings against the person making such a statement as an exception to the hearsay rule. *See, e.g.*, Federal Rules of Evidence 804(b)(3).

15. Background material for this discussion on hearsay comes from law school lecture notes, for which the author gratefully acknowledges Professor (Emeritus) Herbert Peterfreund, J.D., University of San Diego School of Law (1982).

SUGGESTED READING

E. Blount, *M.D.s Who Mind Their P's and Q's Shouldn't Misplace Their Modifiers*. WALL STREET JOURNAL, Jan. 27, 1999, B1.

M.L. BROOKS, EXPLORING MEDICAL LANGUAGE, 4TH ED. (1998), St. Louis, MO: Mosby Year-book, Inc.

D.W. Clifton, *Tolerated Treatment Well May No Longer Be Tolerated*. PT: MAGAZINE OF PHYSICAL THERAPY, 1995, 3 (10): 24–27.

COLLOQUIUM REPORT ON LEGAL ISSUES RELATED TO CLINICAL PRACTICE GUIDELINES (1995), Washington, DC: American Health Lawyers Association.

C.M. DAVIS, PATIENT-PRACTITIONER INTERACTION, 2ND ED. (1994), Thorofare, NJ: Slack, Inc.

GUIDELINES FOR PHYSICAL THERAPY DOCUMENTATION (1993), Alexandria, VA: American Physical Therapy Association.

D.U. Jette, *On Tolerating Treatment Well,* PT: MAGAZINE OF PHYSICAL THERAPY, 1996; 4(4): 13.

G. KETTENBACH, WRITING SOAP NOTES, 2ND ED. (1995), Philadelphia: FA Davis Co

L.O. Kollenberg, *Payment Depends on Documentation,* BIOMECHANICS, 1998 (Feb): 39–43.

T.M. MARRELI & L.H. KRULISH, HOME CARE THERAPY: QUALITY, DOCUMENTATION, AND REIMBURSEMENT (1999), Boca Raton, FL: Marelli & Associates.

F.M. PIERSON, PRINCIPLES AND TECHNIQUES OF PATIENT CARE, 2ND ED. (1998), Philadelphia: WB Saunders Co.

RISK MANAGEMENT PEARLS FOR PHYSICAL THERAPISTS (1993), Alexandria, VA: American Physical Therapy Association.

RISK MANAGEMENT PEARLS FOR PHYSICIANS (1993), Chicago: American Society for Healthcare Risk Management.

R.W. Scott, *Incident Reports: Protecting the Record*, PT: MAGAZINE OF PHYSICAL THERAPY, 1996; 4(9): 24–25.

M.H. STAMER, FUNCTIONAL DOCUMENTATION (1995), Tucson, AZ: Therapy Skill Builders.

D.L. STEWART & S.H. ABELN, DOCUMENTING FUNCTIONAL OUTCOMES IN PHYSICAL THERAPY (1983), St. Louis, MO: Mosby Year-book, Inc.

REVIEW: CASE STUDIES

---

1. You are the Director of Medical Records for ABC Hospital. A staff rehabilitation professional asks your opinion on giving greater em-

phasis to critically important details in the narrative sections of incident reports filed within the system by placing such important details in quotation marks. How do you respond?

2. Dr. A, a neurosurgeon at XYZ Medical Center, refuses to adhere to the facility's required patient care documentation format, which consists of the S-O-A-P-G (subjective-objective-assessment-plan-goals) format for new patient evaluations and the P-S-P (problem-status plan) format for treatment, progress, and re-evaluation notation. As service chief or hospital administrator, how would you convince Dr. A to conform to this practice standard?

SUGGESTED ANSWERS AND DISCUSSION

1. The staff rehabilitation professional is correct in opining that witness statements must appear in quotation marks in the narrative sections of incident reports. To merely paraphrase witnesses' statements would do a disservice to all persons and entities affected by an adverse incident, including patients, providers, quality and safety management committees, administrators, attorneys, and others. However, other information should probably not be placed in quotation marks. Authorities state that the overuse of quotation marks in writing may be indicative of stress on the part of the writer. (*See* B. Carton, *Why Does 'Everybody' Now Put 'Everything' in Quotation Marks?* WALL STREET JOURNAL, March 15, 1999, A1.) In the case of an adverse patient incident in a health care facility that may ripen into a claim or lawsuit, an inference of stressed-out health care professionals made by a patient-plaintiff's attorney at trial may be extended by a sympathetic jury into a presumption of substandard health care delivery. Avoid the overuse of quotation marks in patient care documentation.

2. There are several incremental approaches that can be used to obtain Dr. A's compliance with institutional standards. The best initial approach would probably be to schedule a formal meeting with Dr. A and the service chief and the hospital administrator to educate Dr. A about the need for standardized patient care documentation that is readily comprehensible by other health care professionals in the facility. Such a system, and only such a system, fulfills the primary

purpose of patient care documentation—to communicate pertinent clinical information about patients expeditiously to other health care providers having a need to know.

If noncompliance persists, formal counseling should be undertaken, with appropriate documentation in Dr. A's provider activity file. As a last and drastic resort, retention of clinical privileges can be conditioned on Dr. A's compliance with this vital practice standard. Before adverse action affecting privileges occurs, however, Dr. A should be advised by the hospital attorney about the administrative consequences of an adverse action affecting clinical privileges (i.e., reporting of the action to the National Practitioner Data Bank).

Appendix 2–A

Additional Examples of Patient Care Documentation Formats

Exhibit 2–A–1 Sample S-O-A-P Patient Initial Visit Note

The following is a physical therapist's initial note for an outpatient seen in a private practice setting.

ABC Physical Therapy Clinic
Anytown, USA
May 1, 20xx

S: 47 y o M, college math professor, dx: chronic LBP syndrome (Dr. Brown), referral for "evaluation and treatment." Pt. states that his pain is in the midline lumbar spine; is constant; and occasionally radiates across R buttock to R post thigh to just AK; worse w/sitting and prolonged standing; better w/rest, esp. sleeping on L side. No c/o sensory systems. Neg. B/B. Hx of sx for 1 yr, since fall on ice onto back while shoveling snow at home (Apr. 19, 20xx). Spent 10 days in hospital, undergoing lumbar traction, WFE, MIL and with initial success. Intermittent OP rx since then. (Records w/pt. and reviewed.) No prior back hx; no subsequent injury. Med. hx: AODM, controlled by diet; stomach ulcer, GB surgery, Feb. 1988. Meds: Indocin, Tagamet.

O: Alert, cooperative. Does not appear to be in acute distress. X-ray, L spine, Apr. 23, 20xx: mild facet DJD, otherwise WNL. GMT NL SLE, AROM BLE. L spine AROM: FB full, BB 1/2 w/ pain in midline L spine, SB full B. Reflexes 2+/symm. BLE. SLT intact, symm. BLE and L spine. Neg. SLR to 85 degrees B; neg. Fabere b. SIJ screen WNL. Neg. spasm, TTP, deformity, L spine, Posture WNL. Gait WNL.

A: Chronic LBP syndrome; mild L spine DJD; probable lumbar extension dysfunction; r/o HNP.

P: MH today in clinic, F/B prone active extension exercises, 10–15 reps; postural, lifting, and sleeping hints. I/C obtained for rx. No observed adverse reaction to rx. Cont. w/ home program of MH prn a/ or p/ extension exercises as above, tid X 30 days. Understands all; no questions. Schedule for back school. F/U p/ re-eval. w/ Dr. Brown, or 4 wks, or prn earlier.

—Ron Therapist, PT

Exhibit 2–A–2 Sample Hx-S-O-A-P Patient Evaluation Note

The following is a physical therapist's initial note for a hospitalized inpatient evaluated in a small community hospital.

Anytown Community Hospital
Anytown, USA
Physical Therapy Clinic
May 1, 20xx

Hx: Dx: Chronic LBP syndrome (Dr. Brown). Hx of sx for 1 yr, since fall on ice onto back while shoveling snow at home (Apr. 19, 20xx). Spent 10 days in hospital, undergoing lumbar traction, WFE, MH, and US, with initial success. Intermittent OP rx since then. (Records w/pt. and reviewed.) No prior back hx; no subsequent injury. Med. hx: AODM, controlled by diet; stomach ulcer; GB surgery, Feb. 1988.

S: 47 y o M, college math professor, referred for "evaluation and treatment." Pt. states that his pain is in the midline lumbar spine; is constant; and occasionally radiates across R buttock to R post thigh to just AK; worse w/ sitting and prolonged standing; better w/rest, esp. sleeping on L side. No c/o sensory symptoms. Neg. B/B. Meds: Indocin, Tagamet.

O: Alert, cooperative. Does not appear to be in acute distress. X-ray, L spine, Apr. 23, 20xx: mild facet DJD, otherwise WNL. GMT NL BLE, FAROM BLE. L spine AROM: FB full, BB 1/2 w/ pain in midline L spine, SB full B. Reflexes 2+/symm. BLE. SLT intact, symm. BLE and L spine. Neg. SLR to 85 degrees B; neg. Fabere B. SIJ screen WNL. Neg. spasm, TTP, deformity, L spine. Posture WNL. Gait WNL.

A: Chronic LBP syndrome; mild L spine DJD; probable lumbar extension dysfunction; r/o HNP.

P: MH today in clinic, F/B prone active extension exercises, 10–15 reps; postural, lifting, and sleeping hints. I/C obtained for rx. No adverse reaction to rx noted. Cont. w/ above program in clinic bid X 3–5 days; re-evaluate for home program on discharge. Understands all; no questions. Scheduled for back school May 3, 20xx.   —Ron Therapist, PT

Exhibit 2–A–3 Sample S-O-A-P-G Patient Evaluation Note

The following is a physical therapist's initial note for a hospitalized inpatient evaluated in a comprehensive rehabilitation center.

Multidisciplinary Rehabilitation Center
Anytown, USA
May 1, 20xx

S: 47 y o M, college math professor, dx: chronic LBP syndrome (Dr. Brown), referred for "evaluation and treatment." Pt. states that his pain is in the midline lumbar spine; is constant; and occasionally radiates across R buttock to R post thigh to just AK; worse w/ sitting and prolonged standing; better w/ rest, esp. sleeping on L side. No c/o sensory symptoms. Neg. B/B. Hx of sx for 1 yr, since fall on ice onto back while shoveling snow at home (Apr. 19, 20xx). Spent 10 days in hospital, undergoing lumbar traction, WFE, MH, and US, with initial success. Intermittent OP rx since then. (Records w/ pt. and reviewed.) No prior back hx; no subsequent injury. Med. hx: AODM, controlled by diet; stomach ulcer; GB surgery, Feb. 1988. Meds: Indocin, Tagamet.

O: Alert, cooperative. Does not appear to be in acute distress. X-ray, L spine, Apr. 23, 20xx: mild facet DJD, otherwise WNL. GMT NL BLE, FAROM BLE. L spine AROM: FB full, BB 1/2 w/ pain in midline L spine, SB full B. Reflexes 2+/symm. BLE. SLT intact, symm. BLE and L spine. Neg. SLR to 85 degrees B; neg. Fabere B. SIJ screen WNL. Neg. spasm, TTP, deformity, L spine. Posture WNL. Gait WNL.

A: Chronic LBP syndrome; mild L spine DJD; probable lumbar extension dysfunction; r/o HNP.

P: MH today in clinc, F/B prone active extension exercises, 10–15 reps; postural, lifting, and sleeping hints. I/C obtained for rx. No adverse reaction to rx. Cont. w/ above program in clinic bid X 3–5 days; re-evaluate for home program on discharge. Understands all; no questions. Scheduled for back school May 3, 20xx.

G: Centralize RLE pain X 3 days; decrease LBP 25% X 3–5 days; RTW sx-free in 1 week; increase back extensor mm strength X 4–6 wks; postural awareness; I ADL w/o sx.   —Ron Therapist, PT

Appendix 2–B

Examples of Acceptable Techniques for Patient Care Documentation Error Correction

Exhibit 2–B–1 Example of Appropriate Treatment Entry Error Correction (Lining through Material To Be Deleted and Initialing and Dating the Correction)

Mainline Community Hospital
Mainline, USA
Occupational Therapy Clinic
Dec. 19, 20xx/1400

S: 38 y o F, occupation: comic book illustrator, w/dx of R CTS, s/p CTR (DOS: Dec 10, 20xx). Referred for ROM evaluation and AROM and strengthening program for RUE. P w/o complaints today. R wrist in neutral brace. Meds include Tylenol and Feldene.

O: Alert, cooperative. GMT deferred. AROM out of brace, R wrist: flex: 65 degrees, ext: 60 degrees, RD: 25 degrees, UD: 25 degrees. SLT intact. Wound, volar wrist ~~fully healed~~ healing/covered with Steri-strips. Negative swelling. *RPH 12/19/00*

A: Resolving R CTS, s/p R CTR.

P: Teach pt. R wrist AROM as ordered. I/C obtained. Demonstrated understanding of exercises; to do as home program, 10 reps each direction tid. Cold pack prn before or after exercises. No adverse reaction to rx. F/U 2–3 wks or prn earlier.

G: STG: Increase pain-free AROM R wrist symmetrical w/ L X 2–3 wks. LTG: I pain-free ADL X 1–2 mos, RTW.

—Reginald P. Hasenfus, Jr., OTR/L

Exhibit 2–B–2 Example of Approriate Care Documentation Entry Error Correction (Lining through Material To Be Deleted, Initialing, and Dating the Correction, and Writing Brief Justification for Correction)

Mainline Community Hospital
Mainline, USA
Occupational Therapy Clinic
Dec. 19, 20xx/1400

S: 45 y o F, occupation: comic book illustrator, w/ dx of R CTS, s/p CTR (DOS: Dec. 10, 20xx). Referred for ROM evaluation and AROM and strengthening program for RUE. Pt. w/o complaints today. R wrist in neutral brace. Meds include Motrin and Indocin.

O: Alert, cooperative. GMT deferred. AROM out of brace, R wrist: flex: 65 degrees, ext: 60 degrees, RD; 25 degrees, UD: 25 degrees. SLT intact. Wound, volar wrist healing/covered with Steri-strips. Negative swelling.

A: Resolving R CTS, s/p R CTR.

P: Teach pt. R wrist AROM as ordered. I/C obtained. Demonstrated understanding of exercises; to do as home program, 10 reps each direction tid. Cold pack prn before or after exercises. No adverse reaction to rx. F/U 2–3 wks or prn earlier.

G: STG: Increase pain-free AROM R wrist to symmetrical w/ L X 2–3 wks. LTG: I pain-free ADL X 12 mos, RTW.

—Reginald P. Hasenfus, Jr., OTR/L

~~Bitte, Violet P. SSN. 234-56-7899~~   O-Boyle, Doree M. SSN: 345-67-8901
~~F/DOB. Mar. 30, 195x~~   F/DOB: May 1, 195x

See pt. identifier at right.
RPH
12/19/00

Chapter 3

The Patient Care Record in Legal Proceedings

This chapter focuses on the patient care record as a business and legal document and examines its uses in administrative and legal proceedings. The relative advantages and drawbacks of the patient welfare and defensive foci of patient care documentation are explored. Spoliation, or the intentional alteration or destruction of patient care records, and its consequences are examined. The health professional-patient legal privilege against disclosure of care-related information is also explored. The chapter concludes with a discussion of confidentiality issues concerning patient health information.

PATIENT TREATMENT RECORDS AS BUSINESS AND LEGAL DOCUMENTS

Chapter 2 addressed the principal purposes for which health care professionals document information about patients in patient care records. Although the primary reason for creating and maintaining patient care records is to have a database of clinically pertinent information readily available for use by other health care providers caring for patients now or in the future, many other purposes also exist for the creation of these records. This chapter describes the nature and uses of the patient care record as a business document and a legal document.[1]

As a business document, the patient care record serves a wide range of administrative functions. These include, among others, serving as the basis for justifying reimbursement for health care services from third-party payer entities; creating a database for monitoring quality and establishing appropriate risk management activities; and providing a resource base for research and training.

As a legal document, the patient care record serves, at once, to protect the legal interests of all participants in the health care delivery system, including patients, health care providers and their support staffs, health care clinical managers and administrators, and health care organizations and systems. In health care malpractice litigation, for example, a patient care record can simultaneously be used as a sword by a patient-plaintiff and as a shield by the patient's health care provider-defendant.

PATIENT WELFARE FOCUS OF PATIENT CARE RECORD-KEEPING: ROAD MAP TO QUALITY CARE AND EFFECTIVE RISK MANAGEMENT

Despite its broad range of variegated uses as a legal instrument, health care recordkeeping is not and should not (with limited exceptions) be carried out with a defensive legal focus. Rather, the creation of patient care records should be guided primarily by patient welfare-oriented health care principles. All health care professional disciplines and the overwhelming majority of health care providers have as their altruistic, narrow focus the welfare of the patients under their care, whom they are attempting to restore to optimal health.

Health care professionals documenting entries in patient care records often have little time to ponder carefully over what they write about patients under their care, as such a significant proportion of health care delivery occurs under emergent circumstances or under the time constraints of cost-containment-focused managed care. Even so, health care professionals are acutely focused on their patients and on recording in an objective manner data that will create a historical basis for efficacious continuity of care. They rightly are not primarily focused on self-protection from legal action.

In large part because of this focus and the objectivity inherent in health care recordkeeping, patient care records have always commanded a high degree of credibility in legal proceedings as important evidence of a patient's health status and of the quality and quantity of patient care. There are several reasons why patient care records enjoy such a high degree of respectability as substantive evidence in administrative and legal proceedings. First, assuming that patient care documentation is performed in a timely manner, it probably represents the most accurate objective evidence of a patient's health status at a given point in time. And second, because health care providers document care primarily with the patient's welfare in mind, what they document is largely unbiased.

By analogy, documentation by an attorney of attorney- or attorney–agent-generated information about a client's case is called "attorney work product," which shares many similarities but also has important differences from a health care provider's patient care documentation about a patient. Both classes of professional documentation memorialize the professional's assessment of a client's condition or case. Both enjoy qualified immunity from disclosure to other persons. However, attorney work product does not enjoy the same status as substantive, objective evidence as does patient care documentation.

Attorney work product is, by definition, documentation prepared on a client's behalf in anticipation of litigation. Only by asserting the claim of its potential use in litigation on behalf of a client can attorneys withhold from disclosure to litigation opponents or others the information contained in such documentation. By its very nature, attorney work product documentation is, or at least is deemed to contain, information that is biased in favor of the position advocated on behalf of the client served. Therefore, even if it were not privileged information, attorney work product would not normally qualify in court as substantive evidence of the truth, unlike patient care documentation.

There are serious dangers inherent when health care providers adopt a philosophy of defensive, legally oriented patient care documentation. Where patient care documentation has the appearance of having been written primarily to protect or "cover" providers rather than to record objectively patient status or care, its credibility as substantive evidence of patient status and care becomes suspect. Patient care records written in anticipation of litigation do not usually qualify as substantive evidence about the quality of care rendered.

CREATION AND MAINTENANCE OF PATIENT RECORDS

State and federal statutes, administrative regulations, and organization, system, and accreditation entity standards typically establish the parameters of a health care provider's or organization's duty to create and maintain patient health records. Even in the absence of such regulatory guidance, however, primary health care providers have a common law duty to make and store patient care records. Failure to create a patient care record and maintain it on a patient's behalf for a specified period of time is a breach of duty owed to that patient. And if the breach of that duty can be tied to some sort of patient injury, then an actionable health care malpractice lawsuit for negligent (or intentional) failure to document care or retain records can be successfully pursued by the patient.

How are patient care records stored? Depending on state or federal law, patient care records are stored as originals, on computer or microfilm, or otherwise. State or federal statutory, regulatory, and common law as well as professional association and institutional practice and accreditation standards control or provide guidance on how long a patient care record must be maintained.[2] Different rules often apply to hospitals, other treatment facilities, and individual health care providers. More restrictive rules often apply to special situations, such as infants', children's, and cancer patients' records. Under many state statutory laws, for example, minors' health records must be preserved until some number of years after the minor patients reach age 18 years, the legal age of majority.[3]

Irrespective of any legal patient care record retention requirements, providers and facilities should customarily and routinely keep patients' records at least until the applicable *statute of limitations*, or "time clock" for bringing legal actions incident to care, has expired. Remember, when considering the lengths of various statutes of limitations, that different "time clocks" apply to actions brought by patients under tort (wrong-based) theories of health care malpractice and other potential bases of liability, such as breach of contract, fraud, and criminal law violations (in which statutes of limitations are usually longer).

Some authorities recommend that providers maintain patient records containing significant data until after the deaths of such patients.[4] In addition to the legal requirements for retaining critical patient information, providers may be ethically responsible for preserving this kind of data about their patients to ensure continuity of care. Even for routine information, it may be prudent to retain patient care records for 7 to 10 years, irrespective of whether state or federal law allows their earlier destruction.[5] This is sound advice even in a case in which the provider has disengaged from care for a particular patient.

NONAVAILABILITY OF PATIENT CARE RECORDS AS EVIDENCE OF SPOLIATION

The adverse consequences when health care providers fail to maintain patient care records as prescribed by law, practice standards, or custom are potentially severe. In particular, courts adjudicating health care malpractice cases in which records are unavailable for patients' (and providers') use may permit juries to infer[6] or even presume[7] health care malpractice against providers under the theory of "spoliation" of records.

Spoliation is a legal term of art that describes the intentional destruction or material alteration of a document by a party for the purpose of changing or concealing its original meaning. (Courts normally disallow a patient legal cause of action against a provider or health care organization for negligent, or unintentional, spoliation.[8]) A charge of spoliation of patient treatment records can give rise to civil, criminal, and adverse administrative and professional association actions against a health care provider. As a criminal matter, spoliation can be both a form of fraud and obstruction of justice. If it is planned, discussed, and/or carried out in concert by two or more health care providers, spoliation of a patient care record may also give rise to a civil or criminal action for conspiracy. (*Conspiracy* involves a situation in which two or more people agree to commit an unlawful act. When charged as a criminal action, it is a separate offense from any underlying crime, such as fraud, obstruction of justice, or perjury.)

Also, the wrongful intentional alteration of patient care records with an intent to deceive is an implicit or explicit violation of most, if not all, health care professional ethics codes. A charge of spoliation can result in adverse licensure action, such as suspension or revocation, and imposition of a monetary fine by the provider's state licensing board and reporting of the adverse licensure and/or credentialing action to the National Practitioner Data Bank.[9]

> *"Spoliation" of patient care documentation is the intentional destruction or material alteration of the entry for the purpose of changing or concealing its original meaning.*

Spoliation of patient records can be considered as the civil health care analog to the criminal law concept of "obstruction of justice." The health care provider who intentionally alters or destroys records "obstructs" the effective delivery of patient care by distorting the true account of a patient's course of care.

Health care providers can commit spoliation of patient care records even when they do not have any malicious intent to defraud anyone—patients, their attorneys, legal authorities, or others. For example, consider the hypothetical case in which a patient lodges a complaint against a health care facility, alleging poor quality of care and a resultant adverse outcome. The patient's letter to the facility triggers the flagging of the patient's record and designation of the patient's care as a potentially compensable event.

Now assume that the health care clinicians named in the claim as parties responsible for the patient's care are asked by the facility's administrator to review the patient's record, without being told that the patient was dissatisfied with care. In this hypothetical situation, assume that some providers mistakenly presume that they are being asked to review the record for quality self-assessment.

If the providers see documentation entries that are obviously erroneous or incomplete, they may be inclined or tempted to "correct" the record by adding information without annotating the supplemental material as a new entry or by removing original material and substituting new entries. This is especially tempting when there are blank lines in the original notation or when individual patient care entries are written on separate pages.

This tendency to "correct" patient care documentation entries in hindsight may be a natural instinct, in large part reflective of health care providers' innate concern for ensuring accuracy and clarity in patient care documentation. As was stressed in Chapter 2, such considerations reflect the principal purpose for patient care documentation (i.e., effective communication of pertinent clinical information to others having a need to know).

Assume hypothetically that a treatment entry seemingly requiring clarification appears as follows:

May 3, 20xx

P: Status post right proximal humeral fracture, nondisplaced, Apr. 15, 20xx

S: N-V intact. Minimal swelling and c/o pain. In sling, with arm adducted and internally rotated, held against abdomen. Med: Tylenol 3.

P: To PT for ROM. F/U 2 wks or prn.

G: Promote healing; prevent adhesive capsulitis X 4–6 wks; independent ADL.   —J. Ortho, MD

The above note, when reviewed by Dr. Ortho, might be "corrected" to read as follows, with substitution of a page containing the amended entry in place of the original one:

May 3, 20xx

P: Status post right proximal humeral fracture, nondisplaced, Apr. 15, 20xx.

S: *Doing very well.* N-V intact. Minimal swelling and *minimal* c/o pain. In sling, with arm adducted and internally rotated, and held against abdomen. Med: Tylenol.

P: To PT *within 72 hrs for passive and active assist ROM to pain tolerance only.* F/U 2 wks or prn.

G: Promote healing; prevent adhesive capsulitis X 4–6 wks; independent ADL.   —J. Ortho, MD

The changes, although arguably only minor in nature, make the record appear as if more findings were observed and more detailed orders made than originally appeared. In this case, Dr. Ortho actually believed that he recalled hearing the patient say that she was doing "very well." He also remembered telephoning physical therapy to ask the therapist to examine the patient within 72 hours of referral and to carry out only passive and active assist range of motion with the patient. He just forgot to annotate those items the first time around. Imagine the impression on a judge or jury if the provider in the hypothetical case were on the stand in a health care malpractice trial trying to explain his substituted progress note after the original had been located. Even if the physical therapist corroborated what Dr. Ortho wrote the second time around, the judge might still direct the jury to presume negligence based on spoliation of patient care records.

Health care professionals and administrative employees of health care organizations are not at liberty to alter existing patient care documentation notation, even for the innocent purpose of clarifying an ambiguous or incomplete prior entry. Even though the hypothetical alteration above was performed without any wrongful intent, it would probably be characterized as such by the patient's attorney and might be so construed by the court, if the potentially compensable event (PCE) were to ripen into a health care malpractice legal action.

If the surgeon in the case above forgot to annotate some crucial clinical information that needed to be added to the patient record, then the surgeon should have added the missing information by way of a new entry explaining the prior omission. Such a proper new entry might appear as follows:

> May 4, 20xx
>
> P: Status post right proximal humeral fracture, nondisplaced, Apr. 15, 20xx.
>
> S: Regarding my earlier note of May 3, 20xx, the following examination and follow-up information is added: The patient reported that she was doing "very well" on exam. I coordinated telephonically with physical therapy for her to be seen within 72 hrs for passive and active assist ROM to pain tolerance only.
>
> G: Promote healing; prevent adhesive capsulitis X 4–6 wks; independent ADL.   —J. Ortho, MD

Because of this natural propensity on the part of providers to correct inaccurate patient care record information—whether for self-serving reasons or out of concern for patients or for accuracy—organization/system administrators and risk managers should not routinely permit providers, consultants, or others to review original patient care records involving known PCEs. For the protection of patients, providers, and the organization or system, interested parties should only be given clear, complete photocopies of patient care records to review. In a legal case involving a purportedly lost patient care record entry, the facility administrator and/or risk manager might even be held legally accountable if the original records were in their possession at the time of probable loss.[10]

Unfortunately, unlike the hypothetical case presented above, most spoliation of patient care records probably is not performed unknowingly or innocently. In fact, health law and other authorities express concern that spoliation of health records may be a growing problem.[11] One authority, Dr. Robert Prosser, attributes the increase in the incidence in patient treatment record spoliation during the past five years to a defensive reaction by health care providers to the fear of health care malpractice litigation and liability.[12] Dr. Prosser correctly noted in his article that most clinicians who alter patient treatment entries are competent, well-meaning providers who inadvertently document their good patient care inadequately and often "correct" entries without any intent to deceive.[13]

Clinic, department, and risk managers, and organization/system administrators should educate all clinicians who write in patient records about spoliation and its consequences and, in particular, should emphasize that it is wrong and legally indefensible—irrespective of the motive for doing it. Spoliation of a patient care record is a shortcut to certain settlement of a health care malpractice case—usually on terms unfavorable to health care providers and organizations. Along with such a settlement come the adverse personal consequences to individual providers discussed in Chapter 2, including the possible inclusion of providers' names in the National Practitioner Data Bank. A settlement under these circumstances that would otherwise have been unnecessary is also detrimental to the reputation of the health care organization in the community, adversely affecting its business interests.

Once it is concluded that alteration, destruction, or even negligent loss of patient care records that are under the control of health care providers individually, or the health care facility generally, has taken place, there is good reason to settle a health care malpractice case, rather than go to court. This is so even in the face of clearly disputable patient allegations because of the danger that the court will allow an inference or presumption of negligence and the possibility of a punitive damages award in the event of a finding of liability. Because of these considerations, most insurers of health care professionals settle such cases.

Investigators and document examiners have little trouble spotting patient care entries that have been altered or supplemented without creating a new dated entry. They often need only examine the original records with the naked eye to see signs of alteration. Such signs may include:

- differences in handwriting style within an entry, including different slanting of added words or individual alphabetical letters and mixed cursive and printing handwriting styles
- use of different writing instruments within an entry
- obvious erasures and other forms of obliteration, such as the use of correction liquid or permanent marker
- nonuniform crowding of words, phrases, or symbols within an entry, especially between lines or in the margins of the entry

Signs of substitution of rewritten patient care entries, although often more difficult to detect, may include:

- differences in paper type or quality in the substituted entry and the record generally
- binder holes or other markings that do not match up with the rest of the record
- date and/or time discrepancies
- subsequent entries (by the provider committing spoliation of records or by other providers) that are incongruous or confusing, based on material contained in the substituted entry
- observations or findings in the substituted entry that could not have been observed or known at the purported time of notation
- handwriting style and/or quality of documentation that is inconsistent with documentation exemplars of the writer

For more subtle alterations, document examiners rely on sophisticated scientific detection instruments and techniques. These include, among many others, ultraviolet and infrared light analysis, spectrometry and chromatography, chemical analysis of ink used in treatment entries, fingerprint analysis[14], and computer data retrieval methods.

Defending against an Inference or Presumption of Negligence

When a court in a malpractice case rules as a matter of law that the jury either can infer or must presume negligence against a provider or health care facility based on lost or altered patient care records, the defense attorney normally has the special burden to either dispel the inference or rebut the presumption to prevent imposition of liability. In particular, to rebut a presumption of negligence based on spoliation, the defense must introduce some evidence that negates the presumption that providers or the facility was responsible for the loss of patient records.

What types of evidence might be sufficient to dispel a presumption of spoliation? At the simplest (or perhaps most complex) level, a provider accused of spoliation can testify convincingly that he or she did not alter or destroy patient record entries. The defense can introduce investigators, document examiners, and other scientific expert witnesses during its own case to testify that spoliation did not occur. The defense can also introduce doubt about the source of clear spoliation into the jury's mind if it can show that the patient-plaintiff possessed or controlled his or her own records during the pendency of the legal process.

> *Once a health care provider's defense attorney produces some credible evidence negating a presumption of alteration or destruction of patient records at the hands of the provider, any presumption of negligence based on spoliation is normally dispelled, and the patient-plaintiff's full burden of proving malpractice in order to prevail is restored.*

Segregation of Litigation Patient Care Records

In large part because of the dangers of spoliation—either at the hands of health care providers, patients, or others—facility risk managers should routinely segregate original patient records and other tangible items such as imaging studies, photographs, electronic monitoring tapes, microscopic slides, and tissue samples involving PCEs and secure them to prevent their unauthorized removal. Release of health records or information should be handled centrally by the facility risk manager or health records administrator. Requests for records involving PCEs should be coordinated with the facility's legal counsel before release.

OWNERSHIP OF PATIENT CARE RECORDS

What entity owns patient health records—the health care organization, individual health care providers, or patients? Or do all of them co-own patient records? Under early common law, before state and federal statutory law controlled this area of law, physicians had absolute ownership rights to records of patients under their care. Under this scheme, the patients had no legal right of access to information contained in their records and little or no legal recourse if record access was denied to them.

Under modern patient record statutes, health care providers creating the records still own the physical records. However, in most states, patients have either direct or indirect access to the information contained in them.

Some of the reasons offered by authorities for favoring ready patient access to health records include the following:

- It fosters a closer provider-patient relationship, particularly when there is also good communication generally between health professional and patient.
- Under consumerism principles, the patient has the right to rebut and compel correction of false or inaccurate information contained in his or her patient care record. False information in patient care records can form the basis for denial of health insurance or even employment, if physical performance standards are legitimate requisites to employment.[15] False information can also form the basis for a legal action against the provider or health care organization for defamation or intentional infliction of emotional distress.
- A trend in health care law philosophy holds that, although the health care provider may own the physical record of a patient, the patient has proprietary rights to the ethereal information contained in it because such information is personal to the patient and the patient has an autonomous right to it.

Currently, 28 states, by statute, give patients full access to information contained in their patient care records that are in the possession of individual health care providers and hospitals (excluding mental health records).[16] Patients whose health records are maintained in federal health care facilities also generally have a free right of access to information contained in their records.[17]

In states where direct patient access to health care information is restricted, administrative hurdles to be overcome by patients in order to gain access to their records include: the requirement for a court order before release of records; release only for potentially compensable events or to an attorney; release to the patient only after demonstration of "good cause"; and substitution of a report or summary of care in lieu of actual patient care records, at health care providers' and organizations' discretion.[18]

In some health care systems, patients retain their own patient care records, under what is called an "ambulatory" record system. Such a system of patient care record maintenance may offer important advantages in this era of managed care and cost-containment, including ready access to the records by health care providers caring for the patient; enhancement of patient self-awareness and education about personal health status; and decreased cost for record storage by health care organizations.

Disadvantages also exist in an ambulatory patient care record system, however. These include the danger of spoliation of record entries by patients or their representatives; emotional distress associated with patients reading about, but perhaps not adequately understanding, their health status; and the possibility that patients will have a greater propensity to bring claims or lawsuits based on perceived health care malpractice.

From a patient's perspective, the most effective way to gain release of the patient's own records is to make the request in writing. Oral requests carry less weight.[19] Also, insist on the actual records, rather than a provider's own summary of the information contained therein.

What about ownership of patient care records after dissolution of a clinical practice group or the retirement or death of the custodial health care provider? When a clinical practice dissolves, providers have an ethical and legal obligation to notify their patients of the dissolution and request that the patients provide the retiring providers with the names of substitute health care professionals to whom copies of the patients' records will be forwarded. Original records should be retained by the original health care providers, where allowed by law, at least until the expiration of applicable statutes of limitations for health care malpractice legal actions.

When a health care provider dies, the patients' records normally become the property of the deceased professional's estate. The executor or administrator of the estate must then advertise the availability of copies of the patients' records for transfer to other health care providers. Creditors of the deceased provider may also claim a right to payment of patient bills owed to the provider before his or her death.

How To Handle a Patient Request for Release of Patient Care Record Information

There are many reasons other than seeking a legal review for suspected health care malpractice for which a patient may request his or her health records from a provider or facility. The patient may be transferring to another geographical area of the country or world, or the provider may be moving or retiring from practice and the patient is responding to the provider's request to have records transferred. Nevertheless, patients often request their records to take them to attorneys for legal review for suspected malpractice.[20]

As was explained above, most states require providers to release patient care information to patients or their representatives on request. A prudent patient relations and risk management measure is to have a health care provider or small group of providers request a meeting with the patient to give the patient an opportunity to ask questions about his or her health status or care and have them answered in straightforward, layperson's language by the providers. This form of communication and show of concern may prevent a lawsuit. Such an offer should first be coordinated with the facility risk manager and perhaps with legal counsel to avoid violating the attorney-client privilege in the event that the patient is already represented by legal counsel.

When meeting with a disgruntled patient under such circumstances, providers must exercise caution not to use jargon in speaking to the patient and his or her family/significant others. Rather, they should break down information into simple layperson's English (or Spanish, Vietnamese, etc., as appropriate, with or without an interpreter).

This sort of meeting between provider(s) and patient may be the last best chance to prevent a claim or litigation over perceived substandard care, so it is vital that providers know how to conduct themselves in such circumstances. Facility providers and support staff should attend in-service education on communication skills with patients and perhaps should conduct mock exercises on how to deal effectively with disgruntled patients. This training is the responsibility of the facility risk manager or outside risk management consultant, as appropriate. Managed care and its inherent time constraints make the scheduling of such meetings between providers and patients more difficult. They should, however, be undertaken, because providers are *fiduciaries* (i.e., in a position of special trust, charged to place patient interests above their own) for their patients and because it is in providers' and health care organizations' own risk management best interests.

Ask yourself whether the typical patient would understand the following explanation of his or her diagnosis. "The MRI and electromyographic studies reveal, and my neuromusculoskeletal clinical examination confirms, that you display increased polyphasic potentials in the musculature supplied by your right common peroneal nerve and have point tenderness to palpation over the tibial plateau. My diagnosis, therefore, is to rule out intercortical lesion of the right knee secondary to trauma, with peroneal nerve compression." Probably not.

Just as lawyers learn (or should learn) through continuing legal education courses to break out of "legalese" when speaking to clients, health care professionals must learn to break down health jargon into layperson's language for their patients and their significant others. The esoteric explanation expounded by the surgeon above should have been stated as follows to the patient: "You had a bad fall. I believe you may have broken your right knee. You may also have some nerve damage, involving muscles in your right shin and foot."

Studies have revealed that patients often do not understand even the terms that most health care providers would consider elemental, such as *hypertension*, *oral*, and *asymptomatic*.[21] The failure to communicate clinical information effectively to patients probably leads to disgruntled patients and health care malpractice legal actions more often than explaining terms and parameters of patient examinations, evaluative findings, diagnoses, prognoses, and intervention instructions in simple language at the patients' levels of comprehension, and soliciting and answering patient and family/significant other questions effectively.

The final point regarding release of patient records concerns copying fees. Most statutes permit health care providers and facilities to charge a reasonable or statutory fee for copying records and, in many cases, a reasonable handling fee. Providers and health records administrators should exercise prudence when setting such fees, to prevent already disgruntled patients from becoming even more so. Such anger might just be vented by the patient through filing a health care malpractice lawsuit. Courts, too, closely scrutinize the propriety of health records copying fees.

ADMISSION OF THE PATIENT CARE RECORD IN COURT AS EVIDENCE

Patient care records serve a myriad of functions in legal proceedings in both the pretrial and trial stages of civil and criminal proceedings. In criminal prosecutions, patient records may be used to aid police investigations; determine the extent of injuries or cause of death of a victim; and establish a defendant's competency to stand trial or sanity, among other things. In civil proceedings other than those involving health care malpractice, health records are vital to the administration of justice as well. In motor vehicle or other accident cases and in workers' compensation actions, patient care records are introduced to establish the extent of a party's injuries or disability, to ascertain a party's functional or work capacity,[22] and to justify a plaintiff's request for damages based on the quantity and cost of health care rendered, among other uses.

In health care malpractice cases, patient care records are used as discussed above to prove or disprove patient injury from provider/organization malpractice, and to establish losses, or *damages*. They also are often introduced as substantive evidence of a patient-plaintiff's health status and to evaluate the quantity and quality of care rendered to a patient.

Patient care records typically are requested by a patient or the patient's attorney long before a potentially compensable event ripens into a lawsuit. In states where a court order is required to release treatment records to patients, attorneys may have to seek a court order and "discover" the records from the official custodian of the records through issuance of a legal document called a *subpoena duces tecum*.[23] A *subpoena duces tecum* is an order to the custodian of documents or other physical things that are pertinent to issues in a legal controversy to deliver them to a particular place, such as a copying center, or to bring them when testifying at a legal proceeding, such as a pretrial deposition or a trial.[24]

Patients whose records are subpoenaed have statutory rights of challenge to subpoena of their health records. The subpoenaing party must normally send the patient a "notice of subpoena" and send the health care provider having custody over the records a "certificate of compliance." This certificate is a sworn statement made by the subpoenaing party to the record custodian that the patient received the notice of subpoena. Normally, the record custodian must wait a statutory period of time, for example, 15 days, before forwarding the records to the party with the subpoena, to give the patient sufficient time to mount a challenge to the order to produce, if so desired. In a recent Rhode Island case, the state Supreme Court held that patients whose records are subpoenaed before investigative grand juries also have the right to notice and challenge of the subpoenas.[25]

> *"Subpoena duces tecum": a court order to the custodian of patient treatment records that are pertinent to issues in a legal case to deliver them to a business location or to bring them when testifying at a legal proceeding, such as a pretrial deposition or a trial.*

When used at trial as substantive evidence of patient status or care, a patient care record is hearsay evidence. *Hearsay* evidence is any statement (oral, written, or otherwise) made outside of the setting of a trial offered at trial as substantive evidence of the truth of the matter asserted in that statement. Under the "hearsay rule," absent some recognized exception, hearsay evidence is inadmissible in a court of law.[26]

That does not mean that evidence that would otherwise be excludable hearsay cannot be used for purposes other than offering it for its truth. For example, a written hearsay statement might properly be shown to a witness testifying at trial, whose memory is weak, to refresh the witness's present recollection of an event, without admitting the document into evidence. This use of hearsay evidence is called "present recollection refreshed." A witness is better prepared to answer attorneys' questions and makes a better impression on a judge or jury if the witness prepares for deposition or trial in advance by reviewing pertinent records and other documents that will or may be referenced during such testimony.

In addition, what otherwise would be hearsay evidence may be used on cross-examination (after a witness has testified on direct examination) to impeach the witness by showing that the evidence contradicts the witness' in-court testimony. Hearsay evidence contained in patient treatment records may also be used as the basis or foundation of an expert witness' opinion on an issue in controversy.

> *"Hearsay" evidence includes any statement (oral, written, or otherwise) made outside of the setting of a trial, offered at trial as substantive evidence of the truth of the matter asserted in that statement. Under the "hearsay rule," absent some recognized exception, hearsay evidence is inadmissible in a court of law.*

The Patient Care Record as a Business Document

When patient care records are offered in a health care malpractice trial as hearsay evidence of the truth asserted in them, they are admissible because they are business records, or "records of regularly conducted activity."[27] Under an exception to the hearsay rule,[28] business records are generally admissible as substantive evidence so long as four requirements (which may vary from state to state, and in the federal system) are met:

1. The entries in the record are routinely made as part of a "regular course of business";
2. It is part of the regular practice of the business to make such entries;
3. The entries in the records are made contemporaneously with the events recorded; and
4. The custodian of the record testifies and swears or affirms that all the above requirements apply to the record offered as evidence and "authenticates" the record, making it admissible as evidence.

Patient care records normally meet all the above requirements. Before their admission into evidence, the facility health records administrator or another qualified witness testifies that (1) patient care records are required to be routinely produced in the "regular course" of health care delivery by law, accreditation standards, and custom; (2) patient care entries in health records are customarily made at or near the time of examination or intervention by providers privileged to write in patient records; (3) patient care records under the custodian's control are protected from unauthorized handling and alteration; and (4) the patient care record in issue was not produced in anticipation of litigation.

The custodian of the records must also attest to the authenticity of the records in issue, as is usually evidenced by an authentication page bearing the custodian's signature and stamp. For an example of an authentication page, see Exhibit 3–1.

Normally, the "best evidence rule" requires that the custodian produce the original patient care record in court. Under federal evidence rules, and similar rules in most states, an authenticated photocopy is acceptable "secondary" evidence in lieu of the original record, so long as the custodian's explanation of the original's absence satisfies the court as to the trustworthiness of the record copy.

Health Care Professional-Patient Legal Privileges against Breach of Confidentiality

The health care professional-patient privilege[29] is a testimonial privilege that sometimes precludes the admission of patient care information into evidence in legal proceedings. This evidentiary privilege protecting confidentiality in court is different from the health professional's general duties

Exhibit 3–1 Example of Authentication To Release Patient Care Records

---

[Hospital Letterhead]
Patient Records Division

AFFIDAVIT

State of _____

County/Parish of _____

Before me, the undersigned authority, personally appeared Mr./Ms. _____ , who, being duly sworn, certified as follows:

My name is _____ . I am over age twenty-one, am of sound mind, capable of making the following declaration, and personally acquainted with the facts stated herein:

I am the Health Records Administrator of ABC General Hospital and the custodian of all patient care records for the facility. Attached to this affidavit are (#) pages of clinical record on (patient's full name) from ABC General Hospital. These said pages of records are kept by ABC General Hospital in the regular course of business of the facility for an employee, representative, or physician privileged to practice in ABC General Hospital, with personal knowledge of the events and conditions herein recorded. The entries made in this record were made at or near the time of the events described, or reasonably soon thereafter, and were not transcribed into the record in the anticipation of litigation. The records attached hereto are exact duplicate photocopies of the original. It is a rule of ABC General Hospital not to permit original records to leave the facility.

Sworn and subscribed before me on the _____ day of _____ , 20xx.

_____

Notary Public for the State of _____ . My commission expires _____ .

---

of confidentiality and fidelity owed to a patient, which are examined separately in a later section of this chapter.

Under early common law, the legal system took a utilitarian approach to claims for testimonial privileges. Only those that met the following four requirements were allowed:

- The communication originates in confidence.
- Confidence is essential to the relationship in issue.

- The relationship merits confidentiality.
- The harm that would result from disclosure of the confidential communication outweighs the benefit of preserving it.

No health care professional-patient privilege was recognized in common law. Today, most states authorize by statute at least physician- and mental health professional-patient privileges. Some others authorize evidentiary privileges for other health care professionals.

There are qualifications to any health care professional-patient privilege. It belongs to the patient and not to the health care provider. The privilege only applies in situations in which the patient consulted with the provider for care or for a relevant diagnosis in anticipation of intervention. It may not apply in other situations, for example, in which a patient undergoes a functional capacity evaluation pursuant to a court order or in which a health care professional is consulted by the patient (and not by the patient's attorney) for testimony as an expert at trial. The privilege also may not normally apply in administrative workers' compensation actions as to injuries that are at issue in the proceedings. (Note, however, that even in situations in which a testimonial privilege is inapplicable or waived, a treating health care provider still has an ethical and legal [depending on state law] obligation to obtain patient consent before releasing patient care records.)

The health care professional-patient privilege is subject to many exceptions. Of importance to health professionals is the exception that applies to cases in which a patient's physical or mental condition is in issue in a legal case, such as in motor vehicle or other accident cases.

For health care malpractice lawsuits, waiver of the privilege also applies, so that health care professionals who are defendants cannot be prevented from testifying about the patient-plaintiff's condition or care. Under such circumstances, the patient is deemed to have waived the privilege by bringing suit.

CONFIDENTIALITY OF PATIENT CARE INFORMATION

For more than 2,000 years, physicians, on entering the practice of medicine, have recited the Hippocratic Oath,[30] which reads:

> You do solemnly swear, each man (or woman)*
> by whatever he (or she)* holds most sacred

That you will be loyal to the Profession of
Medicine and just and generous to its members
That you will lead your lives and practice
your art in uprightness and honor
That into whatever house you shall enter,
it shall be for the good of the sick to the
utmost of your power, your holding
yourselves far aloof from wrong, from
corruption, from the tempting of others to vice
That you will exercise your art solely for
the cure of your patients, and will give
no drug, perform no operation, for a
criminal purpose, even if solicited, far
less suggest it
That whatsoever you shall see or hear of
the lives of men (or women)* which is not
fitting to be spoken, you will keep
inviolably secret [emphasis added]
These things do you swear. Let each man (and
woman)* bow the head in sign of acquiescence
And now, if you will be true to this, your
oath, may prosperity and good repute be ever
yours; the opposite, if you shall prove
yourselves forsworn.

[*Author's additions]

Hippocrates recognized, as have scholars, ethicists, and health care professionals generally throughout the ages, that a sense of trust in the health care provider on the part of a patient concerning the safeguarding of confidential information is crucial to the success of the professional-patient relationship. The duty of confidentiality is what promotes a patient to "open up" to physicians and other health care professionals and reveal innermost secrets that must be disclosed to the provider for accurate diagnosis and efficacious intervention for disease and injury.

According to the philosopher Sissela Bok, author of the book *Lying: Moral Choice in Public and Private Life,*[31] four fundamental ethical principles form the foundation for confidentiality inherent in the health care professional-patient relationship. These include respect for (1) patient autonomy over information pertaining to that individual, (2) interpersonal relationships and the individual patient's right to confide in a professional of choice, (3) the solemnity of a pledge of confidentiality, and (4) the use of the health care professional-patient confidential relationship in meeting compelling societal health needs.[32]

Since the inception of the Hippocratic oath, all health care disciplines and professionals have come to share the same ethical and legal obligation to safeguard confidential information provided to them by their patients. Modernly, the legal duty of health professionals to respect patient confidentiality derives from statutory and common law, administrative (licensure and certification) regulations, and professional association ethics standards.[33]

Also within the scope of patient confidentiality is a patient's constitutional right of privacy regarding issues ranging from the use of contraceptives[34] to terminating a pregnancy.[35] Physicians figure prominently in advising patients contemplating such decisions. In these situations, patients frequently turn to their physicians (and to other primary health care professionals, especially including nurse practitioners and physician assistants) for professional advice and information. The provider's advice to the patient enjoys the same degree of constitutional protection as does the patient's right to seek such advice to make an informed, intelligent decision.[36] The abortion issue is perhaps the most divisive issue facing America (and many other nations) today. More and more, Congress and state legislatures are narrowing a patient's right to choose to terminate a pregnancy, often through statutes that restrict the kind of information that physicians and other primary health care providers can impart to women seeking their advice.[37]

Special confidentiality rules are in effect in many or most states for such issues as a patient's HIV status and documentation involving treatment for drug (including alcohol) abuse, venereal disease, and birth control and abortion advice. Special reporting requirements to state agencies also exist in many jurisdictions for conditions such as HIV/AIDS, other venereal diseases, tuberculosis, and for suspected child, spouse, or elder abuse. These reporting requirements supersede patients' rights to confidentiality concerning information of "compelling state interest."

Other exceptions to the requirement for confidentiality of patient information include requests for patient information from law enforcement agencies and discretionary release of information disclosed by patients to providers where patient's conduct poses an imminent threat of death or serious bodily harm to a third party or national security.[38] Professional association codes of ethics also address these exceptions.[39]

When a health care provider breaches the duty of confidentiality owed to a patient, the patient may have a legal cause of action under the applicable state confidentiality statute. Penalties for violations typically include a civil or administrative monetary fine. Criminal action brought by a state or federal prosecutor is also possible. Disciplinary action under licensing statutes and regulations also is a potential sanction for unauthorized disclosure of a patient's confidences, as is action for a breach of ethics before a professional association of which the provider is a member.

When no statutory remedy exists for violating a patient's confidence, the patient may bring a civil lawsuit against a provider under the common law principle of invasion of privacy. There are four recognized classes of invasion of privacy:

1. unreasonable intrusion on a patient's solitude
2. unauthorized publicity that portrays a patient in a false light in the public eye
3. appropriation (use) of a patient's name or characteristics without consent
4. unauthorized public revelation of private facts about a patient[40]

The branch of invasion of privacy most often associated with misuse of patient care documentation is the one concerning the public disclosure of private patient facts. Unauthorized disclosure of private patient information, whether done verbally or through the transfer of written documents, is an actionable breach of a health care provider's duty of confidentiality. A patient who successfully sues a provider for invasion of privacy may be awarded damages for emotional and psychological harm as well as physical harm suffered. The patient may also win punitive damages, if the violation is egregious.

> *To fulfill your duty as a health care provider to a patient under your care, never release confidential patient information (except where required to do so by law) without: (1) valid written patient authorization, and (2) a written request for release of specified patient information by a named third party, outlining the purpose(s) for the request. A patient should always be informed in a release authorization of his or her right to withdraw consent of further releases of personal information to third parties.*

There is an increasing public concern over the quantity and uses of confidential individual patient health information held by third parties, especially including health insurance entities. Confidential information particularly includes genetic testing results and histories, as such information may lead to illegal workplace, insurance, and other discrimination.[41] In 1996, Congress enacted the Health Insurance Portability and Accountability Act,[42] which, in part, authorizes Congress to establish statutory confidentiality protections for citizens and legal residents. As Congress has failed to act as of the writing of this passage, the Department of Health and Human Services is authorized by the Health Insurance Portability and Accountability Act of 1996 to enact its own patient-protective regulations.[43]

How do private entities gain the right of access to confidential information contained in patient care records? We the people/patients routinely give up our right of confidentiality every time we sign "routine" waivers of confidentiality in the form of patient care record data releases when receiving care, when applying for life or health insurance, when processing health care claims, or for a myriad of other seemingly good reasons. (An example of a patient care record release appears in Exhibit 3–2.)

Consumer advocates urge all individuals to take several steps to ensure that any information on file about them is accurate. First, consumers should inquire of such agencies about any information that they might have on them and request a summary of that information. If it is erroneous, as it sometimes is, consumers should take steps to have the data corrected to prevent denial of employment, insurance, or other rights and benefits. Second, consumers should consider "tailoring" any releases that they authorize in terms of scope of data subject to release and time. In this way, agencies cannot assume a right to collect health-related information about such individuals into perpetuity. States are beginning to limit the duration for release authorizations in the absence of set time limits within actual release instruments. Congress and/or the Department of Health and Human Services should include such a provision in their implementing legislation/regulations related to the Health Insurance Portability and Accountability Act of 1996.

CONCLUSION

Besides their primary function of creating a ready database of clinically pertinent patient health information, patient care records have important

Exhibit 3–2 Example of a Patient Authorization for Release of Patient Care Records

---

AUTHORIZATION FOR RELEASE OF HEALTH INFORMATION

I, (name) _____ , (SSN) _____ , (date of birth) _____ , hereby authorize <u>(name and address of health records custodian)</u> to release <u>(exact description of information to be released)</u> to <u>(name and address of party to whom records are to be released)</u>.

I understand that this authorization empowers the custodian of my health records to release all records included above, including information pertaining to drug and alcohol treatment, psychological evaluation and treatment, and HIV status, as permitted by state/federal law.

The purpose of this authorization is to provide relevant health information to parties to the lawsuit named above.

This authorization is subject to written revocation by me at any time and otherwise is valid for three months from the date of signing.

_____
Date

_____   _____
Street Address   Signature

_____   _____
City, State, ZIP Code   Name (typed or printed)

---

administrative and legal uses, too. They are routinely offered by parties in civil and criminal court cases as substantive evidence of a patient's health status or of the type and quality of care that a patient received. Patient care records are used in virtually every type of administrative and civil legal case, including disability claims cases, workers' compensation cases, personal injury cases, child custody and paternity cases, and health care malpractice cases, just to name a few.

Clinical health care professionals should always document in patient care records as if the entry were being prepared for court because such records may in fact find their way into court. A "patient welfare" approach to patient care documentation is recommended, over a defensive, self-preservation approach. However, the effective self-protective practice of liability risk management is not necessarily the equivalent of defensive documentation.

Spoliation of records involves the intentional alteration or destruction of patient care entries or records, and there is evidence that this practice is growing among health care providers. Documents examiners can easily detect spoliation through gross examination and, where necessary, scientific testing of documents or computer files and systems. If a court finds that a health care provider or other health care organization employee altered or destroyed records, it will probably order the jury to infer or presume negligence against the provider in a health care malpractice case. Punitive damages, not indemnifiable by insurers, may also be awarded against a health care provider/organization-defendant in such cases.

A health care professional's duty to safeguard confidential patient information is similar to but not congruous with the limited health care professional-patient privilege against involuntary disclosure of patient information in legal proceedings. All providers and health-related support personnel owe their patients a special duty of confidentiality. It is primarily because of the trust patients have that their health care providers will safeguard their confidences that they are willing to "open up" to providers during examination and intervention. The scope of this ethical and legal duty is governed by state and federal statutory, regulatory, and case law; state licensure and ethical codes; professional association and accreditation standards; and longstanding custom.

The privilege to withhold confidential patient care information in legal proceedings derives from an evidentiary rule that allows a provider covered by federal or state law to refuse to divulge patient examination, evaluative, diagnostic, prognostic, and intervention-related information on behalf of a patient. The privilege being invoked in such cases belongs exclusively to the patient and not to the health care provider. Exceptions to confidentiality and privilege may include information pertaining to criminal activity; child, spouse, and elder abuse; and findings related to reportable communicable disease.

REFERENCES

1. Background material for the discussion of patient records in legal proceedings derives, in part, from law school lecture notes, for which the author gratefully acknowledges Professor Corey Marco, M.D., J.D., University of San Diego School of Law (1982).

2. For example, in the federal sector (Army hospitals), inpatient treatment records must be stored by major medical centers for five years. *See* Army Regulation 40–66, ¶ 8–5 (July 20, 1992). Similar regulations exist for other military and civilian federal health care facilities under federal law and for state public and private facilities under state law.

3. C.T. Hardy, *Hotline Answers*, PHYSICIAN'S MGMT., May 1992, at 210.

4. Hardy, *Hotline Answers.*

5. Hardy, *Hotline Answers.*

6. In legal terms, an *inference* allows (but does not compel) a conclusion of negligence by a jury based on permissive deductive reasoning that the loss of the patient-plaintiff's treatment records logically occurred at the hands of the defendants, who were at fault.

7. An instruction by a judge to a jury that they are to presume negligence (i.e., a *presumption*) based on lost or altered treatment records could require the jury to assume negligence unless and until the defendants rebutted the presumption with sufficient evidence of their own to the contrary.

8. *See, e.g.,* Proske v. St. Barnabas Medical Center, 1998 WL 35297 (NJ Sup. Ct. App. Div., June 23, 1998).

9. Health Care Quality Improvement Act of 1986, 42 U.S.C. §§ 11101–11152.

10. *See The Vanishing Nurse's Note: Was Risk Manager to Blame?* HOSP. RISK MGMT., February 1991, at 17–21, citing the legal case, Battocchi v. Washington Hospital Center, D.C. Court of Appeals, October 16, 1990. Note that in that case, the designated hospital risk manager vehemently denied ever having possessed the lost treatment note.

11. *See* R.L. Prosser, *Alteration of Medical Records Submitted for Legal Review*, JAMA, 2630–2631 (May 1992).

12. Prosser, *Alteration of Medical Records.*

13. Prosser, *Alteration of Medical Records.*

14. Background material for the discussion on scientific analysis of evidence comes from the author's lecture notes from the LLM Program, TJAGSA, Charlottesville, VA, 1987–88, and from tour of the U.S. Army Criminal Investigation Laboratory, Frankfurt, Germany, undertaken in May 1984. For further elucidation on forensic analysis of documents, *see* D.A. Nygaard & S.J. Deubner, *Altered or "Lost" Medical Records*, TRIAL, June 1988, at 50–55. *See also* S. McInnis, *Signs and Symptoms of Defensive Medical Recordkeeping*, 60 OKLA. BAR J. 2339–2342 (1989).

15. Under the landmark civil rights federal legislation, the Americans with Disabilities Act of 1990, 42 U.S.C. §§ 12101–12213, an employer may not discriminate against a qualified disabled job applicant or employee, unless doing so would create a provable legally sufficient undue hardship for the employer. Title I, ADA. *See* R.W. Scott, *The ADA and You*, CLINICAL MGMT., January/February 1991, at 16–17.

16. M. Chase, *How to Gain Access to Your Medical Files Amid Varied Laws.* WALL STREET J. December 2, 1996, B1

17. *See, eg.,* Army Regulation 40–66, Medical Record Administration, July 20, 1992, ¶ 1–5 ("Record Ownership"), which reads in pertinent part

   a. Army medical records are the property of the Government . . .

   b. Army medical records will remain in the custody of the military MTFs [medical treatment facilities] at all times, except when being transferred directly from one military MTF to another. This medical record is the Government's record of medical care that it has rendered and must be protected. Upon request, the patient may be provided with a copy of his or her record but not the original record. Procedures should ensure conscientious Government control over medical records for good medical care, quality assurance, and risk management.

18. Chase, *How to Gain Access.*

19. Chase, *How to Gain Access.*

20. *See What To Do When Patients Ask for Their Medical Records*, HOSP. RISK MGMT., August 1991, at 104.

21. *See Eliminate Jargon To Improve Communication with Patients,* HOSP. RISK MGMT., October 1990, at 137–139.

22. *See* W.D. Sommerness, Testifying in Court: You and Your Records. In: S.J. ISERNHAGEN, THE COMPREHENSIVE GUIDE TO WORK INJURY MANAGEMENT (1995), Gaithersburg, MD: Aspen Publishers, Inc.

23. A custodian of patient records also has legal recourse if the request for records contained in the *subpoena duces tecum* is overbroad. For example, a request for "all of the patient's medical, dental, and other health records, including billing, payment, and insurance documents for all times, past and current" would be oppressive. The records custodian (health records administrator) could ask the court for a protective order that would require a more tailored subpoena that requests only those records pertinent to conditions related to injuries claimed in the lawsuit. For elucidation on the rights of the records custodian, *see* B.E. Krell & P.L. Hendrix, *Protecting the Record*, CAL. LAW., May 1989, at 86–87.

24. For detailed information on deposition practice, *see* R.W. Scott, HEALTH CARE MALPRACTICE, 2ND ED., (1999), New York: McGraw-Hill, Inc., pp. 109–111.

25. *In Re Doe Grand Jury Proceedings.* No. 97–283-M.P. (R.I. August 4, 1998).

26. *See, e.g.,* Federal Rules of Evidence, Rule 803 (Hearsay Rule), which reads

Hearsay is not admissible except as provided by these rules or by other rules prescribed by the Supreme Court pursuant to statutory authority or by Act of Congress.

The federal rules of evidence apply to legal cases brought in federal court, either involving a "federal question" or having complete "diversity" of citizenship between opposing parties to the suit and a greater than $50,000 amount in controversy. *See* 28 U.S.C. § 1332.

27. *See* Federal Rule of Evidence, 803(6), which reads

The following are not excluded by the hearsay rule, even though the declarant is available as a witness:

(6) A memorandum, report, record, or data compilation, in any form, of acts, events, conditions, opinions, or diagnoses, made at or near the time by, or from information transmitted by, a person with knowledge, if kept in the course of a regularly conducted business activity, and if it were the regular practice of that business activity to make the memorandum, report, record, or data compilation, all as shown by the testimony of the custodian or other qualified witness, unless the source of information or the method or circumstances of preparation indicate lack of trustworthiness. The term "business" as used in this paragraph, includes business, institution, association, profession, occupation, and calling of every kind, whether or not conducted for profit.

28. Federal Rule of Evidence.

29. *See generally* E.W. CLEARY, MCCORMICK'S HANDBOOK ON THE LAW OF EVIDENCE, 2ND ED. (1972), pp. 212–228.

30. R.W. SCOTT, PROFESSIONAL ETHICS: A GUIDE FOR REHABILITATION PROFESSIONALS (1998), St. Louis, MO: Mosby, p. 15.

31. S. BOK, LYING: MORAL CHOICE IN PUBLIC AND PRIVATE LIFE (1989), New York: Vintage Books.

32. *See* M.G. Bissel, *Respect Primary in Patient Confidentiality*, ADVANCE RADIOLOGIC SCI. PROF., March 9, 1992, at 8, citing S. Bok, *Lying: Moral Choice in Public and Private Life* 31, 149, 150, 160 (1989).

33. B. Woodward, *Medical Record Confidentiality and Data Collection: Current Dilemmas*, JOURNAL OF LAW, MEDICINE, AND ETHICS 25(2,3), 88–97 (1997).

34. Griswold v. Connecticut, 381 U.S. 479 (1965).

35. Row v. Wade, 410 U.S. 113 (1973).

36. *See* H.M. Cole, *The Right of Privacy Protects the Doctor-Patient Relationship*, 263 JAMA 858–861 (1990).

37. Cole, *The Right of Privacy.*

38. The lead legal case involving a health care professional's (psychotherapist) duty to warn third parties of the potential danger of serious bodily harm at the hands of patients under his or her care is Tarasoff v. Regents of the University of Cal., 17 Cal.3d 425, 131 Cal. Rptr.14, 551 P.2d 334 (1976).

39. *See, e.g.,* Guide for Professional Conduct, American Physical Therapy Association (1997), Section I2D, which reads:

    Information may be disclosed to appropriate authorities when it is necessary to protect the welfare of an individual or the community. Such disclosure shall be in accordance with applicable law.

40. For more on the invasion of privacy, *see* R.W. SCOTT, HEALTH CARE MALPRACTICE: A PRIMER ON LEGAL ISSUES FOR PROFESSIONALS, 2ND ED. (1990), pp. 64–68.

41. P.S. Miller, *Genetic Discrimination in the Workplace.* JOURNAL OF LAW, MEDICINE, AND ETHICS 26(8), 189–197 (1998).

42. Health Insurance Portability and Accountability Act of 1996, P.L. 104–191.

43. *Congress Wrestles with Complex Issues of Patient Privacy As August Deadline Looms*, P.T. BULLETIN 14(32), 1–2 (1999).

SUGGESTED READING

R.E. Bergmark & M. Parker, *How Confidential Is Confidential?* MANAGED CARE AND AGING (1998): 5(1), 1–2, 8.

E.S. Flores-Troy, *The Genetic Privacy Act: An Analysis of Privacy and Research Concerns*, JOURNAL OF LAW, MEDICINE, AND ETHICS 25(4), 256–272 (1997).

Mandziara v. Canulli. No. 1–97–4644 (Ill. App. Ct., September 24, 1998) (lawsuit for alleged unauthorized possession of patient mental health records).

M.A. Prost, *Protecting Patient Confidentiality*, ADVANCE FOR PHYSICAL THERAPISTS. March 30, 1998, 8–10.

B.E. Ranke, *Documentation in the Age of Litigation*, OT PRACTICE. March 1998, 20–24.

R.W. SCOTT, HEALTH CARE MALPRACTICE: A PRIMER ON LEGAL ISSUES, 2ND ED. (1999).

R.W. SCOTT, PROMOTING LEGAL AWARENESS IN PHYSICAL AND OCCUPATIONAL THERAPY (1998).

M.E. Silber & M.E. Rabler, *Access to Medical Records*. HEALTH LAWYER 1996: 8(6), 10–13.

R.W. Thompson, *Feds Should Regulate Medical Records Privacy, Congress Told*. HR NEWS. November 1998, 7.

REVIEW: CASE STUDIES

1. You are a registered nurse in charge of the afternoon shift in a surgical intensive care unit. X, a comatose patient in the unit, who is on a respirator, just arrested and is being transported to the operating room for heart surgery. One of your staff nurses, F, telephones to check on some missing keys, and, during the conversation, you inform him of patient X's condition. Nurse F suddenly remembers that he forgot to document in the computerized nursing progress notes during his shift that he performed respiratory hygiene and postural drainage on patient X twice during his shift. He asks you to add that information to his end-of-shift note. What do you tell him?

2. J, a paralegal employed by WXY Law Associates, telephones your office, requesting the name, address, and other personal and clinical information about a patient being treated in your clinic for soft tissue injuries sustained in a motor vehicle accident. J claims that he has been in contact with the patient about pursuing a product liability class action lawsuit stemming from a defective automobile part. You are personally familiar with the named patient J seeks information about. Should you release any information to the paralegal?

3. You are the medical librarian at AZ Community Hospital. While conducting a research computer search, you overhear two teenage summer volunteers from the community health office talking to one another about a patient's HIV status. You do not hear the patient's name and are not sure that any name was used. What course of action should you take?

SUGGESTED ANSWERS AND DISCUSSION

1. You should inform nurse F that you cannot add information to his prior treatment documentation. Whether by computer or in writing, intentional alteration of prior documentation entries constitutes illegal spoliation of records. Spoliation can usually be detected by document examiners, even when performed on a computer. If you agree with nurse F to alter his documentation of patient X's care, then you may be liable for "conspiracy" as well as spoliation. If it is critical for nurse F to add the information about patient X's respiratory care performed earlier that day, then nurse F should personally document his prior omission as a new entry. Before doing so in this case, however, nurse F may want to coordinate with the hospital risk manager, because patient X's condition has deteriorated and patient X's case may become a PCE.

2. You should refrain from providing any information to J under the circumstances of this hypothetical case for several reasons. First, while J's employer may have formed an attorney-client relationship with the patient in issue, you are not a party to that agreement. You have a separate legal duty to safeguard the patient's personal information from unlawful disclosure to others. Although some state statutes may allow for unilateral release of nonclinical information about patients to third parties, it would probably be imprudent to do so in today's litigious environment. Second, J's request for information was made over the telephone. Never give patient information out to anyone over the telephone. J's request must be made in writing and should appear on his attorney's letterhead to reference the source of the request. Third, if you do not already have a patient release on file, the written request must be accompanied by an authorization to release clinical information, signed by the patient. Then release only that information within the scope of the patient's authorization and not necessarily all that has been asked for by J. A prudent precaution before releasing the information would be to confirm telephonically with the patient that he or she consents to the release. Be sure to document your conversation with the patient, in the form of a memorandum. The same requirements and precautions are likewise true for insurance company and other requests for patient information.

3. The volunteers have disclosed, in public, private facts about a patient. As librarian, you probably have no official need or right to know such information. This invasion of privacy probably will not be legally actionable, however, if the patient cannot be identified, or if others, besides the librarian—a hospital employee—did not overhear the volunteers' conversation. If the patient can somehow be identified (by the volunteers' description of the patient, for example), and if the patient sues and wins, then the hospital probably will be vicariously liable for damages suffered by the patient for the volunteers' invasion of privacy.

Chapter 4

Informed Consent
Documentation Issues

This chapter examines the concept of patient informed consent to health-related examination and intervention. The history of the development of the law of informed consent is examined, and the sources of authority for requiring patient informed consent are presented. A standardized checklist of disclosure elements for legally sufficient informed consent is offered, with the caveat that this information is illustrative and not necessarily a reflection of the law of any particular state. The chapter ends with a discussion of documentation guidelines for memorializing patient informed consent.

INTRODUCTION

The issue of patient informed consent to examination and intervention is one that is or should be of critical concern to all health care professionals, whether they examine and intervene on behalf of patients with or without a referral from another provider. There are relatively few health care malpractice cases solely involving allegations of lack of informed consent. However, with current practice trends and issues, including direct access practice in physical therapy and other nonphysician disciplines and the time constraints of managed care, the issue of informed consent is made all the more salient.

All primary health care providers have a legal and ethical responsibility to provide their patients with sufficient disclosure information about examination and interventions to allow them to make a knowing, intelligent, and unequivocal decision regarding consent. The concept of informed consent is premised on respect for the patient's rights of autonomy and self-determination (i.e., the inherent right of every patient with legal and mental capacity [or of a legitimate surrogate decision maker] to control the health care decision-making process and decide the intervention(s), if any, that will be carried out on him or her).

LEGAL RECOGNITION OF THE CONCEPT OF INFORMED CONSENT

Informed consent to health care intervention is recognized as a fundamental right in case law[1], by statute, or as a matter of customary practice in virtually every jurisdiction. It is also recognized as such a right by health professional practice, ethics, and health care organization/system accreditation standards.[2]

A number of state legislatures have enacted statutory informed consent procedures that include informed consent forms, signed by patients, for specific surgeries and other medical procedures. A patient's signature on such a form may constitute presumptive legal evidence of patient informed consent. When such a statute is in effect in an informed consent-based health care malpractice case, the patient must usually prove that consent was induced by a misrepresentation of material facts or must produce credible evidence that he or she did not reasonably understand the form in order to rebut such a presumption.

U.S. Supreme Court case decisions interpreting the Constitution also reflect respect for patient self-determination in making important health care decisions. Case law based on the federal constitutional right of privacy[3] has balanced patient autonomy against "compelling state interests" and frequently has ruled in favor of patients and/or their surrogate decision makers on issues such as the withdrawal of life[4] and nutritional support.[5,6]

Health professional associations have also promulgated rules and standards concerning patient informed consent. For example, reflecting the primary care nature of physical therapy practice (including direct access patient evaluation and treatment), the American Physical Therapy Association's core practice documents, the *Guide for Professional Conduct* (Principle 1.4), the *Guidelines for Physical Therapy Documentation* (IA2: General Guidelines: Informed Consent); and the *Standards of Practice for Physical Therapy* (Standard IIIA: Provision of Services: Informed

Consent), all address provider informed consent-related duties in great detail. [Relevant portions of these documents appear in Appendix 4–A.] Similar legal and professional ethical standards apply to, and are memorialized in writing for, all other primary health care disciplines.

The federal Patient Self-Determination Act of 1990[7] also codifies the rights of patients to control health care decision making, both routine and extraordinary. The law binds hospitals, long-term care facilities, and other health care facilities participating in Medicare and Medicaid to its provisions.

The Patient Self-Determination Act provides in pertinent part that

> The requirement of this subsection is that a provider . . . maintain written policies and procedures with respect to all adult individuals receiving medical care . . .
>
> To provide written information to each such individual concerning an individual's rights under State law (whether statutory or as recognized by the courts of the state) to make decisions concerning. . .medical care, including the right to accept or refuse medical or surgical treatment.[8]

Some authorities argue that financial reimbursement for health care services should be tied to proof that the patient (or surrogate decision maker) gave valid informed consent to treatment.[9]

EVOLUTION OF THE LAW OF INFORMED CONSENT

The concept of patient informed consent is largely a result of the consumer rights movement that has swept the Western world since World War II, although it was recognized earlier than that. As early as 1914, a respected jurist, Justice Benjamin Cardozo, wrote in his opinion in the case of *Schloendorff v. Society of New York Hospital* that "every human being of adult years and sound mind has a right to determine what shall be done with his own body; and a surgeon who performs an operation without his patient's consent commits an assault for which he is liable in damages."[10]

For several decades after the *Schloendorff* decision, the care of patients without their consent was treated as an assault or battery, depending on the term used by the particular state. By definition, an *assault* normally encompasses intentional conduct on the part of one person that creates in another an apprehension or anticipation of the application of force. In other words, an assault is a fear of an unwanted touch. The actual application of force, in the form of an unconsented, unprivileged harmful or offensive touch or other physical contact, is, in legal terms, a *battery*. Commonly recognized examples of commission of a battery in the health care setting include striking a patient in anger, amputating the wrong limb or excising the wrong breast during a mastectomy surgery, or administering an ultrasound treatment in the wrong situs.[11]

Assault: the apprehension or anticipation of the application of unauthorized physical force.

Battery: the unconsented, unprivileged harmful or offensive touching of another person.

Sexual assault or battery: the unconsented, unprivileged harmful or offensive intentional touching or attempted touching of the sexual or other intimate parts of another person, for the purpose of sexual arousal or gratification (of either party), or for patient abuse.

For many years, allegations of a lack of patient informed consent continued to be treated as the intentional torts of assault and battery. The precise term *informed consent* only came into common use after it was used by the Kansas Supreme Court in the case of *Natanson v. Kline*.[12] That case concerned a claim by a cancer patient that she was injured by excessive radiation therapy. The patient claimed that she did not understand the nature and consequences of the treatment, and if she had, she would not have consented to it. The justice writing the legal opinion in *Natanson* stated:[13]

> The fundamental distinction between assault and battery on one hand, and negligence such as would constitute malpractice, on the other, is that the former is intentional and the latter unintentional. . . .
>
> We are here concerned with a case where the patient consented to the treatment, but alleges in a malpractice action that the nature and consequences of the risks of the treatment were not properly explained to her. This relates directly to whether the physician has obtained the *informed consent* [emphasis added] of the patient to render the treatment administered. . . .
>
> The courts frequently state that the relation(ship) between the physician and his patient is a fiduciary one, and therefore the physician has an

obligation to make a full and frank disclosure to the patient of all pertinent facts related to his illness. We are here concerned with a case where the physician is charged with treating the patient without consent on the ground the patient was not fully informed of the nature of the treatment or its consequences, and, therefore, any "consent" obtained was ineffective. . . .

In considering the obligation of a physician to disclose and explain to the patient, in language as simple as necessary, the nature of the ailment, the nature of the proposed treatment, the probability of success or of alternatives, and, perhaps, the risks of unfortunate results and unforeseen conditions within the body, we do not think the administration of such an obligation, by imposing liability for malpractice if the treatment were administered without such explanation, where explanation would reasonably be made, presents any insurmountable obstacles.

The appellate court in *Natanson* reversed the trial level court's jury verdict in favor of the defendants and ordered a retrial with instructions to be given by the trial judge about a physician's duty to make disclosures about a patient's illness; the nature of the recommended intervention; and its risks, expected benefits, and alternative interventions to ensure patient informed consent. *Natanson* was one of the first cases to properly label the treatment of a patient without informed consent as health "professional negligence," instead of calling it a "battery."

In another landmark informed consent case, *Canterbury v. Spence*,[14] the federal appeals court refined the concept of informed consent even more and established a new standard for information disclosure by health care providers to patients. In *Canterbury*, which involved a laminectomy patient's claim that the surgeon negligently failed to inform him fully of postoperative complications, Judge Spotswood Robinson III held that:[15]

The patient's reliance upon the physician is a trust of the kind which traditionally has exacted obligations beyond those associated with arms length transactions. [The patient's] dependence upon the physician for information affecting his well-being, in terms of contemplated treatment, is well-nigh abject. . . .

We now find, as a part of the physician's overall obligation to the patient, a similar duty of reasonable disclosure of the choices with respect to proposed therapy and the dangers inherently and potentially involved. . . .

The topics importantly demanding a communication of information are the inherent and potential hazards of the proposed treatment, the alternatives to that treatment, if any, and the results likely if the patient remains untreated. The factors contributing significance to the dangerousness of a medical treatment are, of course, the incidence of injury and the degree of harm threatened. A very small chance of death or serious disablement may well be significant; a potential disability that dramatically outweighs the potential benefit of the therapy or the detriments of the existing malady may summon discussion with the patient.

There is no bright line separating the significant from the insignificant; the answer in any case must abide a rule of reason.

Judge Robinson reversed a trial court *directed* [expedited] *verdict*[16] for the defendants (surgeon and hospital) and ordered a new trial. The *Canterbury* case is revisited in later sections, during discussion of prerequisites to legal action for an allegation of a lack of informed consent, exceptions to the requirement to obtain a patient's informed consent before examination or intervention, and the legal and professional ethical standards for information disclosure.

The *Natanson* and *Canterbury* cases, then, established that the failure on the part of a health care provider to obtain a patient's informed consent to examination or intervention is health professional negligence and not the intentional tort of assault or battery. Care of a patient without the patient's informed consent means that the patient was not given sufficient disclosure information about the process by his or her primary health care provider to make an intelligent, informed choice about whether or not to agree to it.

> *Failure on the part of a health care provider to obtain a patient's informed consent before examination or intervention is a form of health professional negligence, and constitutes substandard care delivery.*

WHEN IS THE FAILURE TO OBTAIN PATIENT INFORMED CONSENT LEGALLY ACTIONABLE?

Although every failure to obtain patient informed consent before examination or intervention is professional negligence (absent some recognized exception to the requirement), not every such breach of duty can result in legal action by the patient. Litigation over informed consent only arises when:

1. an undisclosed risk materializes, resulting in injury to the patient, and
2. the patient establishes (i.e., proves) that he or she would not have consented to examination or intervention had the risk been disclosed.

The court in *Canterbury*[17] discussed the requirement for a causal connection between patient injury and the negligent failure to impart information to the patient, and reasoned that:

> No more than breach of any other legal duty does nonfulfillment of the physician's obligation to disclose alone establish liability to the patient. *An unrevealed risk that should have been made known must materialize, for otherwise the omission, however unpardonable, is legally without consequence. Occurrence of the risk must be harmful to the patient, for negligence unrelated to injury is nonactionable* [emphasis added]. And, as in malpractice actions generally, there must be a causal relationship between the physician's failure to adequately divulge and damage to the patient.
>
> *A causal connection exists when, but only when, disclosure of significant risks incidental to treatment would have resulted in a decision against it* [emphasis added]. The patient obviously has no complaint if he would have submitted to the therapy notwithstanding awareness that the risk was one of its perils. On the other hand, the very purpose of the disclosure rule is to protect the patient against the consequences which, if known, he would have avoided by forgoing the treatment.

Litigation concerning informed consent should never have to occur because obtaining a patient's informed consent is a legal prerequisite to examination and intervention. And because the legal requirements for gaining a patient's informed consent are relatively straightforward, the process is not particularly burdensome for clinicians. Providers simply need to make informed consent an integral part of their patient examinations and intervention processes.

DISCLOSURE ELEMENTS FOR LEGALLY SUFFICIENT PATIENT INFORMED CONSENT

The following elements normally must be disclosed to the patient before examination or intervention, then patient [or surrogate] questions must be actively solicited, and any questions that the patient has satisfactorily answered by a primary health care provider in order to meet the legal requirements for patient informed consent. The exact requirements for informed consent vary from state to state, however. This list that follows does not necessarily represent the law of any particular state. (See your facility or personal attorney for specific advice.)

Patient informed consent to examination involves disclosure and discussion of the patient's medical or other prior relevant diagnosis and the parameters of the intended examination. For a patient's consent to substantive intervention to be legally sufficient, or "informed," the primary health care provider must relate the following elements to the patient in layperson's language at the level of patient understanding:

1. A description of the patient's health problem (diagnosis or evaluative findings) and the recommended intervention.
2. Material risks, if any, associated with the recommended intervention. Material risks include important "decisional" risks (including foreseeable complications associated with the recommended intervention) or precautions that would cause an ordinary, reasonable patient to think carefully when deciding whether to undergo or reject the recommended intervention.
3. Reasonable alternatives, if any, to the proposed intervention (i.e., other effective potential interventions that would be acceptable substitutes under legal standards of practice). The provider must be sure to include discussion of the relative risks and benefits of alternative interventions.
4. Expected benefits, or goals, and prognosis associated with the recommended intervention.

Providers should memorize the above elements and routinely cover each of them with every patient. After the applicable disclosure elements are imparted to a patient, the health care provider must solicit patient questions and answer them to the patient's satisfaction before proceeding on to either examination or intervention.

When the English language is not a patient's primary language (or that of the surrogate decision maker, for patients lacking mental capacity), the provider must use the services of an interpreter to ensure patient comprehension of the informed consent disclosure elements. Careful documenta-

Exhibit 4–1 Example of Informed Consent Documentation Involving an Interpreter for the Patient

---

ABC General Hospital
Rehabilitation Center, Physical Therapy Section

May 23, 20xx/1600

S: 42 y o F, dx multiple sclerosis, wheelchair-bound, referred for "evaluation, facilitative range of motion, and progressive exercise and ambulation, to tolerance." Pt. is Spanish-speaking; Mrs. Gonzales, Red Cross volunteer, acted as interpreter.

O: . . .

A: . . .

P: Begin AAROM today; standing at parallel bars, to tolerance. I obtained informed consent from the pt. in Spanish through Mrs. Gonzales, interpreter. Pt. verbalizes understanding of her diagnosis and my examination findings; the recommended intervention as outlined in Dr. Doe's order; the risks of muscle soreness, fatigue, and the slight risk of joint subluxation associated with exercise; and information about the alternative options of bedrest and limited activity in her wheelchair. I asked for her questions, through Mrs. Gonzales. She wanted to know how long sessions lasted; I told her 45 min. to 1 hr. each, but only to her tolerance. She verbalized satisfaction with the program as outlined and agreed to try it.

G: . . .

—Reggie Hausenfus, PT, #07165733

---

tion is recommended whenever an interpreter is employed during these processes. An example of documenting the services of an interpreter during informed consent disclosure appears in Exhibit 4–1.

Checklist Disclosure Elements for Patient Informed Consent to Intervention

Examination and evaluative findings; diagnosis (or diagnoses)

• *Description of the recommended intervention(s)*

- *Material (decisional) risks of possible harm or foreseeable complications associated with the recommended intervention(s)*
- *Expected benefits (goals) and prognosis*
- *Reasonable alternatives to the recommended intervention, including relative risks, benefits, and prognosis associated with reasonable alternative interventions (or no intervention)*
- *Solicitation of and answers to the patient questions*

As primary health care providers, always bear in mind that any health-related intervention is only a recommended intervention (even if prescribed or ordered by another health care professional) unless and until a patient with legal and mental capacity agrees to it.

DOCUMENTING A PATIENT'S "INFORMED REFUSAL"

In the event that a patient is inclined to refuse examination and/or intervention altogether, the primary health care professional involved in the patient's care must undertake a further step to meet legal requirements for informed consent. In cases involving patient declination of care, a provider must explain to the patient, in an objective fashion, the expected consequences of refusing examination and/or intervention. After such disclosure, a decision by the patient to refuse care would constitute legally "informed refusal." Careful and thorough documentation in the patient care record of the above processes, in informed refusal situations, is always required in case a legal action ensues. An example of how to document patient informed refusal of intervention appears in Exhibit 4–2.

Checklist Disclosure Elements for Patient Informed Refusal of Intervention

- *Examination and evaluative findings, diagnosis*
- *Description of the recommended intervention*
- *Material (decisional) risks associated with the recommended intervention*
- *Expected benefits and prognosis*
- *Reasonable alternatives*
- *Solicitation and satisfactory answering of patient questions*

> • *Explanation of the foreseeable consequences of refusing intervention*
> • *Careful and thorough documentation of the above processes in the patient care record*

CLINICAL MODELS FOR IMPLEMENTING INFORMED CONSENT

Health care professionals may feel a sense of frustration with having the responsibility of going through a litany of checklist elements to obtain patient informed consent for each of their patients, especially in a hurried

---

Exhibit 4–2 Example of Documentation of Patient Informed Refusal of Intervention

---

ABC General Hospital
Rehabilitation Center
Physical Therapy Section

May 23, 20xx/1600

S: 42 y o F, dx multiple sclerosis, wheelchair-bound, referred for "evaluation, facilitative range of motion, and progressive exercise and ambulation, to tolerance."

O: . . .

A: . . .

P: Begin AAROM today; standing at parallel bars, to tolerance. After explanation to pt. of her diagnosis and my evaluative findings; the proposed therapy as outlined in Dr. Doe's order; the risks of muscle soreness, fatigue, and the slight risk of joint subluxation associated with exercise; and the alternative options of bed rest and limited activity in her wheelchair, pt. stated, "I don't want any treatment." I explained to her, in the presence of Holly Wood, PT, the risks of joint contractures, muscle wasting, osteoporosis, and cardiovascular compromise associated with inactivity, and invited her questions about the recommended intervention and my explanation of the risks of forgoing intervention. She still refused to proceed. Pt. transported back to nursing floor; RN in charge and Dr. Doe notified. Will attempt to persuade pt. to change her mind in the A.M.

—Reggie Hausenfus, PT, #07165733

world of managed (or as some might say, minimal) care. Providers may also be confused about how to document in patient care records the fact that patient informed consent has been obtained. Rozovsky[18] correctly asserts that informed consent is a process and not just the *pro forma* adherence to oral or written checklists or preprinted forms. Checklists and careful documentation about patient informed consent, although important, only serve as some evidence that this critically important process took place. That process is ensuring, through good communication, that a patient truly understands the parameters of a proposed treatment and agrees to accept examination and/or intervention.

> *Documentation of patient informed consent, although important, is only some evidence that the critical process of communication between health care provider and patient took place and that the patient truly understood the parameters of examination and/or recommended intervention and agreed to it.*

Several recognized models can be adopted by health care providers to implement patient informed consent.[19] The rules-oriented legalistic model and the traditional medical model focus on strict compliance with regulatory or health professional practice standards, and not on patient autonomy over health care decision making. The normative model focuses on the patient's right to self-determination so much that it defers to patient choice in all circumstances, even when that choice is seemingly irrational. The interactive model, advocated in various forms by the author, and by Katz,[20] Rozovsky, and others, is the patient informed consent model that focuses attention on the *processes* of:

- communication between provider and patient,
- patient comprehension and education, and
- patient participation in, and joint responsibility for, health care decision making.

This model, grounded in mutual trust and respect, recognizes that health care providers and patients come together both as equals and unequals. Although providers normally come into the process with a greater understanding of scientific principles concerning health and disease, their patients usually possess a greater intuition about their own personal health status. Therefore, this model offers the best opportunity, through shared decision making, to simultaneously improve the quality of patient care delivery and to manage the formidable risk of health care malpractice exposure incident to clinical practice.

SPECIAL INFORMED CONSENT ISSUES

Who Must Obtain a Patient's Informed Consent?

Any primary health care provider who provides care for a patient has a legal and professional ethical duty to obtain the patient's informed consent before commencing examination or intervention. For nonphysician primary health care providers, this duty applies whether or not the provider cares for patients with a physician (or other provider) referral. Referring physicians often issue generic referral orders such as "evaluate and treat" and, therefore, practically cannot ascertain the precise interventions that a nonphysician consultant will employ. Also, nonphysician primary health care provider-specialist-consultants typically know more about their practices than do referring entities and are therefore in a better position to explain them to patients and answer patient questions.[21]

> *It is primary health care professionals who bear legal and professional ethical responsibility for gaining patients' informed consent, not referral entities, nor assistants, aides, clerical personnel, or others. This point is particularly important to remember in the extender-oriented managed care environment.*

A health care organization or system may bear vicarious or primary liability for the failure of providers in its facilities to obtain patients' informed consent to examinations and interventions. In addition to being indirectly liable for the conduct of professional employee staff, health care organizations have an independent primary duty to establish practice standards and monitor patient care within their facilities, irrespective of who delivers that care.

How Often Must Informed Consent Be Obtained?

Must informed consent be obtained over and over again for the same patient before each individual intervention? No. Renewed informed consent only needs to be obtained when an original intervention plan is substantially changed or substituted with another plan of care.

Substitute Health Care Providers and the Need for Renewal of Informed Consent

What are the informed consent responsibilities, if any, of substitute providers who take over for a primary health care provider who goes away to a continuing education course or goes on vacation? In a hospital setting, a patient may not have an expectation of exclusive care by a single nonphysician provider in a clinical setting, so that informed consent gained by one provider is valid so long as a substitute provider carries out the same program.

In a private practice setting, however, such as an outpatient physical or occupational therapy clinic, a provider responsible for vacation or other coverage may not be able to rely on the original therapist's disclosure of information and receipt of patient informed consent to intervention, particularly when documentation of informed consent is absent or insufficient to rely on. Under such circumstances, it is advisable to gain patient informed consent independently and document it before providing care for the patient. (This is a gray area in the law of informed consent, without many reported cases.) An example of how to document informed consent as a substitute provider in an outpatient clinical setting appears in Exhibit 4–3.

Exceptions to the Requirements for Informed Consent

Are there any exceptions to the legal requirement to obtain a patient's informed consent before treatment? Yes.

One exception to informed consent is the "emergency doctrine," under which consent typically is not obtained for emergency lifesaving care. This doctrine applies when, for example, a clinical provider performs cardiopulmonary resuscitation on a patient who suffers a myocardial infarction

Exhibit 4–3 Example of Documentation of Informed Consent by a Substitute Health Care Provider

---

ABC General Hospital
Rehabilitation Center
Physical Therapy Section

May 26, 20xx/1600

S: 42 y o F, dx multiple sclerosis, wheelchair-bound, referred on May 23, 20xx, for "evaluation, facilitative range of motion, and progressive exercise and ambulation, to tolerance." Has been to PT Clinic for last 2 days and was treated by Reggie Hausenfus, PT, who had to take emergency vacation to attend his father's funeral. Pt. appears confused by my substitute coverage of PT care.

O: . . .

A: . . .

P: Renewed pt. I/C by explaining my examination/evaluative findings; diagnosis; the course of therapy as outlined in Dr. Doe's order and R. Hausenfus' progress notes; the risks of muscle soreness, fatigue, and the slight risk of joint subluxation associated with exercise; and the alternative options of bed rest and limited activity in her wheelchair. I asked for her questions. She had none and stated that she now understood why another therapist was caring for her today. Cont. w/program, as outlined. Tolerated 45-min session well.

G: . . .

—Carrie Cover, PT, #07263720

---

while in the provider's clinic. Under these circumstances, patient consent generally is presumed. Exceptions to this exception include valid patient advance (or surrogate agent) directives and do-not-resuscitate orders disallowing intervention.

Another exception to informed consent is "therapeutic privilege," under which a health care provider may be excused from disclosing information to a patient who, in the provider's professional judgment, could not psychologically cope with the information disclosed (e.g., when the diagnosis or prognosis involves a life-threatening disease).

A situation that involves a qualification, but not an exception, to the doctrine of informed consent concerns the care of minors (who lack "legal capacity") and adults lacking mental capacity and under conservatorship or guardianship because of such condition. Informed consent in such circumstances is obtained from a legally appointed surrogate decision maker and not from the patient. An exception to the no-legal capacity rule for minors involves minors' rights in some states to make independent decisions concerning such conditions as pregnancy and intervention for drug and alcohol addiction and for venereal disease intervention.

Standards for Disclosure

There are two basic legal standards for disclosure of information for informed consent. Some states employ the professional standard of disclosure, meaning that a health care provider must disclose to the patient that information that another provider of the same profession, acting under the same or similar circumstances, would have disclosed. Legal cases tried in professional-standard jurisdictions often require expert testimony about the information that a defendant's professional peers would consider appropriate for disclosure.

A number of states use a layperson's standard for disclosure. In these states, a provider must disclose all the information that an ordinary, reasonable patient under the same circumstances would deem material in making an informed decision.

The court in *Canterbury*[22] delineated the two standards as follows:

> The larger number of courts, as might be expected, have applied tests framed with reference to prevailing fashion within the medical profession. Some have measured the disclosure by "good medical practice," others what a reasonable practitioner would have bared under the circumstances, and still others by what medical custom in the community would demand. We have explored this rather considerable body of law but are unprepared to follow it. . . .
>
> In our view, the patient's right of self-decision shapes the boundaries of the duty to reveal. That right can be effectively exercised only if the patient possesses enough information to enable an intelligent choice. The scope of the physician's communication to the patient, then, must be measured by the patient's need and that need is the materiality to the patient's decision: all risks potentially affecting the decision must be unmasked. And to safeguard the patient's interest in achieving his own determination on treatment, the law must itself set the standard for adequate disclosure.

Optimally for the patient, exposure of a risk would be mandatory whenever the patient would deem it significant to his decision, either singly or in combination with other risks. Such a requirement, however, would summon the physician to second-guess the patient, whose ideas on materiality could hardly be known to the physician. . . . Consonantly with orthodox negligence doctrine, the physician's liability for nondisclosure is to be determined on the basis of foresight, not hindsight; no less than any other aspect of negligence, the issue of nondisclosure must be approached from the viewpoint of the reasonableness of the physician's divulgence in terms of what he knows or should know to be the patient's informational needs. If, but only if, the fact-finder can say that the physician's communication was unreasonably inadequate is an imposition of liability legally or morally justified. . . .

From these considerations we derive the breadth of the disclosure of risks legally to be required. The scope of the standard is not subjective as to either the physician or the patient; it remains objective with due regard for the patient's informational needs and with suitable leeway for the physician's situation. In broad outline, we agree that "a risk is thus material when a reasonable person, in what the physician knows or should know to be in the patient's position, would be likely to attach significance to the risk or cluster of risks in deciding whether or not to forego the proposed therapy."

The topics importantly demanding a communication of information are:

- the inherent and potential hazards of the proposed treatment,
- the alternatives to that treatment, if any, and
- the results likely if the patient remains untreated.

The factors contributing significance to the dangerousness of a medical technique are, of course, the incidence of injury and the degree of the harm threatened. A very small chance of death or serious disablement may well be significant; a potential disability that dramatically outweighs the potential benefit of the therapy or the detriments of the existing malady may [warrant] discussion with the patient.

There is no bright line separating the significant from the insignificant; the answer in any case must abide a rule of reason. Some dangers—infection, for example—are inherent in any operation; there is no obligation to communicate those of which persons of average sophistication are aware. Even more clearly, the physician bears *no responsibility for discussion of hazards the patient has already discovered or those having no apparent materiality to the patient's decision on therapy* [emphasis added].

Canterbury, then, was the first reported case to change the focus of inquiry in an informed consent-based health care malpractice case from what a reasonable health care provider would disclose to a patient to what an ordinary, reasonable, prudent patient would expect to hear about a recommended intervention: its relative risks, benefits, and prognosis, and similar information about reasonable alternatives, if any.

Informed Consent in the Specialty or Limited Practice Setting: Preventing an Allegation of Patient Abandonment

The issue of liability for patient abandonment is discussed in greater detail in Chapter 6; however, there are informed consent issues involving providers practicing in a specialty or limited practice setting that warrant mentioning in this section.

Legally actionable abandonment of a patient occurs when a health care provider *improperly* unilaterally terminates a professional relationship with a patient. Providers practicing in specialty areas, such as physicians who confine their practices to cosmetic or other types of surgery, or physical therapists who limit their practices to orthopedic or sports physical therapy, need to carefully apprise their patients of the restricted nature of their practices. Then, when the surgery is completed, or the zenith of the patient's rehabilitation has been reached, the specialist can more easily disengage from further care for unrelated patient complaints.

If a claim or lawsuit ensues alleging patient abandonment, thorough documentation of the patient's informed consent to limited scope care may be crucial to avoid health care malpractice liability. An example of how to document patient informed consent to care in a limited scope specialty practice appears in Exhibit 4–4.

Informed Consent as a Risk Management Tool for Preventing Allegations of Battery and Sexual Battery

Unlike most other professional-client relationships, the delivery of health care routinely involves "hands-on" therapy or other intervention. In some disciplines—medicine and surgery; physical, occupational and speech therapy; nursing; and chiropractic; among others—these manual procedures can be very intensive and occasionally uncomfortable. With tech-

Exhibit 4–4 Example of Documentation of Informed Consent by a Health Care Provider in a Speciality (Limited) Practice Setting

---

Doe Occupational Health Center
Specializing in Evaluation and Treatment of Hand Disorders
Halifax, Nova Scotia, Canada

Dec. 1, 20xx/1935

S: 32 y o F, ceramics artist, referred by Dr. Smith for "evaluation and gentle, progressive mobilization, left hand, s/p immobilization of left hand X 6 wks for suspected scaphoid fx. No fx."

O: . . .

A: . . .

P: Paraffin rx X 20 min qd, F/B gentle mobilization, AROM, and mild PREs, to tolerance. I/C to rx obtained. Pt. advised that mine is a limited scope practice, specializing exclusively in hand therapy. Pt. asked if I could evaluate her R shoulder also, which cracks w/shoulder AROM X 3 yrs. Pt. is 3 yrs. s/p L CVA. I told her that a separate referral would be required for an OT or PT to evaluate her R shoulder and that I did not work with patients with shoulder complaints because of the limited scope of my practice to hand care. She verbalized understanding and agreed to seek a referral from Dr. Smith for OT or PT evaluation of her R shoulder at ABC Hospital.

G: . . .

—Aidee El, OT

---

niques such as deep friction massage, myofascial mobilization, and spinal, pelvic, and extremity manipulation, clinicians may work close to patients' private zones (i.e., breasts, buttocks, and genitalia). It is imperative that a patient fully understands any manual therapy procedure before undergoing therapy and gives his or her informed consent to it.

Of the growing number of sexual battery allegations lodged by patients against primary health care providers, many, perhaps, are simply the result of a lack of understanding or a misunderstanding about the nature of the procedure used on the patient.[23] A caring, prudent provider must take the time to explain manual therapy procedures carefully and thoroughly to a patient for whom they are prescribed; solicit and answer any patient questions; and address any patient concerns before, during, or after these procedures. It is especially important to let patients know that they have the absolute right to order a halt to any intervention (from massage to joint mobilization to functional or work capacity evaluation) at any time, for any reason. It is critically important, any time intensive hands-on manual therapy is to be carried out in the vicinity of a patient's private zones of contact, to thoroughly document the informed consent elements explained to the patient in the patient care record. An example of documentation of informed consent for physical therapy manipulation appears in Exhibit 4–5.

> *It is critically important, anytime intensive hands-on manual therapy is to be carried out in the vicinity of a patient's private zones of contact, to thoroughly document the informed consent elements explained to the patient in the patient care record.*

INFORMED CONSENT DOCUMENTATION FORMATS

Like other issues in the law of informed consent, the legally correct form for documenting a patient's informed consent to examination and intervention varies from state to state. Some states have specific statutory disclosure requirements for medical and/or surgical procedures and may consider statutory form disclosure presumptive—or even conclusive (irrefutable)—evidence of a patient's informed consent. Other states permit the use of a wide variety of methods for documenting informed consent. (This discussion is intended to be informational and not dispositive on the law of any particular state. Ask your legal counsel whether the form of documentation you use in your clinical practice is legally acceptable in your state and appropriate for your practice setting and circumstances.)

There are many acceptable ways to document patients' informed consent. As a premise, it should be said that primary health care professionals must always use *some* means of memorializing, through documentation, that their patients give their informed consent before examination and intervention. This section illustrates several commonly used methods of documenting patient informed consent to intervention, including use of "boilerplate" consent forms, documentation in short- and long-hand form in patient care records, use of informed consent checklists, and reference to standard operating procedures or broad clinic policy statements.

Boilerplate Consent Forms

There are two types of consent forms: short and long. Both forms are signed (and often each element is initialed) by the patient. The short form

Exhibit 4–5 Example of Documentation of Informed Consent for Intensive Hands-on Physical Therapy Intervention (To Prevent a Sexual Battery Allegation)

M&M Community Hospital
Physical Therapy Center

Aug. 5, 20xx/1315

S: 32 y o F, referred by Dr. Ella for "evaluation and consideration for myofascial mobilization for R sternoclavicular pain X 2 months; s/p sling immobilization x 4 wks for recurrent ant. sh. dislocation." Med. hx includes 3 X recurrent ant. shoulder dislocations secondary to FOOSH; psychiatric treatment last Dec. for depression. No prior surgeries. Meds include Elavil, Norflex, and Motrin.

O: Point tenderness over R S-C joint and over medial R chest. FAROM . . .

A: R sternoclavicular myofascial pain syndrome, secondary to sling immobilization. R breast pathology ruled out by Dr. Ella, per telephonic discussion of pt.'s exam.

P: R sternoclavicular manual myofascial mobilization, including transverse friction massage and joint mobilization. Reviewed informed consent elements with patient and her husband, as follows: (1) explanation of dx, R sternoclavicular myofascial pain syndrome, secondary to sling immobilization; (2) proposed rx, R sternoclavicular manual myofascial mobilization, transverse friction massage, and R S-C joint mobilization (demonstrated technique on myself for pt. and husband); (3) material risks: possible soft tissue tenderness and bruising and discomfort with chest & BUE AROM; and (4) reasonable alternative/adjuncts to mobilization: heat, cryotherapy, and stretching ROM. Pt. had question about the intensity of pain during rx. I told her that she should only experience mild discomfort and should tell me if she experiences any more degree of discomfort, and I will modify my pressure. She and husband understand all; pt. consents to rx as proposed. Conducted 15-min myofascial mobilization session w/pt. Mrs. Jones, Red Cross volunteer, present during initial session. Pt. had no adverse reaction to initial intervention.

G: . . .

—Tom Fields, PT, OCS

simply lists the required components of informed consent, followed by the patient's, provider's, and witness' signatures. Such a format might read:

> I, John Patient, was informed of my examination/evaluative findings, diagnosis, prognosis, and recommended intervention(s). My questions were solicited and answered to my satisfaction. I give my informed consent to the recommended interventions of my primary health care provider.

_____

Patient Signature

_____

Provider Signature

_____

Witness Signature

The long consent form may be "customized" for individual patients and may include specifics about each element of required disclosure. Because the provider is legally bound by whatever appears—or does not appear—on the long consent form, the legal danger of the use of such a form is that an element of disclosure, especially including procedure-related material risks, might be inadvertently omitted from the form. The fact that the provider might, in fact, have imparted the missing information verbally to the patient might not withstand legal scrutiny in an informed consent-based health care malpractice action. An additional consideration in using the long form is the fact that it is relatively time-consuming to complete, making its use under managed care especially unattractive and impractical.

There are recognized problems with standardized patient consent forms (such as hospital admission blanket consent forms), some of which can render them legally ineffective as evidence of patient informed consent to treatment.[24] Often, these forms are overly broad and/or ambiguous. Often drafted by attorneys or administrators, many of these forms cannot be understood by lay people, i.e. by patients. In such cases, courts almost universally resolve any ambiguity in favor of the patient and against the health care provider and organization or system.

The circumstances of a patient signing a consent form may also make the form suspect as substantive evidence of consent. If a patient presents a credible legal case that he or she was quickly handed a form and told to sign it at the height of an emergency and did not understand it, a court or jury may believe the patient and discount the form as evidence.

Finally, providers are warned never to fashion consent forms to limit or exclude provider liability for health care malpractice while the patient is under the provider's care. Such forms amount to *exculpatory contracts,*[25] which courts generally find unconscionable and unacceptable in the health care delivery setting.

Documentation in the Patient Care Record

Documentation of informed consent to examination and intervention in a patient care record (typically during an initial patient visit) also may appear in short and long forms. The patient may or may not be asked to initial or sign the entry, attesting consent, in the record. Exhibit 4–5 is an example of long-form patient care record informed consent documentation.

Informed Consent Checklists or Standard Operating Procedures

Primary health care professionals can normally rely on abbreviated documentation of consent in patient care records when the health care organization or system has established either standard operating procedures for patient informed consent to specific procedures, or specialized informed consent checklists that the primary health care providers (not the patients) sign and date to verify that patient informed consent was obtained. Standard operating procedures or checklists outline all the required disclosure elements necessary to obtain patients' informed consent and should be retained at least until the state's statute of limitations for legal actions has expired.

A sample informed consent policy statement that might appear in a department quality management or policies and procedures manual might read:

> This department and its primary and support health care professionals respect the autonomy right of all patients having legal and mental capacity (or valid surrogate decision makers otherwise) to receive sufficient disclosure information about prospective examinations and recommended interventions so as to enable them to make knowing,

informed choices about whether to accept or reject them. Such disclosure universally includes information related to:

1. The patient's health problem and the parameters of any proposed patient history and physical examination.
2. Post-examination, the evaluative findings and diagnosis of the patient, and information about the recommended intervention(s).
3. Material risks, if any, associated with the recommended intervention(s). [Material risks include important "decisional" risks (including foreseeable complications associated with the recommended intervention) or precautions that would cause an ordinary, reasonable patient to think carefully when deciding whether to undergo or reject the recommended intervention].
4. All reasonable alternatives, if any, to the proposed intervention(s) (i.e., other effective potential interventions that would be acceptable substitutes under legal standards of practice). The provider must be sure to include discussion of the relative risks and benefits of alternative interventions.
5. Expected benefits, or goals, and prognosis associated with the recommended intervention(s).

After such disclosure of information is made, patient questions are actively solicited and answered to the patient's satisfaction by the primary health care professional, and examination and/or intervention does not proceed unless and until the patient formally assents to it/them.

Memoranda for Record

On an *ad hoc* basis, primary health care professionals may wish to create office memoranda that memorialize informed consent disclosure and patient assent for individual patients, which may or may not be filed in the patient's care records. Such memoranda are typically created for special cases (e.g., active litigation patients, or patients who express strong dissatisfaction with the department or facility/system offering care). Memoranda might be created in cases in which patient informed consent is not routinely individually documented in detail in patient care records, and where, in these special cases, detail about the informed consent process is deemed advisable.

MANAGED CARE INFORMED CONSENT DOCUMENTATION ISSUES

Managed care has created at least three special informed consent documentation issues, which bear mentioning here. First, there is a public perception—correct or incorrect—that managed care organizations have created "gag clauses" in provider employment contracts that disallow employee-providers from disclosing to patients reasonable alternatives to recommended health care interventions not offered routinely within the organization or system. Such contractual provisions, to the extent that they exist, derogate from health care provider and organization respect for patient autonomy over health care decision making and are unethical in their application. Health professional codes of ethics and state and federal statutes and administrative regulations have largely made their usage nonexistent. Second, health care professionals whose compensation is variable, dependent on how much money they save their employing health care organizations, or those with research interests in the patient's care, should disclose such facts to patients under their care,[26] and should consider adding the following disclaimer to the informed consent communication process (if true):

> I will not violate my special duty of trust and fidelity owed to you as a patient, nor will I compromise the quality of your care, because I receive variable incentive pay from my employer for helping to contain health care costs (or because I am concurrently conducting research on your condition).

The third and final point under managed care is that legal and health professional ethical duties incumbent upon primary health care providers have not changed significantly to accommodate the business of managed care. While it may seem to be a time burden to routinely make informed consent disclosure to patients (and to document it, when appropriate or required), it is imperative to do so, out of respect for patient autonomy—the same autonomy right that each of us would wish respected were we the patient.

CONCLUSION

The law of informed consent may seem complicated; however, meeting legal and professional ethical standards for disclosure is not only mandatory but also relatively easy to do. Every primary health care provider, regardless of level of care or practice setting, is required by law to gain patients' informed consent to examination and intervention.

Although the elements of legally sufficient informed patient consent vary from state to state, there is a core checklist of typically required disclosure information. The checklist includes examination/evaluative findings, diagnosis, prognosis, and information about recommended and alternative interventions, including their relative material (decisional) risks and expected benefits. Patient (or surrogate decision maker) questions must be actively solicited and satisfactorily answered. Providers must always remember to communicate this and all information to patients in a language (including sign) that patients understand, and at their level of understanding. Minimize the use of health professional jargon!

There are many acceptable formats for documenting that patient informed consent was obtained before examination and intervention. These range from reference to clinic, departmental, or organization/system policies and procedures to detailed documentation on consent forms or in patient care records. Careful attention to the processes of documentation of patient informed consent serves simultaneously to improve the quality of patient care and to manage health care malpractice risk exposure in clinical practice.

REFERENCES

1. Two legal case decisions that derogate from this norm are: Spence v. Todaro, No. 94–3757 (E.D. Pa. 1994) (physical therapy) and Friter & Friter v. Iolab Corp., 607 A.2d 1111 (Pa. Super. Ct., 1992) (clinical laboratory scientists), in which judges ruled that, under Pennsylvania law, patient informed consent is only required for operative procedures.

2. *See, e.g.,* Joint Commission on Accreditation of Healthcare Organizations, *Patient Rights and Organization Ethics*, ch. RI, in COMPREHENSIVE ACCREDITATION MANUAL FOR HOSPITALS (1999).

3. The federal constitutional right to privacy was introduced in Chapter 3 concerning the rights to make decisions about contraception and abortion.

4. *See In re* Quinlin, 355 A.2d 647 (N.J. 1976).

5. *See* Bouvia v. Super. Ct., 225 Cal. Rptr. 297, 179 Cal. App. 3d 1127 (1986).

6. *See* Cruzan v. Director, Dep't of Health, 110 Sup. Ct. 2841 (1990).

7. The Patient Self-Determination Act (PSA), part of the Omnibus Budget Reconciliation Act of 1990, Pub. L. No. 101–508, November 5, 1990, became effective on December 1, 1991. The PSA is codified in 42 U.S.C. §§ 1395 and 1396. For more information about the PSA, *see* Chapter 6. *See also* R.W. Scott, *Guaranteeing Patient Rights: It's the Law*, ADVANCE FOR DIRECTORS IN REHABILITATION, September/October 1992, at 43–44.

8. The Patient Self-Determination Act, 42 U.S.C. § 1395cc (f) (1) (A) (i).

9. *See* M. Gunderson, *Eliminating Conflicts of Interest in Managed Care Organization Through Disclosure and Consent.* JOURNAL OF LAW, MEDICINE, AND ETHICS 25(2,3), 192–201 (1997).

10. Schloendorff v. Soc. of N.Y. Hosp., 105 N.E. 92 (N.Y. 1914).

11. For more information about assault and battery, including sexual battery, in the health care setting, *see* R.W. SCOTT, HEALTH CARE MALPRACTICE: A PRIMER ON LEGAL ISSUES FOR PROFESSIONALS, 2ND ED., 56–58 (1999).

12. Natanson v. Kline, 186 Kan. 393, 350 P.2d 1093 (1960).

13. Natanson v. Kline, 186 Kan. 393, 350 P.2d 1093.

14. Canterbury v. Spence, 464 F.2d 772 (D.C. Cir., 1972), *cert. denied*, 409 U.S. 1064 (1974). The term *cert. denied*, as used here, indicates that the U.S. Supreme Court refused, as a matter of discretion, to hear the case on appeal.

15. Canterbury v. Spence.

16. A "directed verdict" means that the party with the burden to prove the case (usually the plaintiff) has failed to present a *prima facie* case (i.e., one on which the plaintiff could prevail), requiring the judge to refuse to allow the case to go to the jury for their consideration. For more detail, *see* Federal Rule of Civil Procedure 50(a).

17. *See* Canterbury, *supra* note 14.

18. *See* T. Hudson, Informed Consent Problems Become More Complicated, HOSPITALS, March 20, 1991. 38–40.

19. *See* J. KATZ, THE SILENT WORLD OF DOCTOR AND PATIENT 85–103 (1986).

20. KATZ, THE SILENT WORLD.

21. One specific court case held that the burden of obtaining patient informed consent was squarely on the shoulders of the provider responsible for carrying out a treatment procedure. *See Consent Responsibility Lies with Independent Physician,* HOSP. RISK MGMT., October 1990, at 134–137, citing the case of Petriello v. Kalman, 215 Conn. 377 (June 19, 1990). Rozovsky is in accord. "Informed consent should be carried out by the person carrying out the procedure." Hudson, *supra* note 18, at 40.

22. *See* Canterbury, *supra* note 14.

23. Some patients, particularly those individuals who have suffered sexual abuse, will interpret any touch—even a therapeutic touch—as sexual. Providers carrying out manual procedures on patients must be prepared to deal with these interpretations and any resultant responses by their patients. For an excellent discussion on this sensitive, but important, topic, *see* C.J. MANHEIM & D.K. LAVETT, CRANIOSACRAL THERAPY AND SOMATO-EMOTIONAL RELEASE: THE SELF-HEALING BODY 33–40, 47–51 (1989).

24. For a more detailed discussion of the legal status of patient consent forms, *see* H.F. ROWLAND & A.B. ROWLAND, HOSPITAL CONSENTS FORMS (1992).

25. The classic legal case involving health care exculpatory contracts is Tunkl v. Regents of the Univ. of Cal., 60 Cal. 2d 92 (1963).

26. *See* Moore v. Regents of the Univ. of Cal., 51 Cal. 3d 120, 793 P.2d 479 (1990).

SUGGESTED READING

AMERICAN PHYSICAL THERAPY ASSOCIATION, IA2: GENERAL GUIDELINES: INFORMED CONSENT. GUIDELINES FOR PHYSICAL THERAPY DOCUMENTATION (1993).

AMERICAN PHYSICAL THERAPY ASSOCIATION, PRINCIPLE 1.4. GUIDE FOR PROFESSIONAL CONDUCT. (1999).

AMERICAN PHYSICAL THERAPY ASSOCIATION. STANDARD IIIA: PROVISION OF SERVICES: INFORMED CONSENT, STANDARDS OF PRACTICE FOR PHYSICAL THERAPY (1997).

Council on Ethical and Judicial Affairs: Ethical Issues in Managed Care. JAMA. 1995; 273:330–335.

J.F. Merz, P. Sanker, & S.S. Yoo, *Hospital Consent for Disclosure of Medicaid Information*, JOURNAL OF LAW, MEDICINE, AND ETHICS, 26(3), 241–248 (1998).

F.A. ROZOVSKY, CONSENT TO TREATMENT, 2ND ED.(1990).

R.W. Scott, *Guaranteeing Patient Rights: It's the Law*, ADVANCE FOR DIRECTORS IN REHABILITATION, September/October 1992, 43–44.

R.W. Scott, *Informed Consent*, CLINICAL MANAGEMENT. May/June 1991, at 12–14.

R.W. SCOTT, PROFESSIONAL ETHICS: A GUIDE FOR REHABILITATION PROFESSIONALS. (1998).

REVIEW: CASE STUDIES

---

1. E, a physical therapist employed by ABC General Hospital, treats F, a female patient referred for "evaluation and treatment" for her complaint of right sternoclavicular pain. E examines patient F and decides to use myofascial mobilization techniques to release local adhesions. The intervention caused patient F some moderate discomfort, and E moderated his manual pressure over patient F's sternum each time she voiced any complaints of discomfort. At home that evening, patient F began to experience right breast discomfort, and she and her husband discussed E's manual techniques. Angered by what they believed to have been a sexual battery, patient F and her husband file a complaint against ABC. How might this situation have been prevented?

2. Patient M is admitted to XYZ Rehabilitation Center for short-term stroke rehabilitation. Patient M displays mild aphasia; has moderate loss of function of his right (dominant) hand; and is brought to the facility in a wheelchair. As part of the admissions process, patient M's wife, N, is directed to read and sign the facility's standard consent/ release form, which reads in part

   > I hereby agree to hold harmless ABC Rehabilitation Center and its agents, employees, and volunteers, for any injury suffered by me incident to my care, except that liability is not waived for acts or omissions amounting to gross negligence, recklessness, or intentional misconduct.

During the admission intake process, a volunteer transporting M by wheelchair runs M's left leg into a door frame, fracturing M's leg. Liability?

SUGGESTED ANSWERS AND DISCUSSION

1. This complaint could have been prevented if E had taken the time to explain carefully to patient F his evaluative findings concerning her condition; the nature of myofascial mobilization; the risks and complications associated with it, such as soft tissue discomfort, erythema, and perhaps mild bruising; and the viable alternatives to myofascial mobilization, such as heat, ice, and stretching and postural exercises. E then should have shared literature about myofascial mobilization with patient F and solicited and answered her questions. At F's request, E also could have included patient F's husband in the discussion. E should have documented the processes used to obtain F's informed consent to examination and intervention. For procedures that bring a provider's hands in close proximity to a patient's private zones of contact, prudence would also dictate the offer of a chaperone the same gender as the patient.

2. Patient M has an actionable cause of action for negligence against XYZ Rehabilitation Center. Hospitals are normally vicariously liable for the negligence of their volunteers, who are treated as employees for the purpose of such a determination. The "consent/release" form that patient M's wife was required to sign on admission is an exculpatory contract that has no legal effect. Health care facilities cannot limit their liability for professional or ordinary negligence incident to health care activities through such an attempted waiver of liability. *See* Tunkl v. Regents of the University of California, 60 Cal. 2d 92 (1963). Depending on state law, the facility might have been able to require patient M to take a claim to some sort of alternative dispute resolution, such as arbitration, instead of filing a lawsuit. However, such an agreement should be made separate and apart from any consent forms a patient is asked to sign.

Appendix 4–A

American Physical Therapy Association Guidelines for Informed Consent

GUIDE FOR PROFESSIONAL CONDUCT

Principle 1

1.4 Informed Consent
Physical therapists shall obtain patient informed consent before treatment.

GUIDELINES FOR PHYSICAL THERAPY DOCUMENTATION

I. General Guidelines

2. Informed consent: As required by the APTA *Standards of Practice for Physical Therapy and the Accompanying Criteria*
   2.1 The physical therapist has sole responsibility for providing information to the patient and for obtaining the patient's informed consent in accordance with jurisdictional law before initiating physical therapy.
   2.2 Those deemed competent to give consent are competent adults. When the adult is not competent, and in the case of minors, a parent or legal guardian consents as the surrogate decision maker.
   2.3 The information provided to the patient should include the following: (a) a clear description of the treatment ordered or recommended, (b) material (decisional) risks associated with the proposed treatment, (c) expected benefits of treatment, (d) com-

parison of the benefits and risks possible with and without treatment, and (e) reasonable alternatives to the recommended treatment. The physical therapist should solicit questions from the patient and provide answers. The patient should be asked to acknowledge understanding and consent before treatment proceeds.

Examples of ways in which to accomplish this documentation:

Ex 2.3.1 Signature of patient/guardian on long or short consent form.

Ex 2.3.2 Notation/entry of what was explained by the physical therapist or the physical therapist assistant in the official record.

Ex 2.3.3 Filing of a completed consent checklist signed by the patient.

STANDARDS OF PRACTICE FOR PHYSICAL THERAPY AND THE ACCOMPANYING CRITERIA

III. Provision of Services

A. Informed Consent

The physical therapist has sole responsibility for providing information to the patient/client and for obtaining the patient's/client's informed consent in accordance with jurisdictional law before initiating physical therapy.

Criteria

The information provided to the patient/client should include the following:

- A clear description of the proposed intervention/treatment.
- A statement of material (decisional) risks associated with the proposed intervention/treatment.
- A statement of expected benefits of the proposed intervention/treatment.
- A comparison of the benefits and risks possible both with and without intervention/treatment.
- An explanation of reasonable alternatives to the recommended intervention/treatment.

Informed consent requires:
- Consent by a competent adult.
- Consent by a parent/legal guardian as the surrogate decision maker when the adult patient/client is not competent or when the patient/client is a minor.
- The patient's/client's acknowledgment of understanding and consent before the intervention/treatment proceeds.

Chapter 5

Documentation Issues in Patient Care Quality and Risk Management Activities

This chapter examines the processes of patient care-related quality and liability risk management. While the concept of liability risk management is straightforward, "quality management" is addressed as a generic concept, rather than in a manner that presents a template for compliance with any particular accreditation or oversight entity's administrative requirements. Providers, organizations, and systems, however, must carefully adhere to these specific requirements, as applicable, to achieve and maintain accreditation and/or certification.

INTRODUCTION

The process of quality management of health care delivery is ever evolving. Once referred to as "quality assurance," the systematic management of the quality of patient care delivery now goes by one of many labels including *quality improvement*,[1] *quality assessment and improvement*,[2] *continuous quality improvement*,[3] *total quality management*,[4] *promoting quality/managing risk*,[5] *improving organizational effectiveness*, and *process improvement*, among others. The change in emphasis in health care quality management away from the impossible task of "assuring" quality to continuously striving to improve the quality of health care delivery is based in large part on the industrial model of total quality management developed by W. Edwards Deming, who consulted with and helped revitalize Japanese industry after World War II.[6]

The term *quality* is not easily defined. Its most important attribute is probably how the purchasers or users of goods and services (including patients and clients who receive health professional services) characterize the products and services they receive. In that respect, modern quality management is "customer-driven." Quality, though, is more than just the consumer's perception of how "good" a supplier's product or service is. It is also a reflection of how the professionals making the product or rendering the service feel, collectively and individually, about their work product. Quality is also the characterization of reputation and prestige afforded to one's work product by competitors, third-party payers, accreditation and oversight entities, and relevant others.

A comprehensive health care quality management program has, among others, the following characteristics:

1. It is patient-focused.
2. It requires top management commitment, vision, and leadership to be effective.
3. It requires a daily commitment by the entire organization/system to excellence and to continuous incremental improvement in the quality of patient care delivery.
4. It uses scientific and quantifiable methods to measure, evaluate, and improve processes of patient care delivery and patient care outcomes.[7]
5. It empowers employees, working collectively in small multidisciplinary, cross-departmental teams, to proactively define and solve organizational problems and seek out opportunities for improvement of processes and outcomes of patient care.
6. It is based on a written plan of action.
7. It recognizes as normal the process variations along the continuum of quality patient care delivery.
8. It celebrates successes and rewards high-quality performance.
9. It redirects the focus of correction from individuals to processes and outcomes, and demands collective responsibility both for successes and failures.
10. It requires ongoing, systematic training, education, and development.
11. It does not "settle" for minimally acceptable patient care standards, processes, and outcomes. (Minimally acceptable quality patient care is a benchmark only for the legal standard of care, i.e., for determining whether health care malpractice has occurred or not. It is inappropriate for determining whether optimal quality patient care has been delivered.)

COMPONENTS OF A HEALTH CARE QUALITY MANAGEMENT PROGRAM

A comprehensive health care quality management program consists of at least the following component parts:

- patient care process and outcome measurement and evaluation activities
- patient care documentation and health care information management[8]
- credentialing and/or competency assessment activities involving all health care providers
- resource utilization management
- liability risk management activities[9]

Patient Care Outcome Measurement and Evaluation Activities

Patient care process and outcome measurement and evaluation encompasses the systematic evaluation of selected clinical indicators concerning important recurrent aspects of patient care. Patient care process and outcome measurement and evaluation activities track patient-health care provider professional interactions along a continuum from intake, through examination, evaluation, formulation of diagnoses and prognoses, intervention, patient/family/significant other education, discharge, post-discharge activities, and follow-up, in every conceivable patient care setting, from hospital to outpatient to long-term care to a patient home environment. To concentrate improvement efforts where they will have the most effect, patient care process and outcome measurement and evaluation activities focus on patient care activities that are high risk, high volume, or problem prone.

Patient Care Documentation and Health Information Management

This book is primarily about patient care documentation issues. The fundamental premise of the book is that documentation of patient care activities is as important as the rendition of patient care itself.

Documentation has lifelong importance to the patient, who depends on an accurate, clear, timely, thorough historical record of his or her health status, for current and future health care needs. It is equally important to the individual health care providers and health care organizations, for whom the patient care record memorializes the nature and quality of care rendered to the patient.

Documentation of patient care is crucial to the survival of a health care organization because it forms the basis for third-party reimbursement and, in the form of a patient health record, serves as a business record, admissible in court as evidence of the nature and quality of patient care rendered in the facility. Documentation in a facility's quality management program also serves as evidence of compliance with laws, regulations, and accreditation standards, and helps prevent imposition of "corporate liability" against an organization or system for failing to monitor the quality of patient care rendered within the organization or system, and for failing to effectively maximize patient, visitor, and staff safety in its facilities, among other nondelegable duties. Finally, patient care documentation serves important societal interests, including use in clinical research on disease and injury.

Provider Credentialing and Competency Assessment Activities

For a variety of reasons, health care organizations need to assess the competence and character of their health care providers, support staff, and others working in their facilities. Health care facilities owe a special duty of care to patients cared for within their facilities, and are vicariously, or indirectly, liable for the negligence and other wrongful acts of employees acting within the scope of their employment. Under the legal theory of "corporate liability," health care organizations are also primarily liable to patients for failure to monitor the competence of professional and support personnel, whether the patient care is rendered by employees or independent contractors.

Along with credentials privileging processes, health care organizations are responsible for ensuring the continuing competence of all of their staff. Included under this responsibility are training, continuing education, cardiopulmonary resuscitation certification and recertification (as appropriate), among other activities.

Resource Utilization Management

In the current managed care cost-containment-focused health care environment, the effective management of health care resources—human and nonhuman—is critical to a health care organization's or system's survival. Important areas of concern for resource and clinical managers include equitable patient access to available services and length of care and post-discharge care, among others.

Liability Risk Management Activities

Liability risk management encompasses a wide range of variegated activities, including, in addition to striving toward optimal quality health professional service delivery:

- patient, visitor, and staff safety activities
- patient, visitor, staff, and public injury prevention, reporting, and investigation
- infection control and waste management
- calibration and maintenance of equipment
- patient satisfaction surveys

Liability risk management is an integral part of an overall quality management program. It shares similarities with other component activities, such as the patient care outcome measurement and evaluation function but is also characterized by fundamental differences that distinguish it from other quality management activities.

In terms of similarities to other quality management activities, liability risk management processes employ a similar methodology, including the identification of important aspects of care, development of measurement indicators that are examined on an ongoing basis, the systematic reporting of results, and the correction of identified problems. As with all other quality management activities, liability risk management processes have the effect of continuously improving and optimizing quality patient care delivery within facilities, organizations, and systems.

Liability risk management activities differ, however, from the other quality management program components in several key respects. The focus of risk management activities is a legal rather than patient focus. The principal purpose of risk management activities is to protect the facility by preventing or minimizing financial losses from legal actions arising from patient care or other activities conducted in the facility. Although risk management activities tend to promote optimal quality patient care, their focus is on "minimally acceptable standards of clinical practice," i.e., the legal standard of care—the legal benchmark in malpractice actions delineating negligent and non-negligent patient care. Risk management activities also differ from the other component quality management activities with regard to their sphere of participant inclusiveness. Patient care process and outcome measurement and evaluation, credentialing and competency assessment, and resource utilization management are all internal processes that involve primarily health care clinicians and administrators; whereas risk management activities include professionals outside of health care delivery and administration, particularly in-house and consulting legal counsel.

Of particular interest to health care facility risk managers is the management of potentially compensable events, involving adverse outcomes of patient care and alleged or actual injuries or other adverse events. Risk managers are also responsible for managing claims against the organization, and potential and pendent legal and administrative actions. Risk management, however, is more than just reactive in nature. Risk managers attempt to prevent potentially compensable events from arising through such processes as occurrence screening of potential risk situations. These situations include facility-incurred trauma, complications, and infection; unplanned return patient visits or surgery; unscheduled readmissions within a specified time period after a prior admission; and unfavorable trends in patient satisfaction surveys.

CONFIDENTIALITY CONSIDERATIONS IN PATIENT CARE QUALITY MANAGEMENT

Quality assurance or management documents normally enjoy a degree of protection from disclosure or release to patients, their attorneys, and others, under statutory and/or common law. Different rules may apply to patient care and related documentation maintained by health care organizations primarily governed under federal or state law, or both.

Under common law, quality management-related documentation enjoys qualified protection either because it is classified as "self-evaluative" material, whose purpose is to improve the quality of patient care delivery now or in the future or, in the case of incident reporting documentation, because it is prepared at the direction of a health care facility attorney or other official in anticipation of litigation and falls under "attorney-client privilege."

So that no question can arise about whether documentation is in fact quality management-related documentation, organization and department quality and risk managers should ensure that such documents are prominently labeled as "quality assurance," "quality improvement," or "quality management" documentation (as appropriate under individual state law), and display the warning that such documentation is not for release to third parties.

RISK MANAGEMENT PATIENT CARE RECORD REVIEW

One of the most interesting duties of a health care organization risk manager is to conduct a treatment record review, on request, for an attorney preparing to defend the facility against a malpractice or other legal action. This review is critically important to the defense of a claim or lawsuit and must be performed in a systematic, accurate, objective, thorough, and concise manner. The reviewer should ask the attorney requesting the review to provide a copy of the patient-plaintiff's complaint, so that the reviewer is familiar with the patient's precise allegations against the health care organization and/or its providers.

The risk manager conducting a litigation record review must remain impartial and produce a report that is free of bias if it is to be useful to legal counsel. Attorneys generally prefer that a record review report be summarized chronologically and that it contains appropriate headings and sub-headings. Many attorneys do not mind and some even expect the candid opinions of the reviewer concerning potential liability and damages (extent of injury) issues.

Risk managers analyzing patient care records for possible litigation must be sure, when writing up their reports, to label the work product (from first draft to final report) as "attorney-client work product, prepared for, and at the direction of, the facility attorney in anticipation of and in preparation for litigation." This disclaimer (or similar language, according to individual state law) maximizes the likelihood that the report is protected from disclosure to a patient-plaintiff's attorney under pretrial discovery rules.

Exhibit 5–1 presents an example of an outline format for a patient care record review litigation report.

Exhibit 5–1 Example of a Risk Management Treatment Record Review Report Format

XYZ General Hospital
Anytown, USA

Risk Management Patient Treatment Record Review Report

1. Patient's name: _____
2. Admission (or treatment) date(s): _____
3. Admission (treatment) diagnoses: _____
4. Clinical resume (chronological): _____
5. Summary of patient allegation(s): _____
6. Synopsis of investigation/interviews: _____
7. Analysis of liability: _____
8. Damages (injury) assessment: _____
9. Other information and issues: _____
10. "Attorney-client work product, prepared for and at the direction of the facility attorney in anticipation of and in preparation for litigation."

_____
Signature block and title of reviewer

_____
Date report submitted

MONITORING INFORMED CONSENT AS A QUALITY IMPROVEMENT INDICATOR

An area of special concern and confusion for many health care providers is patient informed consent to examination and intervention. This is a complicated area of health care malpractice law, often characterized by state-specific statutory and common law disclosure elements that must be imparted to patients, as well as a wide range of potential documentation formats to memorialize informed consent processes.

More and more, health care providers who obtain patient informed consent to examination and intervention on a recurring basis are utilizing audiovisual aids to educate patients about processes and options.[10] These supplements or alternatives to consent forms can take the form of descriptive pamphlets, individual or small-group classes, audio- and videotape presentations, and computer-generated passive and interactive presentations. These kinds of presentation formats for informed consent information enhance primary health care provider-patient communication and patient comprehension and set the stage for focused discussion after the presentation on specific patient concerns.[11]

As a supplement to or substitute for consent forms as the standard means of documenting patient informed consent, many providers and organizations or systems are employing review questionnaires, completed either on paper or on computer, to ensure that patients truly understand the material risks and benefits of and alternatives to proposed interventions.[12] One study concluded that patient recollection of facts about health care treatment procedures is enhanced after patient education and administration of a review quiz on informed consent items.[13] Education and testing strengthen the patient's knowledge base from which to control the treatment decision-making process intelligently.

Primary health care professionals from every health care discipline should consider developing patient educational programs about recurring procedures and therapeutic interventions and supplement them with appropriate audiovisual aids. Review questionnaires should also be developed to ensure that patients understand what they are "consenting" to. These processes and documents serve to memorialize the informed consent process and may be admissible evidence of what was said to and done for a patient during informed consent disclosure.[14]

Providers also should consider monitoring informed consent disclosure procedures as part of quality and risk management programs in their organizations. A sample indicator for informed consent might be, "Patients will give informed consent before examination or intervention commences." This indicator can be monitored through patient record review of informed consent documentation, direct observation of audiovisual patient education programs and discussion with selected patients about their contents, administration of questionnaires or quizzes to patients after informed consent disclosure, and general patient interviews. An example of a generic informed consent patient questionnaire appears in Exhibit 5–2.

CONCLUSION

Every health care organization has a primary legal duty to oversee and direct patient care delivery and promote optimal patient, visitor, and staff safety in the facility. This is carried out through a formal, systematic,

Exhibit 5–2 Example of a Generic Informed Consent Patient Questionnaire

---

Please answer the following questions to the best of your ability. Your answers and comments will be kept strictly confidential.

1. What health problem are you being treated for?
2. What is your health care provider's name?
3. Did your health care provider obtain your informed consent to treatment? (If "no," skip to question 9.)
4. What treatment did your health care provider recommend for your condition?
5. What benefits would this treatment offer?
6. Are there serious risks associated with the proposed treatment? If so, what are they?
7. Are there any other treatment options for your condition? If so, what are they?
8. Did your health care provider use any audiovisual aids (e.g., pamphlets, videos) to help explain your condition and/or treatment? If so, what kinds of audiovisual aids were used? Were they helpful to you in making your decision about treatment?
9. Did you ask any questions about your treatment before accepting it? (Please indicate if you declined treatment.)
10. Were you satisfied with your provider's explanation of your condition and treatment options? Did you feel like *you* were in control of the decision-making process?
11. Please feel free to offer any other comments or make suggestions for improving our service. Thank you for taking the time to complete this questionnaire.

---

comprehensive quality management program. Quality management encompasses patient care process and outcome measurement and evaluation activities, such as peer review and clinical indicator studies; staff credentialing/privileging and competency review activities; resource utilization management; patient care documentation and health information and liability risk management activities.

The Office of the Inspector General (OIG) within the Health Care Financing Administration (HCFA) recently issued a report[15] critical of hospital accreditation survey processes. In particular, OIG recommended that patient records for review be randomly selected by surveyors, rather than hand picked by facilities, which may tend to skew results.[16]

Although the "buzz words"—quality assurance, quality improvement, continuous quality improvement, and total quality management, among others—may be accreditation entity-specific and change with the times, the basic concept remains the same: to provide optimal quality patient care and to protect health care providers, organizations and systems from unwarranted liability exposure and losses. Quality management activities are coordinated at the organization and department levels by quality improvement coordinators. An optimally effective quality management program is patient-focused; guided and strongly supported by top management; and empowering of individual entrepreneurs at the lowest operational levels, who are best equipped to suggest opportunities both to improve care and minimize risk.

REFERENCES

Note: The general outline of a model health care quality/risk management program presented in this section is not intended to replicate any particular program of any organization, system, professional association, or accreditation entity. The concepts presented are generic in nature, although the model program is intended to be comprehensive.

1. *See* ARMY MEDICAL SPECIALIST CORPS, QUALITY IMPROVEMENT MANUAL (1992).

2. Joint Commission on Accreditation of Healthcare Organizations, *Improving Organizational Performance, ch. PI*, in COMPREHENSIVE ACCREDITATION MANUAL FOR HOSPITALS (1999).

3. *See* D.M. Berwick, *Continuous Improvement as an Ideal in Health Care*, 320 N. ENGL. J. MED. 53–56 (1989).

4. "Total quality management," as described by the Federal Quality Institute, is "a strategic integrated management system for achieving customer satisfaction, which involves all managers and employees, and uses quantitative methods to improve an organization's processes."

5. The American Physical Therapy Association's (APTA) former quality management education program, in which the author was the founding legal faculty member, was called "Promoting Quality/Managing Risk." The program is now managed by the AON Insurance Group.

6. *See* M. WALTON, THE DEMING MANAGEMENT METHOD, 1–21 (1986).

7. *See* WALTON, DEMING MANAGEMENT, Chap. 20, ("Doing It with Data").

8. J.D. LIEBLER, ED., HEALTH INFORMATION MANAGEMENT MANUAL (1998), Gaithersburg, MD: Aspen Publishers, Inc.

9. HEALTH CARE FACILITIES RISK MANAGEMENT: FORMS, CHECKLISTS, AND GUIDELINES (1998), Gaithersburg, MD: Aspen Publishers, Inc.

10. *See, e.g.*, R.C. Sechrest, *Educating Your Patient with Multimedia*, PHYSICIANS & COMPUTERS, October 1991, at 18–26.

11. For an excellent review article on improving health care provider-patient communications, *see* J.G. Carroll, *Improving Physician-Patient Communications,* PHYSICIANS & COMPUTERS, June 1991, at 18–25.

12. *See* R. Winslow, *Videos, Questionnaires Aim To Expand Role of Patients in Treatment Decisions,* WALL ST. J., February 25, 1992, at B1, B6.

13. *See* M.M. Hutson & J.D. Blaha, *Patients' Recall of Preoperative Instruction for Informed Consent for an Operation*, 73-A J. BONE & JOINT SURGERY 160–162 (1991).

14. *See* G.R. ANDERSON & V.A. GLESNES-ANDERSON, HEALTH CARE ETHICS: A GUIDE FOR DECISION MAKERS, 210 (1987).

15. J. Appleby, *Hospital Oversight Criticized*, USA TODAY, July 21, 1999, p. 1A.

16. D. Thornlow, BOJ EXPRESS, GEORGE WASHINGTON UNIVERSITY HOSPITAL, July 20, 1999, 1–2.

SUGGESTED READING

D.M. Berwick, *Continuous Improvement as an Ideal in Health Care*, N.E. J. OF MEDICINE. 1989; 320:53–56.

Joint Commission on Accreditation of Healthcare Organizations, *Comprehensive Accreditation Manual for Hospitals Organizations* (1999).

M.S. Malecki, *RM's Careful Review of Record Can Be a Boost to Hospital's Attorney*, HOSPITAL RISK MANAGEMENT, March 1991, 1–3.

R.W. SCOTT, HEALTH CARE MALPRACTICE: A PRIMER ON LEGAL ISSUES, 2ND ED. (1999).

S.C. Withrow, C.G. Hullquist, & K.S. McKenney, *OIG Makes a False Claim: Alleged Upcoding of DRG 416*, HEALTH CARE FRAUD AND ABUSE NEWSLETTER (1999), 2(6), pp. 1–3.

W. Woodruff, *The Confidentiality of Medical Quality Assurance Records*, ARMY LAWYER 5 (May 1987).

REVIEW ACTIVITIES

1. Design an instrument to review primary health care provider compliance with informed consent policies in your organization. Be sure to include indicators of compliance with managed care-era standards, including: non-compliance with gag clause restrictions and disclosure by providers to patients of potential conflicts of interest (such as receipt of variable incentive compensation for minimizing organization/system cost outlays).

2. Design a five-question multiple choice review quiz for patients undergoing a recurrent intervention carried out in your clinic, covering the substantive aspects of the procedure that the patients should be aware of before agreeing to its use on them. Implement the quiz as a means of assessing provider-patient communication during informed consent processes.

Appendix 5–A

Example of a Peer Review Work Sheet for Evaluation of Interdisciplinary Primary Health Care Professionals in a Rehabilitation Setting

ABC Rehabilitation Center
Peer Record Review Work Sheet

Patient's Name _____

Inpatient?   Y   N
Current status:
_____ Undergoing rehabilitation
_____ Discharged with in-clinic intervention. *Discharged to:*
         (home, long-term care facility, etc.)
_____ Discharged secondary to nonattendance
_____ Other (specify): _____

Primary health care provider's name: _____

1. Are initial examination, progress, and discharge notes
    written in the appropriate format?   Y   N
    (If "no," specify the deficiencies noted.)
    _____

2. Are objective findings (e.g., for range of motion,
    muscle strength, girths) written in quantitative terms,
    whenever possible?   Y   N

3. Are evaluative findings and diagnoses based on
    documented objective findings?   Y   N

4. (When applicable) Does the plan of care include or
    address any specific intervention requested or ordered
    by a referring physician?   Y   N

5. Are patient care goals reflective of patient needs and
    desires, and written in quantitative terms, with time
    frames for their achievement?   Y   N

6. In the reviewer's opinion, were patient care activities
    adequately documented? (If not, explain)   Y   N
    _____

7. Additional reviewer comments:

_____   _____

Reviewer's Signature and Stamp   Date of Review

Appendix 5–B

Example of a Patient Satisfaction Survey

ABC Rehabilitation Center
Patient Satisfaction Survey

Please help us improve our service to you and others by answering the following questions and then depositing the anonymous survey in the survey box in the patient dressing room. Thank you for your input.

1. Please rate our service overall: Excellent   Good   Fair   Poor

2. How would you rate the following?

   Check-in time: Excellent   Good   Fair   Poor

   Timeliness of being seen by therapist: Excellent   Good   Fair   Poor

3. How would you rate the attitude of our staff?

   Receptionist: Excellent   Good   Fair   Poor

   Therapist: Excellent   Good   Fair   Poor

   Assistant and/or aide/volunteer (please specify which):   Excellent   Good   Fair   Poor

Comments (optional): _____

4. If any members of our staff were particulary helpful to you, please let us know so we can recognize them and show our appreciation.

5. In your own words, what did you learn about managing your condition or problem?

_____

Thank you again for your comments.
Rehab Staff and Management

Chapter 6

Current Issues in Patient Care Documentation

This chapter presents a capsule summary of several of the important health care documentation problem areas that providers might encounter in clinical practice. Among the issues addressed are advance directives and the Patient Self-Determination Act; adverse incident documentation issues; clinical practice standards and guidelines as evidence of the legal standard of care; computerized, photographic, and video-format patient health records; documenting the care of sexual assault patients; documenting the use of physical restraints; legal issues associated with reimbursement documentation; mandatory reporting requirements, including child, spouse, and elder abuse, occupational and communicable diseases, and defective medical devices; patient discharge documentation; patient noncompliance, disengagement, and abandonment; withdrawal of life support/DNR guidelines; and telehealth documentation issues.

ADVANCE DIRECTIVES AND THE PATIENT SELF-DETERMINATION ACT

The Patient Self-Determination Act[1,2] (hereinafter "Act"), signed into law by former President Bush in November 1990, codifies a patient's common law right to control health care decisions—both routine and extraordinary. When it became effective on December 1, 1991, the Act bound hospitals, health maintenance organizations, long-term care facilities, and other health care entities participating in Medicare and Medicaid to its provisions.

The fundamental purpose of the Act is to ensure that providers and health care organizations provide patient education about informed consent and the right of patients to make "advance directives." *Advance directives* include legal instruments such as the *living will*[3] and *durable power of attorney for health care decision making,*[4] which memorialize patient desires concerning life-sustaining measures to be taken and decision making should the patient subsequently become legally incapacitated.

A key concept underlying the Act is respect for a patient's right to give informed consent to health-related examination and intervention. Under this process, a health care provider must provide the patient with relevant disclosure information about a proposed examination and/or intervention to allow the patient to analyze the options and make an informed choice about whether to accept or reject examination and/or a recommended intervention (or insist on another reasonable alternative intervention— even under managed care).

Although the Act does not create any new substantive patient rights, it does impose burdensome procedural obligations on health care organizations and providers covered by the law. Among other requirements, the Act[5] requires a covered health care provider or facility to

(A) provide written information [to patients] concerning:
  (i) an individual's rights under State Law (whether statutory or as recognized by the courts of the State) to make decisions concerning . . . medical care, including the right to accept or refuse medical or surgical treatment and the right to formulate advance directives . . . and
  (ii) the written policies of the provider or organization respecting the implementation of such rights;
(B) document in the individual's medical record whether or not the individual has executed an advance directive. . . .
  (2) The written information described in paragraph (1)(A) shall be provided to an adult individual:
    (a) in the case of a hospital, at the time of the individual's admission as an inpatient,
    (b) In the case of a skilled nursing facility, at the time of the individual's admission as a resident,
    (c) In the case of a home health agency, in advance of the individual coming under the care of the agency.

Before any substantive care is undertaken, then, in any patient care setting, a patient must receive *written* information about the right to make informed decisions regarding examination and intervention and the right (consistent with state law) to make advance directives regarding future care in the event of the patient's incapacitation. Also, a covered health care facility must provide the patient with a written copy of the facility's policy on implementing the requirements of the Act.

In addition to its disclosure obligations discussed above, a health care organization covered by the Act has documentation responsibilities as well. The facility must annotate in a patient's care record whether the patient has signed an advance directive regarding future care.

Larsen and Eaton carried out an exhaustive study of the Act and reported[6] that the Act has been relatively unsuccessful in safeguarding the rights of patients to make, and have enforced, advance directives concerning health care. The reasons cited for the lack of success of the Act include:

- Lack of individual awareness on the part of primary health care professionals of the existence of the Act,
- Reluctance on the part of patients and long-term care facility residents to execute advance directives, and
- Recalcitrance on the part of health care providers and organizations to honor valid advance patient directives, in part because they substitute their own values for those of patients or fear liability exposure.

ADVERSE INCIDENT DOCUMENTATION ISSUES

The incident report is used by health care clinicians, clinical managers, quality and risk management coordinators, organization and system administrators, and corporate attorneys to document and report adverse events that may have adverse legal and/or quality management implications for the health care organization/system and its providers. Incident reports are used to document adverse events involving patients, visitors, staff, or any other persons—including trespassers and others who may be on facility property without authorization.

Documentation of adverse incidents serves two main purposes. First, by reporting a suspected or actual injury or highlighting a safety concern, the incident report serves to alert management of a potential problem that may warrant corrective action. Thus, the incident report serves as a basis for continuous quality improvement in the facility. Second, the incident report memorializes important facts about an alleged incident that create a record for use in further investigation, in the event that a legal action results from the incident. In this respect, the incident report protects facility and health care provider business and legal interests.

Even with facility guidelines or statutory requirements in effect, health care providers "on the front line" may be confused about when to generate an incident report. Because incident reports are confidential, no incident should be considered too minor to report. At the other end of the scale, major incidents that involve police or firefighter intervention also require a facility incident report, in addition to any official police or fire report that might be generated.

Regarding the contents of an incident report form, the following should be included:

- Administrative data about the patient, including, at a minimum, patient name and address, date of birth, gender, admission and incident dates, and patient status (inpatient, outpatient, or emergency).
- Patient diagnosis and a brief summary of care rendered to the patient. (*Note*: If the incident involves someone other than a patient, then the information required for patients would not be completed.)
- Type of incident (e.g., premises [e.g., wet floor], equipment, medication, exercise, modality, wound debridement, surgery, etc.).
- Condition of person affected after the occurrence: no apparent injury, minor injury, major injury, death.
- Course of action undertaken.
- Witnesses, if any.
- Description of the event. All facility staff must receive training from the facility risk manager about how to write an incident report. This summary of an adverse event must:
  1. be concise, yet thorough
  2. document objectively what was observed firsthand by the writer of the report
  3. delineate in quotes (hearsay) statements attributable to another person
  4. not contain any speculation as to the possible cause of an occurrence or injury
- Typed or printed name and title and signature of the writer of the report.
- Date report completed and date submitted to the facility risk manager.

An incident report also should be identified either as a "confidential quality assurance/improvement report" or as a "document prepared at the direction of the facility attorney in anticipation of or in preparation for litigation," according to state or federal legal requirements. The specific language to be used should be decided by the facility attorney, administrators, and risk manager(s), because, in some jurisdictions, one designation (i.e., quality improvement or litigation) may afford greater confidentiality than the other. Under federal law and the law of many states, for example, quality assurance documentation may be virtually immune from disclosure to third parties, whereas documents prepared for litigation may enjoy only qualified immunity and may be subject to release to a patient-plaintiff if the document is essential to the plaintiff's case and the information contained therein cannot be obtained through any other means.[7]

When an adverse incident involving patient injury occurs, a provider should also document concisely and objectively in the patient care record a summary of patient injury and intervention to aid the victim. Do not mention the incident report in the concomitant patient care record entry. An example of an incident report appears as Exhibit 6–1. A hypothetical problem involving incident reporting is presented in the review case studies section at the end of the chapter.

CLINICAL PRACTICE GUIDELINES AS EVIDENCE OF THE LEGAL STANDARD OF CARE

In addition to expert testimony on the legal standard of care, many health care malpractice attorneys are turning to clinical practice guidelines and protocols to establish required practice standards in legal cases. These guidelines can take the form of federal or state statutory or regulatory requirements, professional association and accreditation standards, and health care organization internal policies, protocols, and procedures.

Often, patient and defense attorneys turn first to internal facility policy and procedures manuals for information on standards of practice in effect in the facility. Providers in the facility are presumed to know and to follow guidelines established in these protocols. If a provider fails to conform to procedures outlined in a protocol, then that fact alone may constitute substantial evidence that the provider breached the required standard of care.

Exhibit 6–1 Example of an Incident Report

Quality Assurance Risk Management Report

WARNING: The information contained in this quality assurance document is confidential and subject to privilege under applicable state and federal law. Penalties may apply for unauthorized release. Do not file or refer to this document in any patient treatment record.

1. (Date/Time/Location of Incident) _____
2. (Name/Age/Gender of Person[s] Involved) _____
3. (If Incident Involved a Patient, State Patient's Principal Diagnosis and Name[s] of Attending Physician[s]) _____
4. (Description of Event) _____
5. (Condition of Patient and/or Other Persons Affected, After Occurence) _____
6. (Name[s], Address[es], Phone Number[s] of Witness[es], If Any, and Each Witness's Description of Event _____
7. (Brief Description of Treatment Rendered, If Any) _____
8. (Name, Title, and Position of Person Completing Form)_____
9. (Signature of Preparer and Date of Report) _____

Note to Preparer of Report: Forward through department or service chief to facility risk manager within 24 hours. Notify risk manager telephonically of event immediately after emergency, if any, is resolved.

For that reason, facilities and clinics that utilize practice guidelines should exercise restraint not to make the protocols too rigid, to the extent possible. For example, in physical therapy, there are many acceptable ways to care for a patient with adhesive capsulitis of the shoulder, including modalities, stretching, active and resistive exercise, passive mobilization, and muscle energy techniques, among others. To limit physical therapists in a clinic to one or two of the above may needlessly create a practice standard that is higher than what the law requires. Wherever possible, a practice standard should contain a clause that allows professional health care clinicians the option of deviating from the standard in individual cases, based on their professional judgment.

The federal and state governments are exploring the use of practice guidelines to establish presumptive or conclusive compliance with legal standards of care as a method of malpractice tort reform. The federal

Agency for Health Care Policy and Research (AHCPR), an agency of the Public Health Service, issued some 41 clinical practice guidelines between 1993 and 1997, however, AHCPR ceased such issuance of guidelines due, in part, to their unintended use by attorneys in health care malpractice legal proceedings as evidence of the legal standard of care.

COMPUTERIZED, PHOTOGRAPHIC, AND VIDEO-FORMAT PATIENT CARE RECORDS

In this age of rapid dissemination of information, more and more patient care information is being stored on computer. There are advantages of computer-generated records for patients and health care providers. For providers, the use of computers to record patient care data can be more efficient than documenting in longhand because many computer software programs offer templates that make patient care documentation seemingly painless. Also, spell check and other error detection features minimize the likelihood of a mistake being made that could affect patient care.

For patients, computerized patient care records offer many advantages over paper records. Patients (may) no longer have to worry about loss of clinical information personal to them. Patient health histories can be retrieved quickly by a provider linked to a patient database in a given health care facility. "Smart (patient identification) cards,"[8] and even patient wristbands containing computerized memory chips, store complete patient health histories, making routine and emergency patient care more efficient and less costly.

There are potential disadvantages of computer-generated patient health records, too. Of primary concern is patient confidentiality. Access to patient databases must be limited to providers and others having an official need and *right* to know the information contained therein. Failure to safeguard patient information stored on computer—such as with a secure password access system—can lead to civil tort liability for breach of patient confidentiality, or even intentional or negligent infliction of emotional distress associated with the unauthorized release of private patient information. Computer users and system managers are also urged to change passwords frequently to prevent unauthorized access to patient care records.

With computerized patient record systems, there is also an increased danger that providers will be tempted to alter or erase prior patient entries, especially in the face of pending health care malpractice actions. Computer fraud experts can readily retrieve "lost" or erased files. Provider education about individual professional responsibility is the key to preventing spoliation of computerized patient care records. Risk managers should also consider installing system controls that do not permit alteration of original completed patient care record entries, but only allow addendums in the form of new notation.

With the impending approach of the millennium, computer experts caution health care organizations and systems to safeguard computerized patient care data and back such data up to prevent losses incident to a "Y2K" snafu. A Scottish health program recently reported that it lost all data from a cancer clinical trial in a Y2K test.[9]

According to Dr. Steve Salvatore, MD, Medical Correspondent for the Cable News Network, the [primary health professional]-computer relationship will be the second most important health professional relationship (behind the health professional-patient relationship) in the 21st century.[10] Some patients are already storing their health records on the Internet, through companies such as PersonalMD.com, AboutMyHealth.net, and drkoop.com (founded by Dr. C. Everett Koop, former United States Surgeon General), among a growing number of others. A key advantage of such systems is ready access of patient historical information for health care provider, for both routine care and emergencies. A principal concern of patients and health professionals about such systems is the potential for a breach of patient privacy by third parties not having the right or a medical need for the information contained therein. Safeguards from encryption to PIN numbers for access to digital trails, indicating who has viewed patient records may help to limit or prevent invasions of privacy.[11]

Photographic documentation of patient status and interventions is also being used increasingly.[12] Surgeons, rehabilitation and wound care therapists, and others use photography to memorialize, among other findings, patient appearance before and after surgery, limb and spinal range of motion, postural alignment, and wound healing. Health record administrators must exercise special precautions to preserve photographic evidence until statutory record retention requirements are met. An additional consideration is the expense, manpower, and time involved in copying photographs for release to patients, their attorneys, insurers, and others.

Video documentation of patient status and interventions is also being used more frequently by health care professionals. A common example is the "day-in-the-life" videotape of a typical rehabilitation day for a tort plaintiff involved in litigation. In one medical malpractice case involving an allegation of negligent placement of a feeding catheter, *Georgacopoulos v. University of Chicago,* the court admitted a day-in-the-life videotape of the patient's "painful physical therapy session."[13] The court established a test for admission of this kind of videotape patient care documentation:

1. The tape must depict an accurate representation of the patient's condition, circumstances, and rehabilitation.
2. The tape's value in the proceedings as relevant and probative evidence must outweigh any inflammatory effect that it might have on the jury.
3. The taped rehabilitation session must not amount to merely cumulative, or repetitive, evidence.
4. The depiction of the patient must be in good taste.[14]

In *Georgacopoulos*, the court concluded that the videotape evidence of the patient-plaintiff's rehabilitation met the required tests and that "the objectionable physical therapy session amounted to only a few minutes."[15]

A serious consideration for health record administrators and risk managers is patient privacy. Videotaping of patient examination and/or intervention in a facility requires explicit written informed consent, signed by the patient and/or the patient's legally appointed representative. Videotape documentation, like photographs and paper and computerized documentation, must be retained in accordance with statutory, institutional, and customary requirements.

DOCUMENTING THE CARE OF SEXUAL ASSAULT PATIENTS

The interview, examination, and care of sexual assault or battery victims require careful coordination of health care and law enforcement personnel. Not only must the patient's immediate and short-term physical and psychological needs be attended to, but important physical and testimonial evidence must be obtained and safeguarded in the patient's legal best interests (i.e., for successful subsequent prosecution of the offender).

Often, a patient who is the victim of a sexual assault will be treated under emergency circumstances, and his or her care will require intervention of a designated sexual assault crisis team. Carefully drafted written policies governing the treatment of sexual assault victims is crucial to minimize additional trauma to the patient and to collect, store, and transfer evidence to law enforcement authorities.

Before carrying out examination and initial treatment of a sexual assault victim, it is important to obtain the patient's informed consent. Depending on the patient's mental status, it may not be feasible to obtain the informed consent in a signed writing. In this case, a member of the crisis team witnessing the informed consent process should summarize the disclosure in the patient's initial examination and intervention documentation.

It is critically important that the examining physician expeditiously record his or her evaluative findings in the patient's emergency medical record. Any statements made by the patient should be included in this documentation and enclosed in quotes. This kind of "hearsay" evidence may be admissible in a legal proceeding as an "excited utterance" or "statement [made] for purposes of medical diagnosis or treatment."[16] Records of sexual assault victims should be maintained separate from general patient care records in a designated special handling file to safeguard the confidentiality of sensitive patient information and to ensure the medicolegal integrity of these records.

Another important issue is chain of custody of laboratory specimens and physical evidence obtained from the victim. Forensic specimens should be appropriately labeled on chain of custody documents after they are obtained by the examining physician and should be safeguarded under lock and key until they are transferred to law enforcement officials having jurisdiction over the criminal case. Patient specimens that are to be used for patient treatment do not normally require the special labeling and handling required for forensic specimens.

DOCUMENTING THE USE OF PATIENT RESTRAINTS

Every day, approximately tens of thousands of hospitalized and long-term care patients in the United States are physically restrained. Many are injured from physical restraints, and some die as a direct result of their use.[17] Because of these considerations, Congress and the Food and Drug Administration have enacted special rules governing the use of physical restraints.

Under interpretive guidelines established pursuant to the Omnibus Reconciliation Act of 1987, health care organizations must justify the use of patient physical restraints in detailed patient care documentation.[18] The

FDA requires manufacturers of physical restraints to label them for use "by prescription only" in an attempt to minimize improper use of restraints.[19]

Because of the inherent danger of misuse and neglect associated with physical restraints, providers must document the following *prior* to using patient restraints:

- that the use of restraints is clinically justified
- that appropriate health care providers have been consulted and that less restrictive alternatives have been attempted and are inadequate
- that the patient's physical and mental conditions have been taken into account when deciding to use restraints

Health care organization administrators and their supporting clinical and legal staff should develop protocols for the proper use of restraints. Appropriate justifications for the use of physical restraints might include:

- combative patient behavior, posing a danger to the patient or others
- patient elopement, where the patient's wandering has the potential to cause patient injury or injury to others
- patient or surrogate request, with physician concurrence

Documentation and policy considerations for using physical restraints include the following (consistent with federal and applicable state law):

- An interdisciplinary committee must develop, implement, and monitor a facility/system restraint reduction system.[20]
- A physician must order the use of physical restraints, except in an emergency. In the absence of a physician on duty, a registered nurse can order their use temporarily, while he or she expeditiously seeks a verbal order from a physician.
- Verbal orders for physical restraints must be countersigned by the physician expeditiously (within 24 hours).
- The physician ordering physical restraints must document in the patient care record the patient behavior justifying the use of restraints; the type of restraint to be used; the time period for its use; the frequency of checks on the patient, including the taking of patient vital signs; and conditions for removal of restraints.

- Restraint orders must be re-evaluated and rewritten at regular short intervals, which vary according to the patient care setting.

LEGAL ISSUES ASSOCIATED WITH REIMBURSEMENT DOCUMENTATION

Business issues, including how-to guidance, associated with third-party reimbursement for patient care are well reported in the health professional literature.[21] These issues involve administrative, not legal, considerations, and change so frequently that their inclusion here is nonproductive.

One important legal issue in health care reimbursement is whether a demand for third-party reimbursement by a health care provider and/or organization constitutes larceny, or theft, by fraud or deception.[22] *Fraud* is defined as a false misrepresentation of a material fact, made with the intent to deceive, which causes another person to take some action detrimental to his or her own (or the public's) interest. A fraudulent misrepresentation can be the basis for administrative, civil, or criminal legal action against the person committing fraud. Larceny by fraud involves theft of money, goods, services, or property by deception.

Elements of fraud:

1. *A misrepresentation of fact,*
2. *made with an intent to deceive,*
3. *on which another person relies to his or her (or the public's) legal detriment.*

Larceny by fraud: theft of money, goods, services, or property by deception.

Health care reimbursement fraud may account for 10 percent or more of aggregate health care expenditures in the United States.[23] The Office of the Inspector General of the federal Department of Health and Human Services (HHS), as well as complementary state agencies, have recently accelerated investigation and prosecution of health care reimbursement fraud by providers and organizations.

Health care providers commit fraud against Medicare, Medicaid, TriCare, commercial third-party payers, workers' compensation agencies, and other entities, through their billing practices. Billing practices that can result in an allegation of fraud include knowingly filing false claims for reimbursement.

Practices that might constitute reimbursement fraud include:

- filing claims for health professional services not actually rendered, such as for patient "no shows," called "phantom billing"
- routine waivers of patient copayments and deductibles under Medicare Part B[24]
- violations of "anti-kickback"[25] and self-referral statutes
- overutilization ("unbundling") of health care-related products and services paid for by third-party payers
- "upcoding," or miscategorizing procedural terminology codes to enhance reimbursement

Inadequate patient care documentation may give rise to, and support an allegation of, third-party reimbursement fraud, leading to liability or settlement of charges with HHS. Penalties for a finding of reimbursement fraud can range from civil fines and liability; criminal convictions, including the imposition of criminal monetary fines; administrative penalties, including exclusion from participation in Medicare, Medicaid,[26] or other third-party payer systems, and adverse licensure action by state licensing agencies; and professional association actions for ethical violations.[27]

MANDATORY REPORTING REQUIREMENTS

Health care providers engaged in primary care delivery are required by every state to report certain findings or good faith suspicions to state or federal authorities, including evidence of child, spouse, or elderly abuse; certain communicable diseases; and defective medical devices. Providers who carry out primary care—especially nonphysician providers, who may not be aware of their reporting obligations—should consult legal counsel to obtain a current summary of their state law on mandatory reporting requirements.

Abuse

Health care professionals have been sued both for the failure to report suspected or actual abuse and for the act of reporting suspected or actual abuse. Some state statutes provide absolute immunity for providers who report abuse found incident to their official health care duties, whereas others offer only a qualified immunity, based on a showing of "good faith." A few states have no statutory abuse reporting requirements, or make such reporting voluntary.

Documentation of findings supporting a conclusion of abuse must be carefully and objectively spelled out in the patient care record. Documentation of the reporting of abuse, however, may be more appropriately memorialized in an office memorandum or in some file other than the patient care record, consistent with state or federal legal requirements. Remember that statements that are made by the patient for the purpose of diagnosis and/or intervention or that constitute "excited utterances" should be carefully transcribed verbatim into the patient care record to protect the patient's health and legal interests because these statements may constitute admissible "hearsay" evidence against a perpetrator in a subsequent civil or criminal legal action.[28]

Providers must be educated about the physical and psychological signs of abuse, including unexplained injuries, malnutrition, withdrawal, and poor socialization. And they must not breach their fiduciary duty owed to patients under their care by failing to report abuse when they see or suspect it.

Occupational and Communicable Diseases

The timely detection, treatment, and monitoring of occupational diseases (e.g., asbestosis, carpal tunnel syndrome, and lead poisoning) and infectious diseases (including tuberculosis and sexually transmitted diseases) is crucial to the maintenance of individual and public health and safety. State legislatures, pursuant to their constitutional "police power" to protect public health, safety, and welfare, mandate that certain occupational and infectious diseases be reported by health care providers (and other professionals) to designated public health agencies at the local or state level. These reporting requirements are permissible exceptions to the duty of confidentiality owed by health care professionals to patients.

As with child, spouse, and elderly abuse, primary health care providers are legally responsible for complying with mandatory disease reporting requirements. As the adage goes, "Ignorance of the law is no excuse for noncompliance." Providers must consult with their legal advisors for up-to-date statutory reporting requirements in their individual states.

Defective Medical Devices

Under the Safe Medical Devices Act of 1990, which became effective on November 28, 1991, health care facilities must report to the FDA and/or equipment manufacturers any cases involving patient injury in which there is a "reasonable suggestion" that a piece of medical equipment contributed to the death or serious injury of the patient.[29] Under this law, a health care organization must designate a person to write such a report (probably the risk manager or safety committee chairperson), which must be submitted within 10 working days of an adverse patient incident involving medical equipment. The report is forwarded directly to the FDA for death cases (as well as to the equipment manufacturer) and to the equipment manufacturer for serious injury cases (or to the FDA, if the identity of the manufacturer is unknown).

These reports enjoy qualified (limited) federal statutory immunity from use in civil litigation. This immunity probably was mandated to encourage reporting of possibly faulty medical devices to federal authorities, so that warnings can be promptly issued to save lives.

PATIENT DISCHARGE DOCUMENTATION

Discharge planning for hospitalized patients is a multidisciplinary, coordinated process that requires careful documentation. Hospital patients often require follow-up outpatient or home care and the coordination of this intervention should be noted in discharge nursing, physical and occupational therapy, social service, physician, and other relevant patient care documentation. In addition to serving to optimize quality patient care, proper notation of discharge instructions and coordinated follow-up care may serve as important evidence of quality and quantity of care rendered, in the event of an ensuing legal health care malpractice action alleging abandonment or other forms of professional negligence.

If home exercise or other interventions are to be used by a patient after discharge from immediate care, then written, personalized handouts should be issued to the patient. The fact that such materials have been issued to the patient and a summary of the teaching imparted to the patient and/or family/significant others should be documented in the patient's discharge note by the appropriate service.

If clinical information about a patient is to be sent to outside agencies or providers to facilitate home or outpatient care, then the patient's consent to release pertinent records should be secured before the patient is discharged. Patient follow-up appointments for re-examination and follow-up care also must be well documented, and the patient given appropriate appointment slips.

For discharged outpatients seen in clinics such as physical or occupational therapy pursuant to physician referral, the therapist responsible for the patient's care should forward a discharge summary to the referring physician on discharge. An example of such a letter appears as Exhibit 6–2.

PATIENT NONCOMPLIANCE, DISENGAGEMENT, AND ABANDONMENT

As part of the implied contract of care between patient and provider, health care clinicians should explain the importance of compliance[30] with instructions to patients during the initial visit and document what is said to the patient and the patient's responses. Providers should have in effect a written policy regarding patient responsibility for compliance with interventions. Providers should also consider including tactful reminders about attendance and compliance policies on patient appointment slips.

Every facility should have a written policy in effect regarding termination of the patient-provider relationship. Failure to comply with interventions and instructions may be a justification for disengaging from care for a patient. Although a provider has almost unlimited discretion to elect whether to *form* a professional relationship with a patient, the provider must comply with certain legal rules to terminate an existing health professional-patient relationship properly.[31]

Termination of the provider-patient relationship is justified when the patient makes a knowing, voluntary election to end the relationship, either unilaterally or jointly with the provider. A provider may unilaterally choose to end the professional relationship with the patient when a cure has resulted from intervention, or when the patient, in the clinician's profes-

Exhibit 6–2 Example of an Outpatient Discharge Report

Physical Therapy Services
ABC Rehabilitation Center
New Wave, California

Date: _____

(Referring Physician's Address)
Subject: Discharge Report
Patient Name: _____

Dr. Dr. _____ :

This letter is a discharge report on your patient, _____ ,
referred on _____ for the following outpatient physical therapy
services: _____ .
* Course and Duration of Treatment: _____
* Summary of Discharge Evaluation: _____
* Home Care Instructions/Needs: _____
* Follow-up Re-evaluation Instructions: _____
* Additional Comments: _____
  _____

Thank you for referring this interesting and pleasant patient to us for care.

Sincerely,
Reggie Hausenfus, PT
Chief Physical Therapist

---

sional judgment, has achieved maximal benefit from intervention. This
latter situation requires careful documentation in the patient care record
that will withstand legal scrutiny in the event of a health care malpractice
action. Also, whenever a clinician has provided patient care pursuant to a
physician referral, the clinician should communicate in writing to the
referring entity that the patient has been discharged.

Patient noncompliance, and even a personality conflict between provider and patient, can form appropriate reasons to discharge or transfer a
patient. Under these circumstances, the provider must:

1. Give advance notice to the patient (and the referring entity, if any) of
   the provider's intent to disengage from care.

2. If continuing care is needed, give the patient a reasonable time before terminating the professional relationship to find a suitable new provider. (A prudent risk management measure would be to assist the patient in finding a suitable substitute provider and document in an office memorandum the steps taken to assist the patient.)
3. On discharge, carefully draft and send to the patient a disengagement letter, coordinated through your facility or personal legal advisor. This type of letter may prevent the health care malpractice statute of limitations from being "tolled," or suspended, because of a patient claim of "continuing care."[32]
4. Carefully document in the patient care record the patient's status at the time of discharge.
5. Expeditiously transfer copies of the patient's records (but not the risk management-focused office memoranda or any incident reports involving the patient) to the follow-on provider and offer to communicate with the new provider telephonically about pertinent clinical information.

WITHDRAWAL OF LIFE SUPPORT/DNR GUIDELINES

The withholding or withdrawal of life-sustaining treatment and support and do-not-resuscitate (DNR) orders are distinct clinical considerations that need to be addressed separately. Both judgments now largely fall within the administrative ambit of the Patient Self-Determination Act, which has already been introduced in this chapter. Some situations, however, fall outside of the jurisdiction of that statute, requiring consideration by providers of other complex statutes, regulations, and common law court precedent. This brief overview of DNR orders is intended only to be a limited introduction to a complicated area of health care law and professional ethics.

A DNR order precludes the otherwise automatic initiation of cardiopulmonary resuscitative efforts for a patient. The order does not affect the provision of any other substantive care such as life support and other treatment decisions.

A DNR order may be appropriate in one of two situations: to respect the free choice of a patient with full mental and legal capacity or the valid decision of a surrogate decision maker, or when, in the judgment of the attending physician, resuscitative efforts would be futile.[33] An order to withhold or withdraw life-sustaining therapeutic interventions may be appropriate for patients who are either terminal or in a persistent vegetative state.[34]

In either case, careful documentation of specific orders by the attending physician is required, as well as careful documentation in the patient's progress notes of:

- the rationale or justification for such a decision
- a brief description of the patient's physical condition and mental/legal capacity to make an advance directive decision
- any discussion about the order with the patient and/or the patient's family and surrogate decision maker, if they are not one and the same
- any input from an institutional ethics committee and/or ethics consultant(s)[35]

Physicians and consultant and supportive providers may have to rely on what is documented in a patient's treatment record about DNR or life-support decisions in defending a wrongful death legal action. In respect of patient autonomy and for the legal protection of providers, this documentation must be accurate and comprehensive.

TELEHEALTH DOCUMENTATION ISSUES

Telehealth involves computerized information transfer systems and technology used to transmit patient care and related data to distant providers having an imminent need for the information conveyed. It poses great promise and potential problems for patients and health care providers and organizations. For patients, providers, and health care organizations, the rapid dissemination of vital patient care or educational or research information to providers may result in more efficacious patient care outcomes that are both more convenient and at lower cost.

Transmission of patient care information via the Internet or similar media carries the same risks of breach of confidentiality as does transmission of any other information through these media, except that the nature of the information potentially compromised is highly personal and sensitive. Adequate steps, including prominent display of privacy warnings within such transmissions, must be undertaken by health care providers and organizations to meet fiduciary duties owed to patients under their care. Whether telehealth or "distance health care delivery" will provide the same (or better) quality of professional service delivery and satisfaction to patients is an open question, whose answer remains to be developed and seen.

For licensed primary health care professionals, the issue of unlicensed practice in states in which providers are not licensed accompanies inter-state telehealth consultation and practice. Penalties for a finding of unli-censed health care practice may include administrative, civil, criminal, and professional association adverse actions. Ways to comply with local licensure requirements include licensure by endorsement and special registration, among others.[36] Malaysia's Telemedicine Act of 1997 and, in the United States, the Federation of State Medical Boards' Model Legisla-tion Regarding Licensure offer guidance for health professional associa-tions and their lobbyists regarding possible solutions to the growing crisis of cross-border licensed health care clinical practice.[37] Providers engaging in telehealth must also comply with FDA regulations concerning their telecommunications technologies, and face the likelihood of non-reim-bursement for services. Currently, federal law (the Balanced Budget Act of 1997) permits limited reimbursement for telehealth consultations by pro-viders to Medicare Part B beneficiaries from rural health professional shortage areas (HPSAs).[38]

More and more, pharmaceuticals are being offered for sale to patients over the Internet. Such practice, while convenient, may violate state licensure and federal prescription laws. In addition, since one-tenth of patient admissions to hospitals involve adverse drug reactions,[39] Internet pharmacies may face liability for health professional negligence (includ-ing patient abandonment) for failing to be available to monitor customers and to offer advice in drug-related emergencies.

CONCLUSION

Health care providers—particularly those primary physician and nonphysician providers examining and intervening on behalf of patients in clinical practice—face complex health care legal issues on a daily basis. Health care organization and system administrators and risk managers should ensure that these clinicians and their support staffs receive ongoing legal instruction on their formidable responsibilities in areas such as patient advance directives, documenting and reporting adverse incidents, documenting the treatment of sexual assault and otherwise abused patients, compliance with mandatory reporting requirements, discharge and disengagement documentation, and ethical and legal considerations surrounding DNR/withdrawal of life support orders, among a myriad of other considerations.

REFERENCES

1. This discussion on the Patient Self-Determination Act is adapted from an earlier article written by the author, entitled *Guaranteeing Patient Rights: It's the Law*, in ADVANCE FOR DIRECTORS IN REHABILITATION, September/October 1992, at 43–44.
2. Omnibus Budget Reconciliation Act of 1990, Tit. IV, § 4206, Congressional Record, October 26, 1990. Pub. L. 101–508, codified at 42 U.S.C. §§ 1395c and 1396a.
3. A *living will* is a legal document, signed by a patient, which states the patient's desires regarding life-sustaining measures to be taken in the event that the patient becomes mentally and legally incapacitated. Living will statutes are in effect in all states. Most states require a patient to be both mentally and legally incapacitated and terminal for a living will to become operative. Some states allow a living will to become activated when a patient is in a "persistent vegetative state."
4. A *durable power of attorney for health care decision making* is a legal document, signed by a patient, that delegates health care decision making to an agent of the patient's choice in the event that the patient becomes mentally and legally incapacitated. The patient executing a durable power of attorney normally may designate anyone—a spouse, relative, or friend—as his or her health care decision maker.
5. The Patient Self-Determination Act, 42 U.S.C. Section 1395cc(f).
6. E.J. Larsen & T.A. Eaton, *The Limits of Advance Directives: A History and Assessment of the Patient Self-Determination Act*. WAKE FOREST LAW REVIEW 32(2):249–293 (1997).
7. R.W. Scott, *Incident Reports: Protecting the Record*, PT: MAGAZINE OF PHYSICAL THERAPY 4(9), 24–25 (1996).
8. See *"Smart Cards" To Provide Data, Rush Payments, Cut Paperwork*, P.T. BULL., November 20, 1991, at 1, 38.
9. K.A. Kearney, *Year 2000 Contingency Planning for Health Care Providers*, HEALTH LAWYER 11(1):8–9, 19 (1998).
10. CNN Headline News, August 14, 1999.
11. M. Chase, *Patients' Next Choice: Whether To Keep Files Stored on the Internet*, WALL STREET JOURNAL, August 16, 1999, B1.
12. One system in use, the Polaroid HealthCam System, was demonstrated at the American Physical Therapy Association's 1993 Combined Sections Meeting, San Antonio, TX, February 3–7, 1993.
13. Georgacopoulos v. University of Chicago, 504 N.E.2d 830 (Ill. App. Ct. 1987), at 832.
14. Georgacopoulos, 504 N.E.2d 830 at 833.

15. Georgacopoulos, 504 N.E.2d 830 at 832.

16. *See, e.g.*, Federal Rules of Evidence 803(2) and 803(4), which read:

The following [is] not excluded by the hearsay rule, even though the declarant is available as a witness:

(2) Excited utterance. A statement relating to a startling event or condition made while the declarant was under the stress of excitement caused by the event or condition.

(4) Statements for purposes of medical diagnosis or treatment. Statements made for purposes of medical diagnosis or treatment and describing medical history, or past or present symptoms, pain, or sensations, or the inception or general character of the cause or external source thereof insofar as reasonably pertinent to diagnosis or treatment.

17. *See FDA Imposes New Restrictions on Use of Restraints,* P.T. BULL., July 1, 1992, at 2.

18. *See* C. Lewis, *How To Handle Upcoming Guidelines,* P.T. BULL., June 27, 1990, at 18.

19. *See FDA Imposes New Restrictions on Use of Restraints, supra* note 17.

20. L.A. Anderson & K. Duhamel, *Restraint-Free Environment: Why the Mystery?* GERINOTES (1997) 4(3): 12.

21. For superlative discussion of reimbursement issues and strategies for rehabilitative and work therapy services, *see* L. Anderson, *"Patient Tolerated Treatment Well,"* GERINOTES (1997) 4(3), 13. ("The most common cause of denials for medical necessity is poor documentation.")

22. For more details about fraud, *see* HEALTH CARE FRAUD AND ABUSE NEWSLETTER, Leader Publications.

23. *See $90 Billion Lost to Fraud, Health-Care Experts Say,* P.T. BULL., March 24, 1993, at 6.

24. *See* L. Charla, *PTs Who Waive Deductibles Face Probe,* P.T. BULL., October 2, 1991, at 3, 37.

25. For health care providers and facilities participating in Medicare and Medicaid, the government has issued guidance on the types of investments and business activities that constitute "safe harbors," protected from allegations of fraud and/or abuse. These include certain investment interests in publicly traded companies; long-term space and equipment rentals, and personal services contracts; sale of a medical practice in anticipation of retirement; professional referral services (with full patient disclosure); warranties; noncash discounts; payments to *bona fide* employees; group purchasing organizations; and routine waiver of Medicare copayments for *hospital inpatient* care. *See* 42 U.S.C. § 13202–7b(b); 42 C.F.R. part 1001.

26. Certain events, such as a prior criminal conviction in state or federal court for Medicare or Medicaid "program-related misconduct" (e.g., for filing false claims for patient care services), will subject a licensed health care provider to mandatory exclusion from participation in the Medicare and Medicaid programs for a period of five years. *See* 42 U.S.C. § 1128(a)(1) [Social Security Act]. For a case example addressing this issue, *see In re* Dow, Docket No. C-92–061, Dec. No. CR222 (A.L.J. decision), reported in CIV. MONEY PENALTIES REP.: MEDICARE/MEDICAID FRAUD & ABUSE, January 1993, at 4–5. The Health Insurance Portability and Accountability Act of 1996 increased penalties

for federal reimbursement fraud to include permanent exclusion from participation in federal reimbursement programs.

27. For example, Principle 5 of the American Physical Therapy Association's *Code of Ethics* states that "physical therapists seek remuneration for their services that is deserved and reasonable." Principle 5.3A further states that "physical therapists shall not directly or indirectly request, receive, or participate in the dividing, transferring, assigning, or rebating of an unearned fee." A violation of this section would subject a physical therapist-APTA member to ethical sanctions.

28. For more information on excited utterances and statements made for the purpose of diagnosis or treatment, *see supra* note 16.

29. The Safe Medical Devices Act of 1990, 21 United States Code §§ 301 note, 321, 360d, and 360hh *et seq.*

30. For an excellent article on psychological aspects of enhancing patient compliance with treatment, *see* N. Clopton & T. McMahon, *Patient Compliance,* CLINICAL MGMT., January/February 1992, at 59–65.

31. For more liability for patient abandonment, *see* R.W. Scott, *Liability for Patient Abandonment,* CLINICAL MGMT., March/April 1992, at 18–19.

32. For more information on disengagement letters (including a sample disengagement letter), *see* J.G. Foonberg, *The Disengagement Letter as a Means of Protecting Yourself from Malpractice Claims,* LAW PRAC. MGMT., May/June 1992, at 58–59.

33. *See* Council on Ethical and Judicial Affairs, American Medical Association, *Guidelines for the Appropriate Use of Do-Not-Resuscitate Orders,* 265 JAMA 1868–1871 (1991).

34. *See* J.M. Luce, *Ethical Principles in Critical Care,* 263 JAMA 696–700 (1990).

35. *See* W.A. Woodruff, *Letting Life Run Its Course: Do-Not-Resuscitate Orders and Withdrawal of Life-Sustaining Treatment,* ARMY LAW, April 1989, at 6–18.

36. A.S. Goldberg, *Taking Healthcare to the Patient–Telemedicine Delivers,* HEALTH LAW DIGEST 27(7), 3–10 (1999).

37. Goldberg, *Taking Healthcare.*

38. Goldberg, *Taking Healthcare.*

39. J. Fischman, *Drug Bazaar: Getting Medicine Off the Web Is Easy, But Dangerous,* U.S. NEWS AND WORLD REPORT, June 21, 1999, 58–62.

SUGGESTED READING

G. Berry, *Keeping Records Secure,* ADVANCE FOR PHYSICAL THERAPISTS 13 (JUNE 1, 1998).

M. Brimer, *Making the Move to Electronic Documentation,* PT: MAGAZINE OF PHYSICAL THERAPY 6(10):58–62 (1998).

A. Coffman, *Filling in the Blanks: Tackling the Resident Assessment Instrument,* GERINOTES (1999) 6(4), 8–12.

Core Principles of Telehealth, FEDERATION FORUM, 16 (Fall 1998).

J.R. Christiansen, *Administrative Simplification and the Forced March into the Digital Future*, HEALTH LAWYER 10(6), 1, 3–7 (1998).

Documentation Tips, GERINOTES (current issue).

J. Erwin, *Keeping Track: Patient Wristbands Hold Medical Records*, HEALTHWEEK, 8 (AUGUST 17, 1998).

C. McLaughlin, *Down to the Wire*, ADVANCE FOR PHYSICAL THERAPISTS, 37–39 (March 30, 1998).

R.W. Scott, *Incident Reports: Protecting the Record*, PT: MAGAZINE OF PHYSICAL THERAPY, 4(9):24–25 (1996).

G.H. Sullivan, *The Right Way to Fill Out an Incident Report*, RN, 51(12):53–55 (1988)

D.P. Vandagriff, *Securing Your Data*, ABA JOURNAL, 58–59 (June 1994).

J. Weiler, *State-of-the-Art Home Care Documentation*, ADVANCE FOR PHYSICAL THERA-PISTS AND PT ASSISTANTS, 8–10, 26 (July 20, 1998).

REVIEW: CASE STUDIES

---

1. X, an outpatient with a diagnosis of left shoulder adhesive capsulitis, arrives at the physical therapy clinic, XYZ Hospital, for his third treatment of "moist heat, followed by passive mobilization and active assistive exercises, followed by ice pack prn." Before applying the heat, the physical therapist assistant, Y, notices a 2-in.-diameter blister at patient X's right acromioclavicular joint and inquires about it. Patient X states that Y had left the heat pack on his shoulder too long during his last treatment 2 days ago, and as a result, he sustained the burn. What does Y do?

2. It is December 26, 20xx. C, an 89-year-old patient, presents to the emergency department of ABC Hospital, Lake Frio, Michigan, for examination and treatment for what her daughter-in-law, D, reports to have been a fall down three stairs onto her outstretched hands this morning. Patient C is reticent when questioned about the fall; however, D volunteers that patient C is frequently disposed to fall and bruise herself. Patient C's symptoms include emaciation, bruising, and scratches over the dorsum of her hands and forearms, and painful bilateral shoulder active-assistive range of motion. Patient C is dressed in a sleeveless cotton dress. As emergency department head nurse, what advice would you offer to the intern evaluating patient C for treatment?

SUGGESTED ANSWERS AND DISCUSSION

1. Y should withhold application of the heat treatment and immediately notify her supervising physical therapist about the incident. Heat pack burns account for a significant proportion of claims and lawsuits against physical therapists. Because Y observed patient X's condition and heard patient X's statement about attribution of cause, Y should write the incident report. In it, she should carefully document what she saw and heard. An appropriate entry describing the occurrence might be:

> Patient X arrived for treatment of moist heat and exercise at 1415 hours, Sept. 19, 20xx. After patient X removed his shirt, I noticed a 1 7/8-in.-diameter round blister at his right acromioclavicular joint. The blister's periphery was surrounded with erythema. The wound was dry. Patient X stated to me, "You left the heat pack on too long during my last treatment, and I got burned." I notified Mary Therapist, PT, who examined patient X and ordered his treatment withheld for now. Mary Therapist consulted with Dr. S in the Acute Care Clinic, who agreed to examine patient X this afternoon. Follow-up pending.

Y was correct not to speculate as to the cause of patient X's burn or to admit fault and apologize for it in the incident report. Y's supervisor or the risk manager will determine cause during an investigation, and Y will have the opportunity then to present her case. Also, the patient care record and testimony of others in the clinic about customary practice will provide evidence as to causation.

Y was also astute to avoid arguing with patient X about possible contributory negligence in failing to alert Y that he was burning, etc. Y displayed a caring, concerned attitude for patient X's welfare and obtained appropriate follow-up care for him. That empathetic intervention alone may prevent a claim from ever being filed.

A concomitant patient care progress note entry for patient X might read:

> Sept. 19, 20xx/1415 hours: 1 7/8-in.-diameter round erythematous dry blister noted at patient's R A-C jt prior to rx. Notified Mary Therapist, PT, who examined pt. and ordered rx. withheld until examination by Dr. S. Follow-up pending.

2. The examining physician should consider the possibility that patient C is the victim of elder abuse. Patient C displays many of the classic signs of possible abuse, including physical symptoms that do not necessarily conform to the attributed source of injury; withdrawal in the face of questions about her injuries; inappropriate dress for the season; pain symptoms distant from the injury site (shoulders); general deconditioning; a reported history of repetitive falling; and a family member answering questions for her without apparent need. The intern should consult with the facility risk manager and/or legal advisor to ascertain any mandatory reporting requirements and coordinate with social services for further social intervention. The physician should carefully document objective evaluative (including radiologic) findings and transcribe verbatim any statements patient C might make concerning attribution of her injuries. Patient C's record should receive special handling, and her case should be reviewed expeditiously for the need for reporting and/or further intervention.

Epilogue

The fundamental principles underlying this book are (1) that documentation of patient care activities is as important as the actual rendition of care, and (2) that accurate, careful, comprehensive, concise, objective, and timely documentation serves simultaneously to promote optimal quality patient care and to lessen, to the maximal extent possible, the risk of health care malpractice liability associated with clinical health care delivery. Documentation and health care information management are the responsibilities of every health care professional and clinical manager, not just of medical records specialists.

This book was written to fill a perceived void in the professional literature regarding legal aspects of patient care documentation and was designed to present a comprehensive overview of salient legal concepts for health care clinicians who document patient care or act based on the documentation of other providers. The issues addressed herein involve complex legal and ethical considerations, and their solutions require close coordination and consultation among health care providers, administrators, risk managers, legal advisors, and pertinent others.

The sample documentation formats offered in this book are intended solely as informational and illustrative general legal principles and not as specific guidance for any particular provider. In that regard, the formats are a good starting point from which to build clinical models and forms for such important requirements as patient informed consent and quality and risk management programs. Be sure to consult with your legal advisor before implementing any of the suggested documentation formats to ensure compliance with state or federal law, as applicable.

Because the complex array of statutory, regulatory, and judge-made law for each state is different and ever-evolving, health care providers, clinical managers, and administrators have the formidable task of staying abreast of health care law issues in order to simultaneously provide optimal quality patient care and protect themselves from health care malpractice liability exposure. Because this task is so Herculean, health professionals must consult regularly with legal advisors and should include attorneys as important advisory members of health care decision-making teams.

Important changes in health care documentation management are in motion. Computerization of health information management systems is ongoing; telehealth is impending. Patient care data collection systems (such as OASIS) to be required in home patient care for Medicare-certified home health agencies are ever-evolving and changing.

Irrespective of any and all changes in health care delivery that may occur—including the rise and (potential) fall of managed care—health care clinicians and administrators will continue to rely on patient care documentation to facilitate optimal quality patient care. It is because good patient care documentation can mean the difference between patient life and death that providers must strive toward zero defects in what they write to uphold their sacred duty and trust to the patients whose health, well-being, and lives they hold in their hands.

Abandonment—a situation wherein a health care provider improperly unilaterally terminates a professional relationship with a patient.

Apparent agency—a situation in which a court will impose vicarious liability on an employer for the actions of a contractor working for the employer because the contractor is indistinguishable from an employee in the eyes of the public.

Assault—the apprehension or anticipation of the application of unauthorized physical force.

Battery—the unconsented, unprivileged harmful or offensive touching of another person.

Beyond a reasonable doubt—the standard (burden) of proof in a criminal case, by which the government must prove a criminal defendant's guilt to the satisfaction of a jury or judge.

Collateral source rule—a legal rule related to (money) damages determination in a civil case under which a jury is prevented from knowing about a plaintiff's collateral sources of recovery for injuries, such as insurance payments and partial payments in settlement from other defendants in the case.

Comparative fault—consideration by a judge or jury, not just of a defendant's conduct, but also that of the plaintiff in a civil lawsuit. If the plaintiff failed to exercise that degree of reasonable care expected by society to protect oneself from harm, the plaintiff's (money) damages for injury at the defendant's hands may be reduced or even eliminated.

Compensatory damages—money awarded by a court to a tort plaintiff to make the plaintiff "whole," such as for lost wages or salary (present and future), medical expenses (present and future), pain and suffering, and loss of enjoyment of life.

Complaint—a formal legal document specifying an incident allegedly causing patient-plaintiff injury and the amount of (money) damages sought.

Criminal action—public action brought by the government for a wrong or wrongs against society as a whole.

Defamation—a communication to a third party of an untrue statement about a person that damages the defamed person's good reputation in the community. Two classifications of defamation are slander (oral defamation) and libel (written or other forms of defamation).

Deponent—a person undergoing deposition.

Deposition—a pretrial "discovery" device consisting of sworn testimony of a party or potential party to a lawsuit, or of a fact or expert witness.

Directed verdict—a situation in which the party with the burden to prove a legal case fails to present a *prima facie* case (i.e., one on which the party could prevail), requiring the judge to refuse to allow the case to go to the jury for its consideration.

Durable power of attorney for health care—a legal document, signed by a patient, that delegates health care treatment decision making to an agent of the patient's choice in the event that the patient becomes legally incompetent.

Emergency doctrine—an exception to the requirement to obtain patient informed consent before treatment for emergency lifesaving care.

Exculpatory contract—a contract between a patient and health care provider in which the provider attempts to limit or eliminate his or her liability for ordinary or professional negligence incident to care.

Expert witness—a witness possessing expertise concerning a relevant issue in a legal case, based on special knowledge, skill, and/or training.

Fact witness—also called a percipient witness or eyewitness, one who possesses relevant firsthand knowledge about the issues and merits of a legal case important to one or both sides.

Fiduciary relationship—a special relationship in which a trustee is expected to put the interests of a beneficiary ahead of his or her own personal interests.

Fraud—a false representation of material (decisional) fact, made with the intent to deceive, which causes another person to take some action detrimental to his or her own (or the public's) interest.

Health care malpractice—an adverse outcome (injury) associated with patient treatment, coupled with a recognized basis for imposing liability, such as professional negligence, failure to achieve a therapeutic promise (breach of contract), or injury from a dangerously defective product (product liability).

Hearsay—any out-of-court statement offered as evidence in court for the truth of the matter asserted in it.

Independent contractor—a worker for whom an employer normally is not vicariously liable, based primarily on the lack of control over the physical details of the contractor's work product.

Inference—a trial rule that allows, but does not compel, a conclusion of negligence by a jury based on permissive deductive reasoning.

Informed consent—providing a patient with sufficient information about a proposed treatment and its reasonable alternatives to allow the patient to make a knowing, intelligent, and unequivocal decision regarding whether to accept or reject the proposed treatment.

Interrogatories—formal written pretrial "discovery" questions posed by one party in a civil case to another, for which answers are required.

Invasion of privacy—an intentional tort having several branches. One, the public disclosure of private facts, involves intentional dissemination of private information about a person to a third party not having a legal right to know the information revealed.

Joint and several liability—among more than one defendant possibly liable to a plaintiff for injury, personal individual responsibility of each defendant for the whole amount of the plaintiff's damages.

Jurisdiction—a court's legal authority to hear a specific legal case and exercise control over the parties.

Larceny by fraud—theft of money, goods, services, or other property by deception.

Living will—a legal document, signed by a patient, that states the patient's desires regarding life-sustaining measures to be taken in the event that the patient becomes legally incompetent.

Monitoring and evaluating patient care (M & E)—the systematic evaluation of selected clinical indicators concerning important aspects of patient care as part of a program to improve quality or organizational performance.

National Practitioner Data Bank—a federal data base maintained under private contract for the Department of Health and Human Services to store information concerning adverse licensure, privileging, and malpractice payments involving licensed health care providers.

Nondelegable duties—duties owed directly by a health care facility to its patients, including the duty to select and retain only competent health care providers; the duty to maintain safe premises and equipment; and the duty to oversee the quality of patient care provided in the facility.

Premises liability—the legal duties of a landowner or occupier to maintain premises that are safe for business visitors and others, as determined by applicable state law.

Preponderance of evidence—the usual standard (burden) of proof in a civil case, in which the party with the burden (usually the plaintiff [party bringing suit]) must prove his or her case by a greater weight of evidence.

Presumption—a trial rule that requires a jury to presume negligence against a defendant unless and until the defendant introduces sufficient evidence to rebut the presumption.

Pro bono publico—the rendition of free of charge or reduced fee services to clients lacking the ability to pay full market value for them.

Professional negligence—delivery of patient care that falls below the standard expected of ordinary reasonable practitioners of the same profession acting under the same or similar circumstances.

Punitive damages—punishment damages imposed upon a civil defendant when the defendant's conduct is deemed egregious.

Res ipsa loquitur—Latin for "the thing speaks for itself." Under this legal doctrine, a patient-plaintiff's burden of proof may be lessened if (1) the patient's injury was the kind that normally does not occur absent negligence, (2) the defendant-provider exercised exclusive control over the treatment or modality that caused the patient injury, and (3) the patient was not contributorily negligent.

Risk management—the process of systematically monitoring health care delivery activities in order to prevent or minimize financial losses from claims or lawsuits arising from patient care or other activities conducted in a health care facility.

Sexual battery—the unconsented, unprivileged harmful or offensive touching of the sexual or other intimate parts of another person, for the purpose of sexual arousal (of either party), gratification, or abuse.

Spoliation—the intentional destruction or material alteration of a document, for the purpose of changing or concealing its original meaning.

Standard of care—the benchmark delineating non-negligent and negligent patient care; a defendant's (party being sued) professional conduct is compared to that of ordinary reasonable peers acting under the same or similar circumstances.

Statement against interest—an out-of-court statement made by a person that is against the declarant's own pecuniary or proprietary interests. A statement against one's own interests is admissible in court as an exception to the hearsay rule.

Statute of limitations—a "time clock" for initiating a lawsuit, after the expiration of which further relief is forever time-barred.

Subpoena duces tecum—a court order to the custodian of documents or other things that are pertinent to issues in a legal case to deliver them for inspection to a business location or to bring them when testifying at a legal proceeding, such as a pretrial deposition or a trial.

Summary judgment—granting a court verdict in favor of a party to the case without a trial, when the pretrial documents demonstrate that there are no material issues of fact to decide by resort to trial.

Summons—formal notification of a lawsuit.

Therapeutic privilege—an exception to the requirement to obtain patient informed consent before treatment for a situation in which an attending physician reasonably believes that the patient could not psychologically cope with the information disclosed.

Tort—a class of civil legal actions that includes most private injuries except breach of contract actions.

Tort reform—legislative and judicial action undertaken in recent decades to decrease the number of tort lawsuits.

Total quality management—a strategic integrated management system for achieving customer satisfaction, which involves all managers and employees, and uses quantitative methods to improve an organization's processes.

Vicarious liability—indirect financial responsibility for the conduct of another person, usually an employee acting within the scope of his or her employment.

Example of an Approved Abbreviation List for a Rehabilitation Service

ABC Rehabilitation Hospital
Physical Rehabilitation Service
Fort McPride, USA

APPROVED ABBREVIATIONS

Note: This list of approved abbreviations is for use facility-wide. No additional abbreviations are authorized for use in patient treatment records. Providers are encouraged to submit requests for additional approved abbreviations to the Abbreviations Committee, ATTN: Dr. J. R. Smedlap, ext. 2457.

A

$\underline{A}$—active, artery, assessment
$\overline{A}$—before
AA—active assist, arteries, Alcoholics Anonymous
AAA—abdominal aortic aneurysm
AAROM—active-assisted range of motion
AB—abortion, antibiotics
ABD—abdominal, abduction

ABG—arterial blood gases
ABN—abnormal
ABO—blood grouping system
AC—acromioclavicular, alternating current, anterior cruciate, assisted control (ventilation), before meals (ante cibum)
ACJ—acromioclavicular joint
ACL—anterior cruciate ligament
ACLR—anterior cruciate ligament reconstruction

ACT—active
ADD—adduction
ADH—antidiuretic hormone
ADL—activities of daily living
AD LIB—as desired
ADM—admission
AE—above elbow
AER—aerosol
AF—atrial fibrillation, anterior fontanel
AFO—ankle-foot orthosis
AFS—assessment flow sheet
AGA—appropriate for gestational age
AHF—antihemophilic factor
AI—aortic insufficiency
AIDS—acquired immune deficiency syndrome
AIIS—anterior inferior iliac spine
AJ—ankle jerk
AKA—above knee amputation
ALB—albumin
ALTE—apparent life-threatening event
AMA—against medical advice
AMB—ambulation
ANT—anterior
AMP—ampule
AN—antigen
ANES—anesthesia
ANT—anterior
A&O—alert and oriented
AODM—adult-onset diabetes mellitus
AP—ankle pumps, anterior-posterior
APC—atrial premature contraction
AR—aortic regurgitation

ARDS—acute respiratory distress syndrome
ARF—acute renal failure
AROM—active range of motion
ASA—aspirin
ASAP—as soon as possible
ASCAD—atherosclerotic coronary artery disease
ASD—atrial septal defect
ASHD—arteriosclerotic heart disease
ASIS—anterior superior iliac spine
AS TOL—as tolerated
ATFL—anterior talofibular ligament
AVM—arteriovenous malformation
AVN—avascular necrosis
AVR—aortic valve replacement

B

B—bilateral
BA swallow—barium swallow
BAB—Babinski sign
BASO—basophil
BB—back bending
BBB—bundle branch block
BC—blood culture
BDAE—Boston Diagnostic Aphasia Evaluation
BE—below elbow, barium enema
BID—twice daily
BIL—bilateral
BILI—bilirubin
BIW—twice weekly
BK—below the knee

BKA—below-knee amputation
BLA—baseline assessment
BLAD—bladder
BLE—bilateral lower extremities
BM—bowel movement, breast milk
BMT—bone marrow transplant
BP—blood pressure
BPD—bronchopulmonary dysplasia
BPM—beats per minute
BR—breast
BRACH—brachial
BRONCH—bronchoscopy
BRP—bathroom privileges
BS—bedside, bowel sounds, breath sounds
B-STREP—beta hemolytic strep
BSO—bilateral salpingo-oophorectomy
BTB—bone-tendon-bone
BTL—bilateral tubal ligation
BTU—British thermal unit
BUE—bilateral upper extremities
BUN—blood urea nitrogen
BW—birth weight, body weight
BX—biopsy

C

C—cervical
$\overline{C}$—with
C1, 2 . . . 7—cervical spinal levels
C&S—culture and sensitivity
CA—calcium, cancer, coronary artery

CABG—coronary artery bypass graft (3VCABG: 3-vessel coronary artery bypass graft)
CAD—coronary artery disease
CAL—calorie
CAP—capillary
CAPD—continuous ambulatory peritoneal dialysis
CARF—Commission on Accreditation of Rehabilitation Facilities
CATH—cardiac catheterization
CBC—complete blood count
CBD—common bile duct
CBI—continuous bladder irrigation
CBS—chronic brain syndrome
CC—chief complaint, cubic centimeter
CCU—cardiac/constant care unit
CDH—congenital diaphragmatic hernia
CEA—carotid enarterotomy
CFL—calcaneofibular ligament
CHF—congestive heart failure
CHI—closed head injury
CHO—carbohydrates
CHR—chronic
CL—chlorine
CLAV—clavicle
CLD—chronic lung disease
CM—centimeter
CMP—chondromalacia patella
CMV—cytomegalovirus
CN—cranial nerve
CNS—central nervous system
CO—cardiac output
C/O—complains of
COG DEF—cognitive deficit(s)

COGN—cognitive
COLD—chronic obstructive lung disease
CONT—continue(s), continue(d)
COPD—chronic obstructive pulmonary disease
CORT—certified operating room technician
COTA—certified occupational therapist assistant
CP—calf pumps, cerebral palsy, chest pain, cold pack
CPK—creatinine phosphokinase
CPM—continuous passive motion
CPR—cardiopulmonary resuscitation
CPS—Child Protective Services
CPT—chest physical therapy
CR—crutch(es), cardiorespiratory
CRF—chronic renal failure
CRI—chronic renal insufficiency
CRNP—certified registered nurse practitioner
CS—Caesarian section
CSF—cerebrospinal fluid
CSM—circulatory, sensory, motor
CT—computed tomography, cholecystectomy tube
CTN—contraction
CTR—carpal tunnel release
CTS—cardiothoracic surgery, carpal tunnel syndrome
CV—cardiovascular
CVA—cerebral vascular accident, costovertebral angle
CVP—central venous pressure

CVT—cardiovascular technologist
CW—crutch walking (NWB: non-weightbearing; TWB: touch weightbearing; PWB: partial weightbearing; WBAT: weightbearing as tolerated; FWB: full weightbearing)
CWI—crutch walking instruction
CX—cervical
CXR—chest x-ray
CYSTO—cystoscopy

D

D—dorsal, distal
D/3—distal one-third
DA—developmental age
DC—doctor of chiropractic
D/C—direct current, discontinue
D&C—dilation and curretage
DDD—degenerative disc disease
DDS—doctor of dental surgery
DEC—decrease(d)
DEP—dependent
DEPT—department
DF—dorsiflexion
DIP—distal interphalangeal joint
DIST—distal
DJD—degenerative joint disease
DM—diabetes mellitus
DNK—did not keep (appointment)
DO—doctor of osteopathy
DOA—date of admission, dead on arrival
DOE—dyspnea on exertion
DOI—date of injury

DON—department of nursing
DOS—date of surgery
DPC—delayed primary closure
DPT—diphtheria, pertussis, tetanus
DT—delirium tremens
DTD—dated
DTR—deep tendon reflex
DUB—dysfunctional uterine bleeding
DVT—deep vein thrombosis
DX—diagnosis

E

EA—educational age
EAD—end artery disease
EBV—Epstein-Barr virus
ECF—extended care facility
ECG (or EKG)—electrocardiogram
ECHO—echocardiogram
ECMO—extracorporeal membrane oxygenation
E Coli—Escherichia Coli
ED—emergency department
EDX—electrodiagnosis
EEG—electroencephalogram
EENT—eye, ear, nose, and throat
EHR—exercise heart rate
EIL—extension in lying
EIS—extension in standing
ELEV—elevated
EMG—electromyogram
EOS—eosinophils
EOSS—end-of-shift summation
EPITH—epithelium

ER—emergency room, external rotation
ES—electrostimulation
ESR—erythrocyte sedimentation rate
ESRD—end-stage renal disease
ET—endotracheal
ETIOL—etiology
ETOH—ethanol
ETT—endotracheal tube
EV—eversion
EX—exercise
EXPIR—expiration
EXT—extension, external, extract, extremity

F

F—fair (muscle test grade), female
FAB ER—flexion/abduction/external rotation
FAROM—full active range of motion
FB—foreign body, forward bending
F/B—followed by
FBS—fasting blood sugar
FCE—functional capacity evaluation
FE—iron
FES—functional electric stimulation
FFAROM—full functional active range of motion
FFP—flash-frozen plasma
FH—family history
FHM—fetal heart monitor(ing)

FHS—family health services
FHT—fetal heart tones
FIB—fibula
FIL—flexion in lying
FIS—flexion in standing
FLEX—flexion
FOOSH—fall onto outstretched hand
FPROM—full passive range of motion
FREQ—frequency, frequent
FSH—follicle stimulating hormone
FT—feet, foot
FTN—finger-to-nose
FTP—failure to progress
FTSG—full-thickness skin graft
FTT—failure to thrive
F/U—follow-up
FUB—functional uterine bleeding
FUO—fever of unknown origin
FVC—forced vital capacity
FWB—full weight bearing
FX—fracture

G

G—good (muscle test grade), gravida
GA—gestational age
GB—gallbladder
GC—Gonococcus
GCS—Glasgow Coma Scale
GE—gastroenterology
GEL—gelatin
GETA—general endotracheal anesthesia
GI—gastrointestinal

GLOB—globulin
GM—gram
GMO—general medical officer
GMT—gross muscle test
GN—graduate nurse
GP(FP)AL—gravida (number of pregnancies), para (number of pregnancies resulting in live offspring), (number of deliveries at full term, number of premature deliveries), number of abortions (elective or spontaneous), number of living offspring
GS—gluteal setting
GSW—gunshot wound
GT—gait training
GTT—glucose tolerance test
GU—genitourinary
GYN—gynecology

H

H—hemovac
H&H—hemoglobin and hematocrit
H&P—history and physical exam
HA—headache
HB, HGB—hemoglobin
HBIG—hepatitis-B immune globulin
HBP—high blood pressure
HC—head circumference, hydrocephalus, hydrocortisone
HCG—human chorionic gonadotrophin
HCL—hydrochloric acid

HCP—hydrocortisone phonophoresis
HCT—hematocrit
HCV—hepatitis-C virus
HCVD—hypertensive cardiovascular disease
HEDIS—Health Plan Employers Data and Information Set
HEENT—head, eyes, ears, nose, throat
HEMI—herniplegic
HFO—high frequency oscillation
HFPP—high frequency positive pressure (ventilation)
HGH—human growth hormone
HI—head injury
HIS—hospital information system
HIV—human immunodeficiency virus
HMO—health maintenance organization
HNP—herniated nucleus pulposus
HOB—head of bed
HOC—head-on collision
HOH—hard of hearing
HOSP—hospital
HP—hot pack, home program
HPI—history of present illness
HPV—human papilloma virus
HR—heart rate, hour(s)
HS—hamstring muscles, hour of sleep (horasomni)
HSM—hepatosplenomegaly
HSS—hamstring sets (isometric exercise)
HSV—herpes simplex virus
HT—height, Hubbard tank

HTN—hypertension
HVD—hypertensive vascular disease
HVGS—high-voltage galvanic stimulation
HX—history
HYPO—hypodermic

I

I—independent
I&D—incision and drainage
I&O—intake and output
IBW—ideal body weight
IC or I/C—informed consent
ICB—intracranial bleeding
ICF—immediate care facility
ICH—intracerebral hemorrhage
ICP—intracranial pressure
ICT—intermittent cervical traction
ICU—intensive care unit
ID—infectious disease
IDDM—insulin-dependent diabetes mellitus
IDK—internal derangement of the knee
IDM—infant of a diabetic mother
IH—infectious hepatitis
II—image intensifier
IM—ice massage, intermuscular (injection)
IMCN—intermediate care nursery
IMI—inferior myocardial infarction
IMP—impairment, impression

IN—inch(es)
INC—incontinent, increase(d)
INF—inferior
IN SITU—in natural position
INT—intact, internal
INV—inversion
IP—interphalangeal
IPPB—intermittent positive
   pressure breathing
IPT—intermittent pelvic traction
IR—internal rotation
IRREG—irregular
IS—incentive spirometry
ISO—isoenzyme
ISS—injury severity score
IU—international units
IUD—interuterine device
IV—intravenous
IVC—inferior vena cava
IVF—intravenous fluid
IVH—intraventricular
   hemorrhage
IVP—intravenous pyelogram
IVSD—intraventricular septal
   defect

J

JCAHO—Joint Commission on
   the Accreditation of Healthcare
   Organizations
JRA—juvenile rheumatoid
   arthritis
JT—joint

K

K—potassium
KAFO—knee-ankle-foot orthosis

KCAL—kilocalories
KG—kilogram
KJ—knee jerk
KUB—kidney/ureter /bladder

L

L—length
L—left, liter, lumbar
L1, 2 . . . 5—lumbar spinal levels
L/3—lower one-third
LA—left atrium
L&A—light and accommodation
LAC—laceration(s), long arm
   cast
LACR—lacrimation
LAMI—laminectomy
LAP—laparotomy
LAT—lateral, latissimus dorsi
   muscle
LAV—lavatory
LB—low back, pound
LBBB—left bundle branch block
LBP—low back pain
LBW—low birth weight
LC—living children
LCL—lateral collateral ligament
LE—lower extremity
LEUC—leukocyte
LFC—lateral femoral condyle
LGA—large for gestational age
LGE—large
LIG—ligament
LL—left lumbar (scoliosis)
LLC—long leg cast
LLE—left lower extremity
LLL—left lower lobe (of lung)
LLWC—long leg walking cast

LMN—lower motor neuron
LMP—last menstrual period
LMT—lateral meniscus tear
LOC—loss of consciousness
LOM—loss of motion
LOS—length of stay
LP—lumbar puncture
LPM—liters per minute
LPN—licensed practical nurse
LRQ—lower right quadrant
LS—lumbosacral
LT—left, left thoracic (scoliosis),
Levin tube
LTG—long-term goal(s)
LTM—long-term memory
LUE—left upper extremity
LUQ—left upper quadrant
LV—left ventricle
LVE—left ventricular
enlargement
LVH—left ventricular
hypertrophy
LYM—lymphocyte
LYTE—electrolyte

M

M—meter, male
M/3—middle one-third
MA—medical assistance
MA—milliamperes
MAE—moves all extremities
MAMMO—mammogram
MAP—mean airway pressure
MASS—massage
MAX—maximum
MC—managed care, Medicare
MCA—motorcycle accident

MCL—medial collateral
ligament
MCP—metacarpophalangeal
MCTD—mixed connective tissue
disease
MD—medical doctor, muscular
dystrophy
MDI—metered dose inhaler
MED—medical, medication(s)
MEDCO—medcollator
MEDSON—medsonalator
MEQ—milliequivalents
METS—metastases
MFC—medial femoral condyle
MG—milligram, myasthenia
gravis
MH—moist heat
MI—myocardial infarction
MICU—medical intensive care
unit
MID—middle, midline
MIN—minimum, minute(s)
ML—milliliter
MM—millimeter,
meningomyelocele, muscle(s)
MMAI—maximal multiple angle
isometrics
MMT—manual muscle test
MO—month(s)
MOD—moderate, modified
MOM—milk of magnesia
MONO—monocyte
MPS—multiphasic screening
MR—mitral regurgitation
MRI—magnetic resonance
imaging
MRM—modified radical
mastectomy
MRN—medical record number

MS—multiple sclerosis
MSR—muscle stretch reflex
MT—manual (or manipulative) therapy, medical technologist
MTF—medical treatment facility, medial tibial flare
MTP—metatarsophalangeal
MV—millivolt
MVA—motor vehicle accident
MVR—mitral valve replacement
MVT—movement
MYELO—myelogram

N

N—normal (muscle test grade), nitrogen
N/A—not applicable
NAD—no apparent distress
NAR—no apparent reason (or rationale)
NAS—no added salt
NB—newborn
NC—nasal cannula, no change
NCQA—National Committee on Quality Assurance
NCV—nerve conduction velocity
NDB—nursing database
NDT—neurodevelopmental treatment
NEG—negative
NF—National Formulary
NG—nasogastric
NH—nursing home
NHP—nursing home placement
NICU—neonatal intensive care unit
NIDDM—non-insulin-dependent diabetes mellitus

NKA—no known allergies
NKI—no known illnesses/injuries
NL—normal (limits)
NN—nerve(s)
NO, #—number
NOC—night, nightly
N-P—nasopharyngeal
NPO—nothing by mouth (nil per os)
NQWMI—non-Q wave myocardial infarction
NSAID—nonsteroidal anti-inflammatory drug
NSR—normal sinus rhythm
NSS—newborn supplemental screening
NSVD—normal spontaneous vaginal delivery
NTG—nitroglycerine
NWB—non-weight-bearing

O

O—objective
OASIS—Outcome and Assessment Information Set (Medicare home health assessment instrument)
OB—obstetrics, occult blood
OBS—organic brain syndrome
OCT—oxytocin
OD—once daily, overdose, right eye, doctor of optometry
OM—oral motor
OME—oral motor exercise
OOB—out of bed
OOP—out of plaster
OP—outpatient

O&P—ova and parasites
OPD—outpatient department
OPR—outpatient record
OPV—oral polio vaccine
OR—operating room
ORIF—open reduction internal fixation
OS—left eye
OT—occupational therapist/ therapy
OTO—otology
OTR—registered occupational therapist
OX—oximetry
OZ—ounce

P

P—para, plan, poor (muscle test grade), pulse
P—after
P/3—proximal one-third
PA—physician assistant, posterior-anterior
P&A—percussion and auscultation
PAC—premature atrial contraction
PAF—paroxysmal atrial fibrillation
PALP—palpation
PARA—paraplegic
PAT—paroxysmal atrial tachycardia, pre-admission testing
PATH—pathology
PAW—pulmonary artery wedge pressure
PB—lead, periodic breathing

PC—after meals
PCA—patient-controlled anesthesia
PCG—pneumocardiogram
PCL—posterior cruciate ligament
PCV—packed cell volume
PDP—postural drainage and percussion
PDR—Physician's Desk Reference
PE—physical examination, pulmonary embolus
PEEP—positive end expiratory pressure
PED—pediatric
PEN—penicillin
PER—by
PERRLA—pupils equal, round, reactive to light and accommodation
PF—peak flow, plantar flexion
PFJS—patellofemoral joint syndrome
PFR—peak flow rate
PFT—pulmonary function test
PGH—pituitary growth hormone
PH—past history
PID—pelvic inflammatory disease
PIE—pulmonary interstitial emphysema
PINS—posterior interosseous nerve syndrome
PIP—peak inspiratory pressure, proximal interphalangeal joint
PMH—past medical history
PMI—point of maximal intensity, posterior myocardial infarction

PMR—physical medicine and rehabilitation
PMS—physical medicine service
PND—paroxysmal nocturnal dyspnea
PNF—proprioceptive neuromuscular facilitation
PNI—peripheral nerve injury
PO—by mouth (per os)
POC—products of conception
POMR—problem-oriented medical record
POS—positive
POSS—possible
POST—posterior
POST-OP—after surgery
POX—pulse oximetry
PPB—positive pressure breathing
PPN—peripheral parenteral nutrition
PPO—preferred provider organization
PPS—prospective payment system
PRE—progressive resistive exercises
PRE-OP—before surgery
PREP—prepare for
PRM—premature rupture of membranes
PRN—whenever needed
PROB—problem, probable
PROG—progress
PROM—passive range of motion
PRON—pronation
PROX—proximal
PSIS—posterior superior iliac spine

PT—patient, physical therapy, physical training, pint, point, prothrombin time
PTA—physical therapist assistant, prior to admission
PTB—patellar tendon bearing
PTCA—percutaneous transluminal coronary angioplasty
PTFL—posterior talofibular ligament
PTL—pre-term labor
PTP—patient teaching protocol
PUD—peptic ulcer disease
PV—post-voiding
PVC—premature ventricular contraction
PVD—peripheral vascular disease
PVR—pulmonary vascular resistance

Q

Q—every (quaque)
QA—quality assurance
QD—every day
Q4HR—every 4 hours
QH—every hour
QI—quality improvement
QID—four times a day
QIP—quality improvement program
QIT—quality improvement team
QN—every night
QOD—every other day

QRS—ventricular complex (on ECG)

QS—quadriceps muscle sets, quantity sufficient

QUAD—quadriceps muscles, quadriplegic

R

R—respirations, right

RA—rheumatoid arthritis, right atrium

RBA—risks, benefits, (reasonable) alternatives

RBC—red blood cell (count)

RCS—rotator cuff strain

RCT—rotator cuff tear

RD—radial deviation, registered dietician

RDS—respiratory distress syndrome

RE—recheck, regarding

RE-ADM—readmission

RE-ED—re-education

REP—repetition(s)

RESP—respiratory

RH—Rhesus factor

RHD—rheumatic heart disease

RHR—resting heart rate

RL—right lumbar (scoliosis)

RLE—right lower extremity

RLQ—right lower quadrant

RN—registered nurse

RNC—registered nurse certified

RND—radical neck dissection

R/O—rule out

ROM—range of motion, rupture of membranes

ROS—review of systems

RPPS—retropatellar pain syndrome

RR—respiratory rate

RRA—registered record administrator

RSLR—reverse straight leg raise

RST—restart

RT—right, radiation therapy, right thoracic (scoliosis)

RTC—return to clinic

RTR—registered technologist radiology

RTW—return to work

RUE—right upper extremity

RUL—right upper lobe (of lung)

RV—right ventricle

RX—treatment, prescription

S

S—sacral, supervision

$\bar{S}$—without

SS—one-half (semsis)

SA—sino-atrial node

SAA—same as above

SAB—spontaneous abortion

SAC—short arm cast

SACH—solid ankle cushion heel

SAH—subarachnoid hemorrhage

SAHS—short-arc hamstring (exercise)

SAQ—short-arc quad(riceps exercise)

SB—side-bending

SBE—subacute bacterial endocarditis
SBQC—small-based quad cane
SC—subcutaneous
SCAP—scapula(r)
SCFE—slipped capital femoral epiphysis
SCI—spinal cord injury
SCJ—sternoclavicular joint
SCM—sternocleidomastoid
SCP—standard care plan
SD—septal defect
SDH—subdural hematoma
SEC—second(s)
SED RATE—sedimentation rate
SEGS—segmented neutrophils
SEM VES—seminal vesicles
SF—synovial fluid
SGA—small for gestational age
SH—shoulder
SI—seriously ill, sacro-iliac
SIB—sibling(s)
SICU—surgical intensive care unit
SIDS—sudden infant death syndrome
SIG—directions for use
SIW—self-inflicted wound
SL—slight(ly)
SLC—short leg cast
SLE—systemic lupus erythematosus
SLR—straight leg raise
SLSLR—side-lying straight leg raise
SLT—sensation to light touch
SWLC—short leg walking cast
SM—small

SMMAI—submaximal multiple angle isometrics
SN—student nurse
SNF—skilled nursing facility
SOB—shortness of breath
SOP—standard operating procedure
S/P—status-post
SPEC—specimen
SPT—static pelvic traction, student physical therapist
SQ—static quadriceps (isometric exercise), subcutaneously
SR—stimulus response
SS—skin score
SSCP—substernal chest pain
SSE—soap suds enema
SSN—social security number
ST—start
STAPH—staphylococcus
STAT—immediately (statim)
STATUS QUO—same condition
STD—sexually transmitted disease
STG—short-term goal(s)
STM—short-term memory
STS—soft tissue swelling
STSG—split-thickness skin graft
SUP—superior, supination, supine
SURG—surgery
SVC—superior vena cava
SVD—spontaneous vaginal delivery
SVT—supraventricular tachycardia
SW—sterile water, social work(er)

SWD—short-wave diathermy
SX—symptom(s)

T

T—temperature, thoracic, trace
   (muscle test grade)
T1, 2 . . . 12—thoracic spinal
   levels
T&A—tonsillectomy and
   adenoidectomy
TAB—tablet
TACHY—tachycardia
TAH—total abdominal
   hysterectomy
TB—tuberculosis
TBC—total body complaints,
   tuberculosis culture
TBI—traumatic brain injury
TBSP—tablespoon
TENS—transcutaneous electrical
   nerve stimulation
TF—tube feeding
TFM—transverse friction
   massage
TG—triglyceride
TGV—thoracic gas volume
THA—total hip arthroplasty
THR—total hip replacement
TIA—transient ischemic attack
TIB—tibia, tibialis
TIBC—total iron binding
   capacity
TID—three times daily
TIW—three times a week
TKA—total knee arthroplasty
TKR—total knee replacement

T-L—thoracolumbar
TM—tympanic membrane
TMJ—temporomandibular joint
TNR—tonic neck reflex
TO—telephone order
TP—trigger point
TRACH—tracheostomy
TRAM—treatment rating
   assessment matrix
TRFD—transferred
TRP—temperature, pulse,
   respiration
T&S—type and screen
TSH—thyroid stimulating
   hormone
TT—tetanus toxoid, tilt table
TTN—transient tachypnea of
   newborn
TTP—tenderness to palpation
TTW—toe-touch weight bearing
TUR—transurethral resection
TX—traction

U

U/3—upper one-third
UA—urinalysis
UBW—usual body weight
UC&S—urine culture and
   sensitivity
UD—ulnar deviation, unit dose
UE—upper extremity
UMN—upper motor neuron
UNG—ointment
UO—urinary output
URI—upper respiratory infection
US—ultrasound

USN—ultrasonic nebulizer
USP—United States
  Pharmacopoeia
USOH—usual state of health
UT—ureteral catheter
UTI—urinary tract infection
UV—ultraviolet

V

V—vein, void
VA—Veterans' Affairs
VAG—vagina(l)
VBI—vertebral basilar
  insufficiency
VC—vital capacity
VD—venereal disease
VE—vaginal examination
VENT—ventilation, ventilator,
  ventral
VER—visually evoked response
VF—ventricular fibrillation
VFSS—video fluoroscopy
  swallowing study
VIT—vitamin
VLBW—very low birth weight
VMO—vastus medialis oblique
  muscle
VMS—variable muscle
  stimulator
VMT—voluntary muscle test
VO—verbal order
VOL—volume, voluntary,
  volunteer
VP—ventriculo-parietal (shunt)
VPC—ventricular premature
  contraction
VS—vital signs, volts per second
VSD—ventricular septal defect

VSI—very seriously ill
VT—ventricular tachycardia
VTX—vertex
VV—varicose veins, veins

W

W—watts, white
W/—with
WB—weight bearing
WBAT—weight bearing as
  tolerated
WBC—white blood (cell) count
WBQC—wide-based quad cane
WC—wheelchair, work
  conditioning
W/CM2—watts per centimeter
  squared
WFE—William's flexion
  exercises
WFL—within functional limits
WH—work hardening
WIC—women, infants, and
  children
WK—week
WMS—Wechsler Memory Scale
WNL—within normal limits
WNWD—well-nourished, well-
  developed
W/O—without
WP—whirlpool
WT—weight, work therapy

X

X—number of repetitions
X RAYS—Roentgen rays

Y

Y—yes
YD—yard
Y/O—year(s) old
YR—year

SPECIAL SYMBOLS

≈—approximately

Δ —change
♀ —female
> —greater than
↑—increase
< —less than
♂ —male
|| —parallel
1° —primary
re ✔ —recheck
2° —secondary
3° —tertiary

Index

About the Author

Ronald (Ron) W. Scott, JD, MSPT, MSBA, PT, OCS, has been a health care professional since 1969. He was a Navy hospital corpsman during the Vietnam conflict, after which he left military service in 1973 to study physical therapy. Ron earned his Bachelor of Science degree in health-related professions with a certificate in physical therapy at the University of Pittsburgh in 1977. He graduated *summa cum laude* and was the American Physical Therapy Association's Mary McMillan scholar, as well as Pitt's Jessie Wright awardee. Ron then worked as a clinical physical therapist at Mercy Hospital, Pittsburgh, Pennsylvania, until his commission in the Army as a first lieutenant in 1978.

Ron's first assignment as an Army physical therapist was at Fort Leonard Wood, Missouri. After that assignment, he attended the University of San Diego Law School under Army sponsorship, where he concentrated in medical law and jurisprudence and was a law review editor. He graduated *magna cum laude* in May 1983 with a Juris Doctor degree.

Ron's next assignment was as a trial attorney in Frankfurt, Germany, where he prosecuted and defended more than 75 federal felony criminal cases. He also served as Chief, Administrative, Civil, and International Law, for the Army's Third Armored Division.

After his return from Europe in 1987, Ron attended the Army's postdoctoral Master of Laws program at the Judge Advocate General's School on the University of Virginia campus at Charlottesville, where he was a Commandant's List honors graduate. He was then assigned as a tort and health care malpractice claims attorney at the U.S. Army Claims Service, Fort Meade, Maryland, where he supervised the operations of 15 claims offices in 8 western states.

From August 1989 to September 1992, Ron was Chief Physical Therapist and Legal Advisor, Bayne-Jones Army Community Hospital, Fort Polk, Louisiana. During that time, Ron played a crucial role in developing the American Physical Therapy Association's "Promoting Quality/Managing Risk" program, designed to educate physical therapists and other health care professionals about how to simultaneously manage malpractice risk in clinical practice and promote the highest quality patient care. Ron was the program's charter legal faculty coordinator from January 1990 through January 1993.

From September 1992 to July 1994, Ron was an Army major and Chief, Acute Musculoskeletal Care Section, Brooke Army Medical Center, Fort Sam Houston (San Antonio), Texas. During that time, he also served as a legal consultant to the command, staff, Army Health Services Command, and Army Medical Specialist Corps.

Ron is active in the American Physical Therapy Association, having served on its Judicial Committee from 1992–1997; as a faculty member in its "Promoting Quality/Managing Risk" program; as an editorial advisory board member for *PT: The Magazine of Physical Therapy*; as a book reviewer and abstracter for the *Journal of the American Physical Therapy Association*; as Membership Chair, Southcentral District, Pennsylvania Physical Therapy Association; and as editor for the Section on Geriatric's CINAHL-indexed journal, *Issues on Aging*. He is licensed to practice law in Texas and is an active member of the Texas and American Bar Associations (and its Health Law Section), as well as the American Health Lawyers Association and Society for Human Resource Management. Ron is certified as an orthopedic clinical specialist by the American Board of Physical Therapy Specialties.

From May 1994 to August 1998, Ron was Associate Professor (and Interim Chair in 1995–1996) in the Department of Physical Therapy, University of Texas Health Science Center at San Antonio. He currently is Chairperson, Department of Physical Therapy, Lebanon Valley College, Annville, Pennsylvania, where he lives with his wife, Maria Josefa (Pepi). Their two sons, Ron, Jr. and Paul, attend the University of North Texas and Southwest Texas State University, respectively.

In addition to this book, Ron has written more than 80 articles, many on health care malpractice and its prevention. He also has authored *Health Care Malpractice: A Primer on Legal Issues for Professionals,* 2nd edition, 1999, McGraw-Hill; *Professional Ethics: A Guide for Rehabilitation Professionals,* 1998, Mosby; and *Promoting Legal Awareness in Physical and Occupational Therapy,* 1997, Mosby. Ron has presented seminars across the United States and in Canada, Puerto Rico, England, and Ireland on various aspects of health care malpractice prevention to groups of health and legal professionals on more than 125 occasions. He is an adjunct faculty/guest lecturer in the physical therapy programs at Hahnemann University, Pennsylvania; Husson College, Maine; Slippery Rock University, Pennsylvania; and the University of Indianapolis, Indiana.